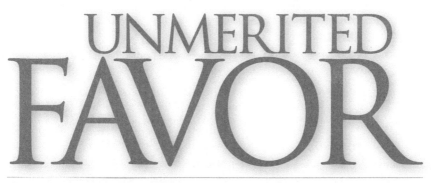

UNMERITED FAVOR

Your supernatural advantage for a successful life

JOSEPH PRINCE

Most STRANG COMMUNICATIONS BOOK GROUP products are available at special quantity discounts for bulk purchase for sales promotions, premiums, fund-raising, and educational needs. For details, write Strang Communications Book Group, 600 Rinehart Road, Lake Mary, Florida 32746, or telephone (407) 333-0600.

UNMERITED FAVOR by Joseph Prince
Published by Charisma House
A Strang Company
600 Rinehart Road
Lake Mary, Florida 32746
www.strangbookgroup.com

Unless otherwise noted, all Scripture quotations are from the New King James Version of the Bible. Copyright © 1979, 1980, 1982 by Thomas Nelson, Inc., publishers. Used by permission.

Scripture quotations marked AMP are from the Amplified Bible. Old Testament copyright © 1965, 1987 by the Zondervan Corporation. The Amplified New Testament copyright © 1954, 1958, 1987 by the Lockman Foundation. Used by permission.

Scripture quotations marked KJV are from the King James Version of the Bible.

Scripture quotations marked NAS are from the New American Standard Bible. Copyright © 1960, 1962, 1963, 1968, 1971, 1972, 1973, 1975, 1977 by the Lockman Foundation. Used by permission. (www.Lockman.org)

Scripture quotations marked NIV are from the Holy Bible, New International Version. Copyright © 1973, 1978, 1984, International Bible Society. Used by permission.

Scripture quotations marked TLB are from The Living Bible. Copyright © 1971. Used by permission of Tyndale House Publishers, Inc., Wheaton, IL 60189. All rights reserved.

Library of Congress Cataloging-in-Publication Data:
Prince, Joseph.
  Unmerited favor / by Joseph Prince.
     p. cm.
  Includes bibliographical references.
  ISBN 978-1-59979-939-1
  1. Grace (Theology)--Biblical teaching. I. Title.
  BS680.G7P75 2009
  234--dc22
                                    2009041177

Published in association with:
Joseph Prince Teaching Resources
www.destined2reign.com

10 11 12 13 14 — 10 9 8 7 6 5 4 3
Printed in the United States of America

Dedication

This book is lovingly dedicated to:

Wendy
After all these years, I still look forward to coming home to you. If I had to choose again, it would still be you.

Jessica
You are the reason Daddy feels incredibly blessed.

Darren
Your wisdom has given this ministry wings.

New Creation Church
You help me see why Jesus loves the church and calls her His bride. Thank you for all your support and love.

Contents

Introduction

This book is all about Jesus. It is about His passionate love for you and His desire for you to experience success in your life. But before we go on, let me ask you this question: **Do you believe that Jesus is interested in your success?**

Take a moment to reflect on this.

My friend, I am so glad that we have the opportunity to talk about this today because I want you to know that Jesus delights in blessing you. It is His good pleasure to see you blessed in every area of your life![1] Now, don't put a limit on His blessings in your life. The blessings of the Lord are not (as some may erroneously believe) just seen in material things. Jesus is infinitely interested in your **total** well-being. He is interested in your family, career, fulfillment in life, marriage, ministry, and boy, does the list go on!

When it comes to your desires, hopes and dreams, there is no detail that is too minuscule, minute or insignificant for Jesus. Trust me, if it matters to you, it matters to Him! Even if you went to Him in prayer to remove that small pimple on your nose, He is not going to look at you and reply mockingly, "Hey buddy, don't you know that I've got a whole universe to run? Come to Me when you have a bigger prayer request." No way! A thousand times no! Jesus will never ridicule or deride your concerns as petty. He is never dismissive or condescending. He is not like some of your so-called "friends," who may delight in poking fun at your shortcomings. If it bothers you, it bothers Him.

Jesus is someone whom you can be completely real with. You can hang out with Him and be yourself, with no pretense and no play-acting. Jesus is ever-loving toward you and you can talk to Him about anything. He enjoys conversing with you about your dreams, aspirations and hopes. He wants to heal you of things in your past that you may be struggling with. He is interested in your present challenges. He wants to weep with you when you are down and rejoice with you in all your victories.

Jesus is love and tenderness personified. Be careful not to confuse His tenderness with the effeminate and weak images that you have seen depicted in some religious paintings of Him. He is tenderness and strength wrapped up in one. He is meekness and majesty, manhood and deity, velvet and steel. You see, sometimes, when we attempt to be assertive and strong, we bulldoze over people's feelings and end up hurting them with our words. When we attempt to be tender, we overdose on niceness and reduce ourselves to doormats to be taken advantage of by others.

Let's turn away from ourselves and look at Jesus. He could sternly force a pack of scheming Pharisees to back off in one instance, challenging them by saying, "He who is without sin among you, let him throw a stone at her first."[2] In the very next moment, this same Jesus could look straight into the eyes of a broken woman caught in adultery, and with compassion resonating deeply in His voice, ask her, "Woman, where are those accusers of yours? Has no one condemned you? Neither do I condemn you; go and sin no more."[3]

This is our God!

He embodies all the heroic qualities that humanity pines for. But instead of seeking Jesus, many in the world have settled for cheap Hollywood imitations of heroism based on artificial ideals of "manliness."

In one moment, a tired Jesus could be fast asleep in a wind-swept fisherman's boat, oblivious to the rough Galilean waters crashing against the hapless vessel. But in the very next moment, you see Him staring unflinchingly at the boisterous waves, His well-toned carpenter's arms raised to the sky. With His single declaration of absolute authority over heaven and earth, the waves submitted and calmed instantaneously into a placid mirror of stillness.[4]

Jesus is 100 percent Man and at the same time 100 percent God. As Man, He understands and identifies with all that you have gone through, are going through and will ever go through in this life. He knows, for example, what it means to be fatigued after a long day. But as a loving God, all His power, authority and resources are on your side.

Do you know that you are important to Jesus? Know with full assurance in your heart that Jesus knows you perfectly, and yet accepts and loves you perfectly. When you begin to understand that, you will realize that it is truly that unmerited favor, that favor from Jesus that you know you do not deserve, did not merit and cannot earn for yourself, that will perfect every imperfection and weakness in your life. If you are facing challenges, such as lack in any area, addictions, fears, sicknesses or broken relationships, Jesus' unmerited favor will protect, deliver, prosper, bring restoration to and provide for you. His unmerited favor will transform you into wholeness, and it is the goodness of God, not your striving and self-efforts, that will lead you to live victoriously for His glory.

Several years ago, I shared with my church that there are essentially two ways in which you can go about your life. The first is to depend entirely on your self-efforts, and the other is to depend completely on the unmerited favor and blessings of God. As for me and my house, the choice is absolutely clear. I am leaning strong on His unmerited favor in every area of my life—my marriage, family, church and anything else that I may be involved in.

Now, *you* have a choice to make—to live your life based entirely on your own efforts, or based entirely on the unmerited favor of Jesus. There are only two ways—either you are depending on "deserved favor" through your self-efforts, or you are blessed by grace, which is **unmerited favor**, through the cross and the obedience of Jesus Christ! The first is the world's way. The second is God's way.

The world's way to success is based on meritocracy. All religions are also based on this same principle of merit. God's way to success in the new covenant is in direct contradiction to that, and is based on His unmerited favor. You can't earn it. You can't deserve it. And you certainly can't merit it. It comes by way of God's grace and by the power of what was accomplished at Calvary. It goes against the grain of every world system you have ever learned or depended upon. God's ways are higher and they always lead to good and abiding success.

My friend, there is no middle road. You cannot mix your own efforts with God's grace. Choose His unmerited favor and all the glory redounds to Jesus. Every success, opportunity, blessing or breakthrough, be it in your health, family or career—success in every aspect of your life—comes by His unmerited favor. It is never you!

"Now Pastor Prince, shouldn't there be a part for man to perform and another part for God to fulfill? Shouldn't man do his best and let God do the rest?"

I am so glad that you asked this question!

You see, when people say that man has a part to play, what they end up doing is to come up with a list of requirements that man needs to fulfill to qualify for God's blessings. They say things like, "In order for God to answer your prayers, you have to do this and do that, and not do this and not do that." And all the while, this list of do's and don'ts to qualify one for God's blessings keeps growing.

Now, let's stop right here. Doesn't this list of requirements that you have to fulfill so that God will bless you sound awfully familiar to you? I believe that many of those who insist on these requirements are well-meaning, sincere people. But what they are doing is pointing others back to the old covenant of the law, whether knowingly or unknowingly!

That's how the law of Moses works. Under the old covenant, God's blessings were contingent on man's fulfillment of a list of requirements. But we are no longer under the old covenant of the law.

This is not Christianity. The **new covenant** that we are under today is based completely on the removal of our sins by the blood of Jesus! "For if the blood of bulls and goats and the ashes of a heifer, sprinkling the unclean, sanctifies for the purifying of the flesh, **how much more shall the blood of Christ**, who through the eternal Spirit offered Himself without spot to God, cleanse your conscience from **dead works** to serve the living God?"[5] Depending on your own efforts to deserve favor from God is considered "dead works." It is God's desire for us to depend wholly on the unmerited favor of Jesus.

Just to make it clear, it is not Joseph Prince who is finding fault with the old covenant. God Himself said, "For if that first covenant [the covenant of law] had been faultless, then no place would have been sought for a second [the covenant of grace]."[6] The Christian life today is not a religion based on what you are doing or not doing. The reality is that the Christian life is not a religion at all. It is about having a relationship based completely on receiving WHAT GOD HIMSELF HAS DONE ON THE CROSS! When you receive completely what Jesus has **done** for you, your "doing" will flow effortlessly.

Hear what the great apostle of grace, Paul, had to say about this: "But by the grace of God I am what I am, and His grace toward me was not in vain; but I labored more abundantly than they all, yet not I, but the grace [unmerited favor] of God which was with me."[7] So my friend, in answer to your question, I would say don't worry about what "man's part" is. Focus, like Paul, entirely on Jesus' part—His grace and His unmerited favor upon your life—and you will end up being energized by the Lord to pray more, read the Bible more and serve both God and your community more, simply because the unmerited favor of God is not in vain in your life. You will also realize that even the outworking of all that you do is not of yourself, but it is by His grace overflowing in you.

Some people think that grace will compromise God's holiness. Absolutely not! The standards that grace sets are much higher than the standards of the law of Moses. When you are under grace, you will effortlessly fulfill and even superexceed the expectations of the law of Moses! Come on, are you getting this? If you can understand what I am saying in this introduction, you have already been blessed!

Now, let me bring this introduction to a close. I don't know about you, but I feel the presence of Jesus as I write this to you. I have released what He has put in my heart for you. I want to give you a scripture premise for this book, because you may be asking why a book that's supposed to be about unmerited favor is turning out to be all about Jesus!

If you have the Amplified Bible, turn with me to 2 Peter 1:2. It is important that you see this in God's Word yourself:

> **May grace (God's favor) and peace** (which is perfect well-being, all necessary good, all spiritual prosperity, and freedom from fears and agitating passions and moral conflicts) **be multiplied to you in** [the full, personal, precise, and correct] **knowledge of God and of Jesus our Lord.**
>
> —2 PETER 1:2, AMP

It really is that simple. The unmerited favor of God will flow like a mighty torrential river into every parched area of your life, be it your physical body, marriage, career or finances, **when you see Jesus**! The more you increase in the knowledge of our loving Savior Jesus Christ and His finished work at the cross, the more God's unmerited favor will be multiplied in your life. And it is His unmerited favor that will cause you to enjoy success beyond your natural intelligence, qualifications and ability!

There are many quality writings by great men of God on favor, but what I want you to see in this book is that God's unmerited favor is not a topic. It is not a teaching. GOD'S UNMERITED FAVOR IS THE GOSPEL! God's unmerited favor is not a subject. It is a PERSON, AND HIS NAME IS JESUS. When you have Jesus, you have unmerited favor! Jesus and unmerited favor do not exist separately. Unmerited favor is embodied in His entire being and in His finished work at Calvary.

It is unfortunate that the word "grace" in the modern church has been made into a theological subject or classified as a doctrine. In the modern vernacular, the word "grace" has also been abused and devalued. For example, you are given "five minutes' grace" before parking charges are levied when you drive into the parking lot of many shopping malls. How that cheapens the word "grace"!

To help the modern reader understand the fullness of grace, I am going to use the words "unmerited favor" and "grace" interchangeably in this book because grace is the undeserved, unearned and unmerited favor of God. To help you see grace in a fresh and new light, whenever I quote scriptures in this book and the word "grace" appears, I will add in parentheses, "unmerited favor." I want you to begin to understand and see grace (unmerited favor) in its fullness.

This book is about your supernatural advantage for a successful life. By the end of this book, I trust that you will indeed begin to believe that Jesus is personally interested in your success. You are His precious child and He wants to see you succeed and reign in life. When you believe that, you will also start to depend on His unmerited favor for success in every area of your life.

It is my prayer that as you dive into the pages of this book, you will start seeing more of Jesus and start experiencing His unmerited favor in an unprecedented way. Get ready to experience God's supernatural success through His unmerited favor today! buddy,

Chapter 1

The Definition Of Success

he sweltering Egyptian sun blazes down on the bustling market. The distinctive scent of aromatic spices wafts over the countless rows of merchants calling out their wares and treasures brought here from far and wide. Looking over the crowd, you will find a colorful assortment of people: Dancers, musicians, thieves, busy housewives, pickpockets and wealthy landlords, all gathered here shopping, bargaining, eyeing over and sifting through the countless objects on display. Everything, from the intricate creations of precious metals to livestock, has a price. In fact, a slave can be yours for 20 pieces of silver. There are no rules here for fair exchange. A top bid will get you what you desire. An inferior one will leave you empty-handed.

Amid this hustle and bustle in the main square by the fountain stands a young man of about 17 years old, his neck and his hands bound firmly with coarse ropes. From the rope burns across his wrists and around his neck, you can tell that the merchants have not been kind as they hurried to reach the market in time to put their prize on display. They have heard a rumor that Potiphar, a high-ranking official from Pharaoh's court, is planning to make a purchase today.

The young man is dazed from so many days of walking. His legs keep buckling beneath him, his arms are weary from the constant tugging and his mouth is parched from the dry desert winds. He is in a foreign land where the people speak in an incomprehensible tongue. With nothing to his name, not even a loincloth to cover his modesty, he is bound and displayed, completely naked. In a short while, he would be inspected like an animal against his will, and sold into a lifetime of slavery.

And yet, God Himself calls this young man, named Joseph, a successful man!

Now, think about this for a moment, and imagine yourself in the scene of this Egyptian market. If you were among the many curious spectators and bystanders in the main square, would you consider this young man who is about to be sold into slavery "a successful man"?

Of course not!

Yet, God says in His own words that Joseph was a successful man.

> Now Joseph had been taken down to Egypt. And Potiphar, an officer of Pharaoh, captain of the guard, an Egyptian, bought him from the Ishmaelites who had taken him down there. **The Lord was with Joseph, and he was a successful man**; and he was in the house of his master the Egyptian.
>
> —Genesis 39:1–2

Success Is A Result Of Who You Have

God's definition of success is contrary to the world's definition. Corporate America measures success based on what **you** have done, what **you** have accomplished and what **you** have accumulated. It is based entirely on **you** focusing all your time, energy and resources in meriting titles and collecting accomplishments.

Now, we have witnessed how this self-indulgent accumulation has led to the subprime crisis, the decimation of investment banks and a widespread international financial meltdown.

My friend, I want to encourage you to begin to see that the world's model of success is unstable and built upon a foundation that is shakable. It may have the outward appearance of the good life, but it is temporal, and we have all seen for ourselves how the world's transient wealth can dissipate like smoke and easily slip away like the shifting sands in the desert.

It is the presence of the Lord in your life that makes you a success!

From Genesis 39:2, it is clear that success is not **what** you have, but rather **who** you have! Joseph literally had nothing materially, but at the same time, he had everything because the Lord was with him. The material things that you have accumulated or are feverishly trying to amass do not make you a success. It is the presence of the Lord in your life that makes you a success!

We need to learn to stop pursuing things and to start pursuing Him. God sees your relationship with Him as the only thing that you need for every success in your life. I can't imagine starting in a worse place than Joseph. He was completely naked. He had nothing! No bank accounts, no educational qualifications, no natural connections with people of influence, nothing. Thank God the Bible records a picture of Joseph who began with nothing, so that you and I can have hope today. If you think that like Joseph, you have nothing, well, you can start believing in the power of the presence of the Lord in your life. Start looking to Jesus and claim that promise in that scripture for yourself!

Let me show you how you can personalize this promise in your life. Insert your name here into God's promise for you:

"The Lord is with _____, and I am a successful person."

Now, read this aloud to yourself. Read it out loud a hundred times if you have to, and begin to see this as your reality. Stick this promise on your mirror, and every morning when you brush your teeth, remind yourself that today, as you go to work, as you go to school, as you start the day caring for your children at home (or do whatever it is that you need to do), the Lord is with you. And because He is with you, YOU ARE ALREADY A SUCCESS! When you have Jesus in your life, you are no longer trying to be a success; you ARE a success!

Saving You Is God's Job Description

Let me share with you a powerful truth hidden in the birth of Jesus. When Mary was engaged to Joseph, before they shared any intimacy as husband and wife, she was found to be with child through the Holy Spirit. Joseph, being a just man and not willing to make Mary a public spectacle, thought of a way to "put her away secretly."[1]

Bear in mind that at that point, Joseph did not yet know that the unborn child was of the Holy Spirit. He thought that Mary had committed fornication. Yet, this righteous man was not willing to expose her publicly. In those days, if you were found to have had sexual relations before marriage, they would stone you to death. That was the culture and law of the Jewish people at that time. But Joseph loved his wife-to-be, Mary, and wanted to protect her dignity and preserve her life as best he could.

Now, as Joseph was contemplating these things, an angel of the Lord appeared to him in a dream, saying, "Joseph, son of David, do not be afraid to take to you Mary your wife, for that which is conceived in her is of the Holy Spirit. And she will bring forth a Son, and you shall call His name **Jesus**, for He will save His people from their sins."[2] The name "Jesus" is *Yeshua* in Hebrew, which contains an abbreviation for *Yahweh*, the name of God in Hebrew. So the name "Jesus" literally means *"Yahweh is our Savior"* or *"The Lord is our Savior"*! What a beautiful name!

Every time you call the name of Jesus, the name that is above every other name, you are calling God Himself to save you. Saving you is Jesus' job description! Whatever the challenge or circumstance, whatever crisis you are in—physically, financially or emotionally—you can call on the name of Jesus and Almighty God Himself will save you!

My friend, you can take time to know the names of God, which He revealed under the old covenant, such as *Elohim*, *El Shaddai*, *El Elyon*, *Jehovah-Jireh*, *Jehovah-Rophe* and *Jehovah-*

Nissi. You can do a complete study on the names of God. I am not against that at all. I teach on the names of God in my church as well, but all these names will mean nothing to you if you don't know that God Almighty Himself, Jesus, wants to save you first from all your sins, then from all your challenges.

God can be all powerful, but if you are not confident that He is interested in your success, His power would mean nothing to you. So, you don't have to memorize all the names of God from the old covenant. What you need is a full revelation that Jesus, in the new covenant, is your *Savior*! What is Tiger Woods famous for? Golf! What is David Beckham famous for? Soccer! (No, he's famous for product endorsements!) What is Jesus famous for? Saving you!

Jesus is your Savior!

That's not all, my friend. The Bible goes on to say that "all this was done that it might be fulfilled which was spoken by the Lord through the prophet Isaiah, saying: 'Behold, the virgin shall be with child, and bear a Son, and they shall call His name **Immanuel**,' which is translated, 'God with us.'"[3] Now, it is very interesting for us to note that Jesus' name is not just Jesus! His name is also Immanuel, meaning the Almighty God is with us.

Jesus Is Immanuel, The Almighty God With Us

A precious brother shared with me that even as a believer years ago, he had a problem with alcohol, and every night he would be out drinking to the point that he could not even remember how he got home the next day. He tried everything he could to stop drinking, but failed over and over again.

One day, he went out with some friends for a game of squash, and after the game, he laid down on the ground to rest. As he was resting, he felt Jesus' presence come upon him, and in that very moment, the Lord broke his addiction to alcohol and completely removed his desire to drink!

Today, this brother whom the Lord delivered from alcoholism is a key leader in my church. Isn't it just like God to take the weak things of the world to confound the mighty, and the foolish things of the world to confound the wise?

You know, all our struggling, willpower, discipline and self-effort cannot do what the presence of the Lord can do in an instant. And who is to say that as we are talking about Jesus now, His presence will not take away something that is destructive in your life? You see, you are transformed not by struggling. You are transformed by beholding Jesus and believing that He loves you and wants to save you.

Now, what does it mean to say "God with us"? We must understand it the same way the Hebrew people would have understood it. There is something beautiful here—this is the secret of Immanuel! The Jewish mind understands that when the Lord is **with you**, you become successful in every endeavor in your life. Don't just take my word for it. Look through the chronicles of Jewish history. The Bible records that whenever the Lord was **with them** in battle, the children of Israel were never defeated, and every military campaign ended in overwhelming success.

In fact, in the battle for Jericho, the city was theirs with just a shout![4] Why? The Lord was with them. Even in battles when they were outnumbered, they triumphed because the Lord was with them. It is no different in the modern context. When the Bible says that Jesus is with you, He is with you to help you, assist you, turn things around for you and make good things happen for you. He is not with you, as some wrongly believe, to condemn, judge or find fault! When Almighty God is with you, good things will happen in you, around you and through you. I have seen that time and time again!

When Almighty God is with you, good things will happen in you, around you and through you.

I learned the truth of what it means to have the Lord with me early on in my teens. One of the first truths that the Holy Spirit taught me was Genesis 39:2—"The Lord was with Joseph, and he was a successful man..." So you know what? I began to claim that verse every day and I would say out loud, "Jesus is with me, so everything I do will succeed." I was practicing the presence of Jesus. It is one thing to give mental assent that Jesus is with you, but it is another thing to start being conscious of Jesus' presence. You can start practicing His presence by speaking it out.

Practice His Presence And See His Power

Do you know that the best time to thank Jesus for His presence is when you don't "feel" His presence? When it comes to the presence of Jesus, don't go by your feelings. Feelings can be deceptive. Go by His promise that He is Immanuel!

Have you heard the story of a groom who approached his

pastor almost immediately after his wedding ceremony? He went up to his pastor and said, "Pastor, can I talk to you for a second?"

"Sure," the pastor replied.

The groom said, "You know what, I don't **feel** married."

The pastor grabbed him by the collar and growled, "Listen, boy. You ARE married whether you feel it or not, understand? Just take it by faith that you are married!"

Feelings aren't based on truth. God's Word is truth!

You see, my friend, you can't go by your feelings. You go by the truth and the truth is this: God promised, "I will never leave you nor forsake you."[5] So the best time to practice His presence is precisely when you **feel** like Jesus is 100,000 miles away. Remember that feelings aren't based on truth. God's Word is truth!

Anyway, soon after I graduated from high school, I took on a part-time job to teach in an elementary school where I was placed in charge of a class of 10-year-olds. I remember one day, when I was practicing His presence, I knelt down in my living room and prayed, "Lord, I just thank You that You are always with me." As I was on my knees, the Lord told me to pray specifically for one of the girls in my class who had been absent from school that day.

Now, it is very common for kids to miss class now and then for various reasons, and I had never been led by the Lord to pray specifically for any of them. This girl was the first! The Lord told me very clearly to pray for His protection to be over this girl and to cover her with His precious blood.

The next day, there was a big commotion in the school and I found out that the girl had been kidnapped by a notorious serial killer that very afternoon that the Lord had told me to pray for her. The killer, Adrian Lim, had kidnapped several children to be offered up as sacrifices to the devil. He believed that Satan would give him power when he offered the blood of these children to him.

Over the next couple of days, this girl from my class was all over our national media because she had been miraculously released. Sadly, she was the only girl released. All the other kidnapped girls had been brutally murdered.

When she returned to class, I asked her how she came to be freed. She told me that her kidnapper was chanting over her when suddenly he stopped and told her, "The gods do not want you." She was quickly released that evening. Of course, you and I know why the "gods" didn't want her—she was covered and protected by Jesus' blood!

Listen to what I am saying here. In America today and around the world, the devil is trying to destroy a new generation because he is afraid that the young people of the new millennium are going to take over the world for Jesus. That is why we have to cover our children with Jesus' protection.

I am sharing all this with you because I want you to see the importance and power of practicing His presence. As a teacher during that time, my class was my responsibility, just like my congregation is my responsibility today. Think with me: How in the world, with my finite knowledge and intelligence, could I have known that one of my students was in grave danger? It is not possible! But because the Lord, who knows all things, was with me, He made me a successful teacher.

Similarly, whatever role or vocation you are in, whether you are a schoolteacher, business leader or homemaker, I want you to know that Jesus is with you and He wants to make you a success. Now, remember, all this happened to me before I became a full-time pastor, so please don't think that this unmerited favor from Jesus is only for pastors. Beloved, His unmerited favor is for you. The Lord Immanuel is **with you**.

Whatever role you are in, Jesus is with you and
He wants to make you a success.

You see, it is not us; it is Him. If Jesus is with us, He will give us success in all that we do and cause us to have good results in every area of our lives to the glory of God. If God can do it for Joseph, a young man sold into slavery, He can do it for you! Let this be your reality:

"The Lord is with _____, and I am a successful person."

As you become conscious of how Jesus is with you, you'll see Him leading you to success in all that you need to do!

Chapter 2

Everything You Touch Is Blessed

B y now, I hope you can see that God's definition of success is contrary to the world's. The world looks at **what** you have, while God sees **who** you have. The world's system is based on what you have done, while God looks at what Jesus has done on the cross for you. It sounds simple, but don't dismiss it just because it's simple. The gospel is simple, and it takes theologians to complicate it!

You can make a choice to live your life depending on yourself to merit, earn, accomplish, fight for and accumulate wealth and success according to the world's definition, or you can make a decision today to live your life depending wholly and completely on Jesus, His merit and His accomplishment on the cross for your every success. It essentially comes down to the question of dependence. Who are you depending on today—yourself or Jesus? Do you want to fight for yourself, or do you want Almighty God, the Creator of the heavens and earth, to fight for you?

You see, when you depend on yourself, **you** carry all the stress, burdens and anxieties that your circumstances may present you. But if your dependence is on Jesus for every success in your life, the Bible records a beautiful promise for you: "Be anxious for nothing, but in everything by prayer and supplication, with thanksgiving, let your requests be made known to God; and the peace of God, which surpasses all understanding, will guard your hearts and minds through Christ Jesus."[1] When Jesus is your source of success, there is no stress and God's peace will garrison your heart and mind. The word "peace" in Hebrew is *shalom*. Its meaning includes peace, prosperity, health, completeness, soundness and safety. What a powerful fortress we have in Jesus!

In A Crisis? Jesus Can Rescue You

My friend, the circumstances around you may appear bleak. Your bank account may have dried up. You may have lost your source of income due to corporate restructuring and you may have no idea how you are going to pay next month's rent. Perhaps your home may be up for foreclosure soon. You may be mired in credit card debt, and the friends that you once trusted may have disappointed you. Maybe you have just received a devastating medical report. The whole world seems to be crashing down around you, and you feel crushed, frustrated and disappointed.

Now, what can you do? Beloved, now is the time for you to turn away from yourself and look to Jesus. In your frustration, you may be wondering, "What can Jesus do for me? Can He rescue me from the crisis that I am in?" The answer is sure—yes, He can! That's what He did for Joseph and He can certainly do the same for you!

Joseph—The Apple Of His Father's Eye

Let's continue to draw powerful truths from the life of Joseph in the Bible. His story begins in Genesis 37. His father made no secret about the fact that he loved Joseph more than all his other children, and made an exquisite tunic of many colors that was given to Joseph only. The Hebrew words for "tunic of…colors" are *kethoneth pac*. The phrase means a coat of pieces of various colors. The coat is a long tunic with sleeves worn by young men and maidens of the better class, a dress of distinction.[2] Thus, this tunic was distinct from the ordinary laborer's garb worn by his older brothers. Joseph's tunic was not woven out of the coarse linen used for normal clothing, but was skillfully woven from fine, high-grade linen. Why is this important? It is important because it did not only mean that Joseph had better-looking clothes compared to his brothers, but it also meant that the tunic was a sign to all that Joseph enjoyed a higher status in his father's eyes.

This fine linen tunic set Joseph apart from his brothers in terms of their responsibilities in the family. It meant that unlike his brothers, Joseph did not need to work in the fields and tend the flock. All he had to do was to attend to his father and bring his father pleasure. What an awesome job description! That is why we find that Joseph was mostly by his father's side while his brothers were laboring under the sweltering sun.

Joseph's tunic, therefore, speaks of a special position of favor and rest with his father. It is no wonder then, that every time Joseph's brothers saw him wearing this tunic, they were reminded that their father loved Joseph more than any of them. Filled with jealousy and envy, they hated Joseph and could not speak peaceably with him. Furthermore, Joseph shared with his brothers the two dreams that he had received from the Lord and these dreams only exacerbated their hatred toward him. They ridiculed his dreams angrily and mocked him saying, "Shall you indeed reign over us? Or shall you indeed have dominion over us?"[3]

Joseph Betrayed By His Brothers

One day, as Joseph's brothers were out tending their father's sheep in the fields of Dothan, they saw Joseph approaching from a distance and waving innocently at them. They knew that he was sent by their father to check on them, and they burned with resentment as they recalled how this little squealer brought a bad report to Jacob the last time he had come to spy on them.

Overcome with rage and compounded jealousy toward Joseph, his brothers conspired to kill him. They said to one another, "Look, this dreamer is coming! Come therefore, let us now kill him and cast him into some pit; and we shall say, 'Some wild beast has devoured him.' We shall see what will become of his dreams!"[4]

Bright-eyed and unsuspecting, Joseph headed toward his brothers, ready to embrace them. Without warning, his brothers seized him and violently stripped him of his beautiful tunic. Struggling frantically all the while, he was dragged toward a nearby pit and shoved into its cavernous depths.

Any notion that his brothers were perhaps playing a prank on him dissipated from Joseph's mind when they returned awhile later, only to heave his gagged and bound body into the hands of a gang of Midianite traders on their way to Egypt. The next time we see Joseph, he is trussed up in ropes and sold like a piece of meat in an Egyptian market.

It's Not The End When The Lord Is With You

Do you know of anyone who is in a worse situation than Joseph was at this point? His whole world appeared to have collapsed around him. Just a few days earlier, he was in his father's embrace but now, his own brothers had betrayed him. All that he owned had been stripped from him. He was reduced to nothing more than a slave in a foreign land.

It is not what you have. It is who you have that makes all the difference.

Was this the end of Joseph? In the natural scheme of things, it sure looked like it was. But even with the odds stacked up against Joseph, the Lord was far from finished. We learned in the previous chapter that even in this dire situation, the Lord was with Joseph, and at this dark and bleak juncture in Joseph's life, the Lord called him a successful man! Remember, it is not what you have. It is **who** you have that makes all the difference.

"How can the Lord make a young slave with not a single cent or possession to his name succeed?"

Well, let's continue with Joseph's story. Genesis 39:3 tells us, **"And his master [Potiphar] saw that the Lord was with him [Joseph] and that the Lord made all he did to prosper in his**

hand." This is a powerful statement and it offers a promise that you can believe Jesus for, in every area of your life. Can you imagine every project, assignment and even errand that you undertake becoming prosperous? Your hands become hands of blessing. You touch your family members and they are blessed. Your company may be struggling to manage a difficult project, but once it is placed in your hands, the project becomes blessed. You become a blessing waiting to happen to someone, waiting to happen to something, everywhere you go!

God's Presence In All That We Do

Now, how will this happen? The Lord Jesus will make it happen when you depend on Him in the same way that Joseph depended on Him. Joseph had nothing. He could not trust in his skills or experience (he had never been a slave), nor could he trust in his natural connections (his father was out of the picture because he believed that Joseph had been killed by a wild animal). All Joseph had was the Lord's presence, and he depended on the Lord to manifest His presence, His power and His glory through him!

When God's presence is made manifest in your life,
that's when His glory shines forth through you.

That's what you and I need—a manifestation of His presence in everything that we do! You see, it is one thing to have His presence (all Christians have His presence because they have accepted Him as their personal Lord and Savior), but when His presence is **made manifest** in your life, that's when His glory shines forth through you!

Even Potiphar, A Heathen, Could See It

Don't forget that Joseph's master, Potiphar, was not a believer in God. He was an Egyptian who worshipped idols. Yet, when the manifested presence of the Lord shone gloriously through the work of Joseph's hands, even this unbelieving heathen could see the tangible results of the Lord's special anointing, power and blessing upon Joseph's life. Potiphar marveled and could not but acknowledge that the Lord was with Joseph, and that "the Lord made all he did to prosper in his hand."

Now, isn't it interesting that Potiphar did not merely conclude that Joseph was a good worker? Instead, Potiphar could see that it was not Joseph's skills, but rather, his God who was prospering all that Joseph set his hands to. Genesis 39:3 tells us that "the Lord made all he did to prosper in his hand." This could not have been "spiritual discernment" on Potiphar's part—he was not a believer and had no spiritual discernment when it came to the things of God. So this tells me that Potiphar must have witnessed tangible results that were really out of this world. He must have seen results that were so spectacular that he knew they were beyond that of an ordinary human being!

Perhaps Potiphar ordered Joseph to dig new wells for his household and every well that Joseph dug yielded water even in the midst of a drought. Perhaps the field that Joseph tended yielded crops that were shockingly bigger than the crops in the surrounding fields. Perhaps Potiphar saw how Joseph called upon his God when the children in the house were suffering from some epidemic in the land, and they were all healed. Whatever the case was, Potiphar knew that the prosperous results he had witnessed were not a result of Joseph's natural abilities. They had to be due to the fact that the Lord was with Joseph, and God made all he did to prosper in his hand. Isn't that beautiful?

Desire To Have The Jesus-Kind Of Results

My personal prayer and desire for my ministry is to have the same kind of results that Joseph had. In everything that I do, I want people to see Jesus and Jesus alone! When I pray for a sick child, I certainly do not want the results that my own hands can produce. If the results are what Joseph Prince alone can produce, I can guarantee you that the child will remain sick. No, I want the results that only Jesus can produce! When I preach about Jesus and His finished work, my prayer is that my church congregation and those who are watching our broadcasts around the world would hear not what **I** have to say, but rather, what **Jesus** is speaking to their hearts through me.

Desire the results that only Jesus can produce!

I am but a vessel, and my words alone have no power. But at His Word, sinners get born again and are saved for all eternity. Sick bodies are healed. Demons flee, marriages are restored and families brought together. Debts are supernaturally cancelled, fears disappear in His perfect love, hearts are encouraged, hope is restored and joy is renewed. Now, THAT is the Jesus-kind of results that I want, and by His amazing and unmerited favor, we have seen all these blessings happening in our church week after week!

Not Our Doing But God's Unmerited Favor

Sadly, the world and even some Christians do not understand what it means to depend on Jesus. For instance, some people think that Joseph Prince somehow grew New Creation Church from 150 members to over 19,000 members today because of some clever strategy or comprehensive 10-year growth plan. A senior Christian pioneer in my country once asked me what I was doing to grow the church. I replied that it was all by grace—Jesus' unmerited favor. He replied, "Yes, yes, I know that it's by grace, but really, what are you doing?"

When you stop doing and start depending on God's divine favor, you will begin to experience the Jesus-kind of results.

Unfortunately, in many Christian circles, "grace" has become a cliché. You see, people are occupied with "doing." They always want to know what you are doing right to get the results that you have. The point of this book is to encourage you to not focus on what you are doing, but to focus on beholding Jesus. Stop trying to merit God's blessings and start depending on Jesus' unmerited favor for every success in your life. When you stop doing and start depending on His divine favor, trust me, you will begin to experience the Jesus-kind of results.

In the same way, I am believing for the Jesus-kind of results in *your* life as I write this book. I do not want you to read what I have to say to you. I want you to receive what I believe Jesus has put in my heart for you. I am but a pointer and I am writing this book to point you to the person of Jesus! It is His manifested presence, His glorious power working in your heart and through your hands that will cause everything you touch to prosper with the Jesus-kind of results, such that even your harshest critic will have to conclude that the Lord is with you and is prospering the work of your hands!

Beloved, stop looking at your outward circumstances or the position you are in. Whether your employer is a believer or not, Jesus can make ALL that you do prosper when you depend on His unmerited favor in your career! And believe me, when that begins to happen, your employer will sit up and notice that there is something special about you. You will stand out in a crowd! Remember that the same Lord who was with Joseph is with you today. His name is Jesus and because Jesus is **with** you, you can expect good success in everything that you do!

Because Jesus is with you, expect good success in everything that you do!

For example, when you are placed over a sales project, believe that your sales team will hit record levels of sales never achieved before in your organization. When you are overseeing the finances of a company, believe that you will find legal ways to help your company save on operating expenses and increase its cash flow like never before. When you are placed in a business development role, believe that Jesus will cause doors that have always been closed to your company to be opened to you because of His unmerited favor upon your life. Perhaps your company is just a small IT start-up in the Silicon Valley, but for some reason, all the big boys in Microsoft, IBM and Oracle like you. They can't put their finger on it, but there is just something special about you that makes them compete to find ways to collaborate with you, leaving you spoiled for choice!

> *Depend on Jesus and Jesus alone, if you*
> *want to experience His success.*

My friend, that's the unmerited favor of God in action. In the natural, you may be unqualified and inexperienced, but remember that all your disqualifications exist in the realm of the natural. You, beloved, live and operate in the supernatural realm! The Lord Jesus is with you 100 percent. You are a successful person in the Lord's eyes and as you depend on Him, He will cause everything that your hands touch to prosper.

Without Him, We Cannot. Without Us, He Will Not

Before I end this chapter, I want to teach you a powerful principle to help you understand God's heart for your success. I trust that by now, you have no doubt in your heart that Jesus is infinitely interested in your success. However, you may be wondering, "If that's the case, why isn't every Christian I know experiencing the Jesus-kind of success in their lives?"

In more than two decades of ministry, I have learned this from the Lord: **Without Him, we cannot. Without us, He will not.** What this simply means is that we need to recognize the fact that if we do not depend on Jesus, there can be no real, long-lasting and abiding success—without Him, we cannot. The Bible tells us that unless the Lord builds the house, we labor in vain.[5] Believers who want to experience His success need to recognize this truth and begin to depend on Jesus and Jesus alone.

There are some believers who may not articulate it, but in their hearts, they believe that without Jesus, they can still succeed. By believing and acting on this, they fall from the high place of God's grace (His unmerited favor) back into the law, back into trying to merit and deserve success by their own efforts. God's Word tells us, "For if you are trying to make yourselves right with God by keeping the law, you have been cut off from Christ! You have fallen away from God's grace [unmerited favor]."[6]

These are strong words of warning. Once you start depending on your own merits and efforts to deserve God's favor, you are back under the system of the law. You are cut off from Christ and have fallen from the place of having His unmerited favor work in your life. Don't misunderstand me, Jesus is still with you (He will never leave you nor forsake you[7]), but by depending on your self-efforts, you effectively cut off His unmerited favor in your life.

So what do I mean when I say, "Without us, He will not"? Well, Jesus is a gentleman. He will not force His unmerited favor and success down your throat. He needs you to allow Him to work in your life. He waits patiently for you to trust Him. He waits patiently for you to depend on His unmerited favor, the way Joseph trusted and depended wholly on the Lord's presence, until His manifested presence took over, and His glory radiated from everything that Joseph touched.

Beloved, let's learn quickly that without Jesus, we cannot succeed, and if we choose not to respond to His unmerited favor, He will not force it on us. God's unmerited favor is ever-flowing toward us and Jesus is waiting for us to come to the end of ourselves. He is waiting for you to stop struggling in your own attempts to somehow "deserve" His favor, and just depend on Him. So start resting in Jesus' unmerited favor and begin experiencing His manifested presence and glory upon everything you touch!

Chapter 3

Becoming Safe For Success

s much as we are interested in the Jesus-kind of **results** in our lives, it is of equal importance that we desire the Jesus-kind of **success**. God does not want us to have success that will crush us. I am sure that you have heard many stories of people who receive a sudden windfall when they come into a large inheritance or strike the first prize in a lottery. However, for some of these people, the sudden wealth did not give them a better life. Instead, in many instances, we know that it corrupted and destroyed their lives.

Often, these people were not able to handle their so-called success, and ended up leaving their wives and allowing their families to break down before their eyes. Perhaps they bought all sorts of things and lived in huge houses. Yet, they still felt a chronic sense of loneliness, emptiness and dissatisfaction. The sad reality is that many of those who chanced upon such sudden wealth squandered it all away, and some even became bankrupt. Such results are clearly not the Jesus-kind of results, nor are they the Jesus-kind of success. Let me make it clear from the onset: God has no problem with you having money, but He does not want money to have you!

"But Pastor Prince, how can you say that God has no problem with us having money? Doesn't the Bible say that money is the root of all evil?"

Hold on a minute, that's not in the Bible. Let's be scripturally accurate. What the Bible says is this: "For **the love of money** is a root of all kinds of evil..."[1] Can you see the difference? Having money does not make you evil. It is the obsession with and intense love of money that lead to all kinds of evil. Just because a person has no money in his pocket does not mean that he is holy. He may well be thinking, dreaming and lusting after money all day long. You don't need to have a lot of money to have the love of money. If a person is always purchasing lottery tickets, going to the casinos and gambling in the stock market, this person clearly has a love for money. He is obsessed with getting more money.

He wants to bless you so that you can be a blessing!

When God called Abraham, He said to him, "...I will bless you...and you shall be a blessing."[2] You and I, who are new covenant believers in Christ, are called the seed of Abraham,[3] and like Abraham, we are called to be a blessing. Now, how can we be a blessing if we are not blessed in the first place? How can we be a blessing to others when we are always flat on our backs with sickness, living from hand to mouth, never having enough for our own family and always having to borrow from others? No way, my friend. God wants you healthy and strong, and He wants you to have more than enough financial resources so that you can be generous with your relatives, friends, community or anyone who needs help. How can you be in a position to help others if you need all the help you can get yourself? It's definitely not God's best for you if you barely have enough for yourself. He wants to bless you so that you can be a blessing!

The Gospel Of Jesus Christ Brings Supernatural Healing And Provision

"Oh, Pastor Prince, now I know that you are one of those health and wealth, prosperity gospel preachers!"

There is no such thing as a "prosperity gospel." There is only one gospel and that is the gospel of Jesus Christ. Through Jesus' finished work on the cross, you can depend on Him for His resurrection life to pulsate and flow in your physical body from the crown of your head to the soles of your feet. Sicknesses and diseases are not from God. On the cross, Jesus bore not just our sins, but also our sicknesses, diseases and infirmities, and "by His stripes we are healed"![4]

That's not all, my friend. On the cross, Jesus bore the curse of poverty! This is what the Word of God declares: "For you know the grace [unmerited favor] of our Lord Jesus Christ, that though He was rich, yet for your sakes He became poor, that you through His poverty might become rich."[5] Read 2 Corinthians 8 for yourself. The entire chapter is about money and being a blessing financially to those who are in need. So don't let anyone tell you that the verse is referring to "spiritual" riches.

One of the things that I always remind my church is this: Always read a verse in its context because when you take the "text" out of its "context," it becomes a con! Don't let anyone con you out of God's blessings in your life. Let me ask you again: How can you be a blessing to anyone when you are always sick and always borrowing from one person to repay another?

Religion is blinding. Religion will tell you that "God" wants you sick to teach you character and patience. Religion will tell you that "God" wants you poor, so that you will learn humility. It sounds so noble, doesn't it? But these are LIES from the pit of hell! Let me tell you this: It is the devil who wants you sick and poor, but the God I know has paid a heavy price to redeem you from the curse of sickness and poverty!

Let's take a step back from all our denominational teachings for a moment. Let's forget about religion and let's focus on **relationship**. As a parent, how would you teach your child character and patience? With sicknesses and diseases? Of course not! There are institutions where we put such parents! Again, as a parent, how would you teach your child humility? By cursing your child with poverty for the rest of his life? No way! Now, isn't it amazing how everything becomes crystal clear when we start thinking from the point of view of a parent, and put our own children in the picture?

When you start to think along the lines of relationship, everything will converge and you will begin to see things from God's perspective. He is our Father and He does not operate on the frequency of religion, where you build character through sickness, and humility through poverty. Our heavenly Father operates on the frequency of relationship, and through His unmerited favor in our lives, we learn character, patience and humility as we rest from our self-efforts and depend on Him.

The more we know our Father, the more we become like Him. This is how God causes us to grow from glory to glory in every area of our lives. It is simply by beholding Him![6]

You know that as parents, we always seek the best things for our children. How much more would our Father in heaven want the best things for us, His precious children? In the same way that you want your children to be healthy, God wants you to enjoy His divine health. And in the same way that you want your children to always have more than enough, God wants you to enjoy His supernatural provision. When He provides, get ready for a net-breaking, boat-sinking load.[7] Get ready for 12 baskets full of leftovers![8] The Bible puts things in perspective most clearly in Matthew 7:11—If you then, as imperfect parents "know how to give good gifts to your children, how much more will your Father who is in heaven give good things to those who ask Him"!

In the same way that you want your children to always have more than enough, God wants you to enjoy His supernatural provision.

Now, take a walk with me to the intensive care unit of any hospital. Look at the people there gasping to draw their next breath and groaning in anguish despite the painkillers being pumped into their ravaged bodies. Look at the inconsolable woman, who has just lost her husband, crying hysterically in the corridor. Then, look me in the eye and tell me that you really think that this is the work of our loving Father.

Then, walk with me through the malaria-infested streets of any slum, and look at the children scavenging through mounds of rubbish and gratefully eating any scrap of discarded food that they can find. Look at the young girls forced into prostitution and the scarred bodies of desperate parents who had no choice but to sell their organs to make ends meet. Then, look me in the eye again, and tell me that you believe poverty is from our Father.

Come on! Even the world has more common sense then some Christians! Look at what people like Bill and Melinda Gates, Warren Buffett and Bono are doing. They are using their fame, resources and time to fight against sickness and poverty. And here, we have believers who are completely blinded by religion, telling us that sickness and poverty are from God. I hope that you are beginning to see how warped and embarrassing this is.

God is not against you having money and material things.
He is against money and things having you.

My friend, get this right: God abhors sickness and He loathes poverty. He gave everything He had to annihilate sickness and poverty when He gave us His only Son, Jesus Christ, to die on the cross for us. He placed all of humanity's sin, as well as the curse of sickness and poverty on the body of Jesus. Right now, humanity only has to respond to Jesus' finished work, and their sins will be forgiven, their physical bodies will be healed and their poverty will indeed be history!

God wants you to be blessed spirit, soul and body. He is not against you having money and material things. But let me make it clear: He is against money and things **having you**. I often tell my church this: Use money and love people. Don't love money and use people. God wants you and your family completely blessed and having more than enough to be a blessing. But at the same time, He wants to be sure that success will not destroy you and cause your family to disintegrate. To be safe for success, keep your heart ablaze with passion for Jesus and His presence, rather than on empty materialistic things.

Safe For Success—Keep Your Eyes On Jesus

The Word of God says, "But seek first the kingdom of God and His righteousness, and all these things shall be added to you."[9] Now, what is the kingdom of God? The apostle Paul tells us in Romans 14:17 that the kingdom of God is not eating and drinking, but "righteousness and peace and joy in the Holy Spirit."

When you keep your eyes fixed on Jesus and pursue the kingdom of God, which is Jesus' righteousness, His peace and His joy, God's Word promises that "all these things" will be added to you. "These things" refer to what you will eat, drink and wear. Jesus tells us that you do not have to be consumed by these concerns. If your Father feeds even the birds of the air, even though they neither sow nor reap nor gather into barns, how much more will He take care of you, who are of much more value to Him than the birds![10]

Beloved, just keep your eyes on Jesus and His finished work on the cross. Not only will He add the things that you need in this life to you, He will also cause you to become safe for success. Now, turn with me to the Book of Jeremiah to see what the Lord says about having riches, wisdom and might.

"Let not a wise man boast of his wisdom, and let not the mighty man boast of his might, let not a rich man boast of his riches; but let him who boasts **boast of this, that he understands and knows Me**, that I am the Lord who exercises lovingkindness, justice, and righteousness on earth; for I delight in these things," declares the Lord.

—JEREMIAH 9:23–24, NAS

Let us be a people who will not depend on our own wisdom, might and riches (in summary, our own merits), but rather, let our boasting (dependence) be in understanding and knowing Jesus. Know that He is gracious and full of unmerited favor toward us. Know that He executes justice against all injustices. Know that He Himself is righteousness and He clothes us with His robes of righteousness. The more you focus on beholding Jesus in all His loveliness and the less you struggle to earn things by your own merits, the more you become safe for greater success in your life.

The more you focus on beholding Jesus in all His loveliness and the less you struggle to earn things by your own merits, the more you become safe for greater success in your life.

Let's continue our study on the life of Joseph. There are still many precious gems hidden in his life that we have not touched on, and I want you to see what it means when a man is safe for success. In the previous chapter, we saw how the Lord's manifested presence in his life made all that Joseph did to prosper. The results that Joseph produced were so spectacular that even Potiphar, an unbeliever with no spiritual discernment, could visibly see that the Lord was with Joseph. Potiphar was no fool. When he saw that whatever Joseph touched flourished in his hand, Joseph "found favor in his sight" and Potiphar quickly promoted Joseph to become the overseer of his house, putting "all that he had" under Joseph's authority. Then, the Bible records that the Lord blessed Potiphar's house "for Joseph's sake," and the blessing of the Lord was on all that Potiphar had in the house and in the field.[11]

My friend, the unmerited favor that you have with the Lord will overflow and lead to favor with the people around you. In your career, when Jesus causes everything that your hand touches to prosper, you will receive favor from your boss, and that will lead to accelerated increase and promotion. Believe that because *you*, child of God, are in the organization, your organization will thrive and be blessed. The Lord will bless the organization that you are in for your sake.

The Difference Between God's Unmerited Favor And Favoritism

We have seen that Joseph was a successful man because the Lord was with him, and because he depended on unmerited favor from God. It is also important for you to recognize that there is a significant difference between **God's unmerited favor** and **favoritism**.

God's unmerited favor is based entirely on Jesus' merit, and we received it through His finished work at the cross. We did nothing to deserve His favor. It is completely unmerited.

Favoritism, however, stinks of self-effort. Individuals who rely on favoritism for promotion have to resort to apple polishing, office politics, manipulative tactics, backstabbing and all kinds of compromises just to get what they want. They use all their efforts to open doors for themselves, and in the process, they lose themselves.

God has a higher and better way for you. It hurts Him to see His own precious children groveling like sycophants just to get ahead in life. If a door closes, so be it! Believe with full confidence that God has a better way for you. You do *not* have to depend on favoritism to keep opportunities open for yourself when you have God's unmerited favor on your side!

That was how Joseph operated. He depended on the Lord for his success, and not on favoritism, which would have required him to compromise his beliefs. When Potiphar's wife kept trying to seduce Joseph to sleep with her, Joseph stood his ground on the firm foundation of unmerited favor. By the way, I believe that Joseph faced a real temptation. Don't forget that Potiphar was a high-ranking officer. He was the captain of the guard, and a man of position, influence and wealth. As a man of the world, he would not have married an ugly woman for her inner beauty and would certainly not have married an 80-year-old grandmother! He would definitely have chosen a young, beautiful woman to be his wife, and she was possibly one of the most beautiful women in the land.

So there is no doubt that she was a real temptation to Joseph, and that is why Joseph had to run! This woman didn't just tempt Joseph once. The Bible tells us that "she spoke to Joseph day by day," enticing him to lie with her.[12] But Joseph refused, saying, "There is no one greater in this house than I, nor has he [Potiphar] kept back anything from me but you, because you are his wife. How then can I do this great wickedness, and sin against **God**?"[13]

From his words, it is clear that Joseph knew the source of his success, favor and blessings. He did not see giving in to Potiphar's wife as a great wickedness and sin against *Potiphar* alone, but against *God* too. He knew that every blessing that he had experienced was a result of **the Lord's** favor on him. He knew that it was not Potiphar who promoted him from a lowly slave to become the overseer of Potiphar's entire estate. It was the Lord!

Have A Living Relationship With Jesus And Walk In His Ways

Now, this is really beautiful. People sometimes ask me, "Pastor Prince, if you don't teach the Ten Commandments to your church, what is going to govern them?" My friend, the Lord Himself will govern them! Look at the life of Joseph. He lived many years before the Ten Commandments were given to Moses on Mount Sinai. Yet, he could look at Potiphar's beautiful wife, who was throwing herself at him, and say, "How...can I do this great wickedness, and sin against God?"

All this took place long before there was a commandment that said, "Thou shalt not commit adultery."[14] The question is, who taught Joseph? Who taught him that adultery was a great wickedness against God? Think about it. He was a young, red-blooded man who was far away from home, and he knew that sleeping with Potiphar's wife would have given him many other perks, if he wanted to depend on favoritism. He could have been bitter with God and with his brothers, who had betrayed him. He could have chosen to take full advantage of the situation that was presenting itself to him, since it appeared as if he had been abandoned by the only people that he cared about. Nobody was around and nobody would know. But guess what? Joseph had a relationship with God. He had a relationship with the King of kings. He knew that the Lord was with him every step of the way and that the Lord had not forsaken him.

Knowing that Jesus is your success makes you safe for success!

You see, we cannot have a relationship with the law, with two cold tablets of stone, but we can have a living relationship with Jesus, and He will put His laws upon our minds and write them on our hearts,[15] causing us to walk in His ways that lead to life. Joseph had no Ten Commandments governing him. All he had was a living relationship with the Lord. He knew that Jesus was His success, and that made him safe for success!

Chapter 4

Success Beyond Your Circumstances

The presence of Jesus is all that you need. It is exciting to enjoy His presence daily in everything that you do. The Bible records the story of a group of friends who broke through the rooftop of a house, so that they could bypass the crowds that were blocking their way to Jesus, and bring their paralytic friend before Jesus to be healed.[1] I love that "whatever it takes" spirit to be in the presence of Jesus. But you know what? Today, we don't have to climb mountains, swim vast oceans or even break through rooftops to be in His presence. Right where you are, Jesus, your Immanuel, is with you!

There is a powerful rhetorical question in the Bible and I encourage you to memorize it:

> If God is for us, who can be against us?
> —ROMANS 8:31

It is unfortunate that there are still some believers today wondering, "Is God really for me?" Well, my friend, the Word of God does NOT say "**maybe** God is for us" or "**hopefully,** God is for us." It simply says, "If God is for us, who can be against us?" Indeed, when God is for you, what opposition can come against you? When God Himself fights for you, defends you and vindicates you, what adversity or adversary can stand against you? There are none! Hallelujah!

"But Pastor Prince, how did God come to be on our side? Even though I am a Christian today, I still fail and fall short of God's holy standards. I still lose my temper on the road now and then, and from time to time, I still get angry with my wife and kids. Why should God be on my side when I fail? Don't you know that God's holy?"

Great question. Let me tell you why. The answer is found at the cross. The blood that Jesus Christ, the Son of God, shed on the cross put God on your side. Today, God can be **for** you even when you fail because Jesus' blood has washed you whiter than snow!

Have you seen Cecil DeMille's movie, *The Ten Commandments*, or the animation, *The Prince Of Egypt*? Do you remember what happened on the night of the Passover? The children of Israel put the blood of the lamb on their doorposts. What did the blood do? The blood put God on their side! None of the families who had applied blood on their doorposts had to fear the death of their firstborn children.

God is for you today because of the blood of the perfect Lamb—Jesus Christ.

Now, think about this for a moment. Were the firstborn children of Israel spared that night because of their perfect behavior and conduct, or were they spared because of the blood of the lamb? Of course, it was because of the blood of the lamb!

In the same way, God does not bless you, as a new covenant believer, based on your perfect behavior and conduct. He is **for you** today because of the blood of the perfect Lamb—Jesus Christ. That is why as believers today, we don't have to fight for ourselves. I like to say it this way: "If God is for us, who can come successfully against us?" Always remember that God is on your side today because of Jesus' blood. His holiness and righteousness that men are afraid of are now on your side because of Jesus' blood. His unmerited favor is on your side and all of heaven's resources are yours because of Jesus' blood! Now, who can come against you? No sickness, no disease, no creditor, no evil accusation, no gossip—no weapon formed against you, can come successfully against you![2]

You Can't Earn God's Favor Because It Is A Free Gift

"Well, Pastor Prince, Jesus is with some people because they do a lot of good. I don't do much good for God or for others, so how can Jesus be with me?"

Some people believe that doing a lot for charity or performing acts of kindness will put God on their side. Somehow, they have this idea that if they have donated significant amounts of money to the poor or volunteered their time to serve in church, all these doings will put them in favor with God and cause Him to be on their side. My friend, let us speak openly about this. God is not with you because of what you do or don't do, or because of what you have done or not done. That kind of thinking still places the focus on **you** and that is religion, not relationship!

All religions focus on you—what you shouldn't do, what you

should do and how often you should do something. Religion is all about you, you, you doing or not doing something in order to earn God's favor and get Him on your side. Christianity becomes a **religion** for Christians who believe that if they spend a lot of time reading the Bible, praying, fasting or volunteering their time in church, they will gain increased favor with God. They think that all their works will cause God to be on their side and answer their prayers.

But do you really think that God's arm can be twisted by your so-called religious works? Let me ask you: Does God answer your prayers because of your merit or Jesus' merit? Is He on your side because of your merit or Jesus' merit? Come on, it's important to get these foundational truths right and not slide in and out of trying to **deserve** God's favor when He wants us to **receive** everything through His unmerited favor. Am I saying that you shouldn't read the Bible, pray, fast or serve the Lord in church? No, a thousand times no! All that I am saying is that when you do these things, do them from a heart that **wants to**, and not from a heart that **has to** because of religious obligations.

Think with me for a moment. Would you like your spouse to spend time with you because he or she wants to, or because he or she *has* to? Do you think that our loving God is any different? Jesus is not interested in your religious works. In fact, He is not interested in religion at all! He is interested in you wanting to spend quality time with Him in His Word, so that He can talk to you, encourage you and impart the necessary wisdom to you for the day. It is not about you fulfilling a daily Bible reading quota, accumulating sufficient prayer minutes or fasting long enough in order to qualify for Jesus' blessings. Absolutely not.

If you do all that, it should be because you have an abiding revelation that Jesus' presence is with you, an understanding that His unmerited favor is toward you and a certainty that He is on your side. And out of that overflowing abundance of appreciation for His love that you are undeserving of, you desire to hear His voice and seek His face. You begin to trust in the Lord with all your heart and lean not on your own understanding. You begin to acknowledge Him in all your ways and allow Him to direct your paths.[3] Isn't it amazing how man, blinded by his self-efforts, can turn something so beautiful, like spending quality time with Jesus, into a work?

The presence of Jesus in your life is a free gift from God.
There is no amount of religious works that
you can perform to merit His favor.

My friend, God is **with you** today because of His precious Son, Jesus. For God so loved the world, He **gave** His only Son, and His name is Immanuel. God **gave** us Jesus. The presence of Jesus in your life is a free gift from God. There is no amount of good that you can do to earn the presence of Jesus. There is no amount of religious works that you can perform to merit His favor. His presence in your life is a free gift. Now, because you did **nothing** to deserve His presence in your life, there is **nothing** you can do that will cause His presence to leave you. Once you have received Jesus into your heart, He will never leave you nor forsake you![4]

"But Pastor Prince, when I fail, doesn't Jesus leave me?"

No, Jesus is right by your side to encourage you and restore you to wholeness. You may say, "But I don't deserve it!" That's right. That's what makes it His **unmerited favor** in your life. There is a beautiful psalm that says, "The steps of a good man are ordered by the Lord, and He delights in his way. Though he fall, he shall not be utterly cast down; for the Lord upholds him with His hand."[5] When you fail, Jesus is there to uphold you. Unlike some of your so-called "friends," He does not just take off. You can count on Him. He is a faithful, dependable and trustworthy friend. Even when you have failed Him, He is right there with you, ready to pick you up and restore you to wholeness. Amen! The Bible talks about a friend who "sticks closer than a brother."[6] That's Jesus!

The Divine Exchange

There was a time under the law in the Old Testament where God would be with you only when you were in complete obedience. But when you failed, He would leave you. Today, however, you and I are under a completely different covenant and God will never leave us. Why? Because of what Jesus did on the cross. At the cross, He became our burnt offering. He bore our sins and carried our punishment. God's judgment against our sins fell upon Jesus, who was forsaken at the cross by His Father so that today, we can have God's constant, unceasing presence in our lives.

Jesus cried out, "My God, My God, why have You forsaken Me?" so that you and I will know exactly what happened on the cross.[7] That is where the divine exchange took place. At the cross, Jesus took our sins and gave up the presence of God, while we took Jesus' righteousness and received the presence of God that Jesus had. God's presence is now ours for eternity. What a divine exchange!

When you are doing right, He is with you. Even when you have failed, He is still with you!

Take a look with me at what the Bible says about our inheritance in Christ: "…For He Himself has said, 'I will **never** leave you nor forsake you.' So we may boldly say: 'The Lord is my helper; I will not fear. What can man do to me?'"[8] What confidence we can have today! Do you know what "never" here means? It means that when you are up, He is with you. When you are down, He is with you. When you are glad, He is with you. When you are sad, He is with you. When you are doing right, He is with you. Even when you have failed, He is still with you! That is what it means when Jesus said that He would **never** leave you nor forsake you!

In case you are still not convinced, let me show you what it says in the original Greek text. When God said, "I will **never** leave you **nor** forsake you," a "double negative"[9] is used to convey the strongest sense of "never" possible in the Greek language. The Greek words *ou me* are used, which in essence means, "never never" or "never ever." And this double negative appears twice in this one statement from the Lord. *Ou me* is used for both "never" and "nor." In other words, God is saying, "I will never never leave you and I will never never forsake you!" The Amplified Bible brings out the strength of what God really meant:

I will not in any way fail you nor give you up nor leave you without support. [I will] not, [I will] not, [I will] not in any degree leave you helpless nor forsake nor let [you] down (relax My hold on you)! [Assuredly not!]

—HEBREWS 13:5, AMP

Wow, that is what Jesus has done for us! He has given us the constant presence of God! My friend, you need to settle it in your heart once and for all—God will **never** leave you! God will **never** forsake you! And if you hear anyone telling you that you can forfeit the presence of God, stop listening. Don't let that person rob you of the certainty of God's presence in your life. When God says "never ever," He *means* "never ever," and our God cannot lie!

Don't Evaluate God's Presence And Unmerited Favor Based On Your Circumstances

Now that you know that God's presence in your life is a guaranteed constant, I want you to recognize that you cannot evaluate God's presence and His unmerited favor in your life based on your circumstances. To help you understand what this means, let's continue our study on the life of Joseph and pick up the story from where we left off in the previous chapter.

Joseph has just refused the advances made by Potiphar's wife, and as the common saying goes, "Hell hath no fury like a woman scorned"! She maliciously accuses Joseph of attempting to rape her, brandishing as "evidence" the garments that Joseph had left in her hands when he fled from her. When Potiphar heard his wife telling her version of the story, his anger was aroused and he seized Joseph, stripped him from the place of authority he had given him and threw him into prison.

Just put yourself in Joseph's shoes. What is happening here? It sounds all too familiar, doesn't it? With the painful memory of his brothers casting him into the pit still fresh in his mind, here he is once again, cast into a dungeon even though he had not done anything wrong. Any average person would be bitter and angry with God! Most people would ask, "Where is God? Why had God brought him this far, only to abandon and forsake him? How could this happen? Where is the justice against this false accusation?"

But Joseph was literally no "average Joe"! He knew that the Lord would never leave him nor forsake him. Joseph considered not his circumstances, but kept his focus on the presence of the Lord. Regardless of whether he was a common slave, an overseer in Potiphar's house or now a prisoner facing the prospect of life imprisonment for a crime he did not even commit, Joseph did not evaluate God's unmerited favor in his life based on his circumstances. Instead of getting bitter, he kept his hope in the Lord. Instead of throwing in the towel and giving up on God and on life, he kept his confidence, knowing that all his success was wrapped up in the presence of the Lord.

And boy, did the Lord deliver him! I want you to read this for yourself to see what the Lord did for Joseph:

> But the Lord was with Joseph and showed him mercy, and He gave him favor in the sight of the

keeper of the prison. And the keeper of the prison committed to Joseph's hand all the prisoners who were in the prison; whatever they did there, it was his doing. The keeper of the prison did not look into anything that was under Joseph's authority, because the Lord was with him; and whatever he did, the Lord made it prosper.

—GENESIS 39:21–23

When You Have God's Unmerited Favor, You Cannot Help But Prosper

When the unmerited favor of God is upon you wherever you are, like it was upon Joseph, (1) you cannot help but find favor, (2) everything that you do cannot help but prosper, and (3) you cannot help but experience increase and promotion beyond your wildest imagination.

Can you see that this was the consistent pattern in Joseph's life? It didn't matter if he was a slave or prisoner. The same applies to you. When the unmerited favor of God is upon you, you are like a rubber ball in a pool of water. Natural circumstances can try to push you down and keep you suppressed under water, but the unmerited favor of God will always cause you to POP right up to the top!

Don't be discouraged by your current circumstances. I know things may sometimes appear bleak, dismal and perhaps, even devastating, but it ain't over, my friend. I wrote this book to tell you that it ain't over! I don't believe for one moment that among the millions of books in publication right now, you are holding this particular one by chance or coincidence. This is a divine appointment and I believe that God is saying this to you: "Don't give up just yet. It ain't over!"

There are many times where the lowest points in your life are actually the launching pads to God's greatest promotion in your life. It was so for Joseph! Let's rewind the tape and observe the fingerprints of the Lord through the ups and downs of Joseph's life. If Joseph had not been betrayed by his brothers, he would not have been sold as a slave. If he had not been sold as a slave, he would not have been in Potiphar's house. If he was not in Potiphar's house, he would not have been thrown into an Egyptian prison meant specifically for the king's prisoners. If he was not in that specific prison, he would not have interpreted the dreams of Pharaoh's officers. If he had not interpreted their dreams, he would not have been summoned to interpret Pharaoh's dream two years later. If he had not interpreted Pharaoh's dream, Pharaoh would not have promoted Joseph to become his prime minister over the entire Egyptian empire!

Your lowest points are launching pads to God's greatest promotions.

This is what Pharaoh said to Joseph: "Inasmuch as God has shown you all this, there is no one as discerning and wise as you. You shall be over my house, and all my people shall be ruled according to your word; only in regard to the throne will I be greater than you…See, I have set you over all the land of Egypt."[10] When we look back, it is clear that the Lord had turned Joseph's darkest hour into his finest hour!

You have seen how God's presence with Joseph and His

unmerited favor caused Joseph to be promoted from the pit to the palace, from the dunghill to Capitol Hill, from the outhouse to the White House. Stop looking at your circumstances and stop allowing them to discourage you. The same Lord who was with Joseph is with you right now. You cannot fail! You can expect to see success beyond your present circumstances!

Chapter 5

Practicing The Presence Of Jesus

et's look at some practical keys on how you can begin to **experience** God's manifested presence in your life by **practicing His presence**. It is one thing to know theoretically that God is with you, but to experience His presence, you have to increase your consciousness of His presence by practicing His presence!

This is not something difficult. In fact, it should be rather effortless. Do you know that even as you have been or are reading about Jesus right now, you have been and you are practicing the presence of Jesus? As you are reading about Jesus and discovering what He says in His Word about you, you have just become effortlessly more conscious of His presence with you right now.

And as you think of Jesus more and more, you will begin to experience a peace you never had, a strength like never before and a joy that you cannot describe with words. Wisdom starts to flow and your decision-making ability is sharpened. Just by being exposed to the presence of the Son of the living God, the breakthrough that you have been struggling for supernaturally occurs.

My friend, trees don't strain and struggle to produce fruit. Instead, with adequate exposure to sunlight and water, fruits are produced effortlessly. Similarly, with adequate exposure to SON-light and the living water of God's Word, good fruits are produced in your life effortlessly. Your victory is a fruit. Your success is a fruit. Your health is a fruit. Family harmony is a fruit. Career success is a fruit. All these good fruits are birthed just by you being in the presence of the Lord! Stress, depression, and anger fade away and no longer dominate your thoughts. Worry has no foothold in your mind. The consciousness of Jesus' perfect love for you removes every vestige of trepidation and fear. You feel and start behaving like the new creation in Christ that you are, regardless of your current circumstances. Hallelujah!

God's Presence Is With You To Make You A Success, Not Find Fault With You

Something very unique and precious happens when you see that the Lord is with you. Trust the Lord to open your eyes to see Him in your situation, and the more you see Him, the more He manifests Himself. If you are in the midst of committing to an important business agreement, I assure you that if you can see the Lord there with you, His wisdom will flow through you, and He will give you supernatural insight to locate any loopholes, details or exit clauses that are missing from that contract that you are about to sign.

Once you involve Jesus and acknowledge His presence, you will sense Him intervening in any decision you are about to make, through the absence or presence of His peace. Everything can appear to be in order on the surface, but somehow, if you sense a discomfort rising up in you every time you think about your decision, my advice to you would be to not rush into it. Once you have involved the Lord, the lack of peace that you feel is often His leading to protect you. You can even be in the midst of an argument with your spouse, but the moment you become conscious of the Lord's presence, your words will change. Somehow, there will be a supernatural restraint that you know is not from yourself. That is also the Lord!

God's presence is with you to direct you, to guide you, to lead you into becoming more like Christ, and to make you a success in every endeavor you undertake.

Before we continue, I just have to say this: It is important for you to eradicate the notion that the Lord is present to **find fault** with you. You may have been raised in an environment where your parents were constantly picking on your faults and pointing out your mistakes, but don't project this characteristic onto the Lord. God knows every idiosyncrasy about you, yet He loves you perfectly because He sees you through the lens of the cross, where His Son has removed **every** failing from your life!

So even your current argument with your spouse is washed by the blood of Jesus. The Lord's presence is with you **not** to judge you or to smack you on the head with a giant bat the moment you fail. No, my friend, His presence is with you to direct you, guide you, lead you into becoming more like Christ, and make you a success in every endeavor you undertake.

No matter where you are, the Lord is with you. Even in the

midst of your fears, while you are alone in your room, He is there with you. The moment you begin to be aware of His presence and cultivate His presence, all your fears, anxieties and worries will melt like butter on a hot day, or as the psalmist David puts it, "The mountains melt like wax at the presence of the Lord…"[1]

You cannot psych yourself out of fear nor can you psych yourself out of worry. You can't just tell yourself, "Come on, stop worrying. There is nothing to worry about." It just doesn't work. The debt will still be staring you in your face and your problems will still be as insurmountable as ever no matter how hard you try to psych yourself up. That is what the world is trying to do, but it does not work. It takes the presence of the Lord to keep you free from worry.

Jesus is not asking you to psych yourself up and live in a state of denial. No way! He is saying to you, "In the midst of your affliction, I am your shield. I am your defender. I am your fortress. I am your refuge. I am your supply. I am your healing. I am your provider. I am your peace. I am your joy. I am your wisdom. I am your strength. I am the glory and the lifter of your head!"[2] Amen! He is not asking you to pretend that the facts are not there. He wants you to realize that HE IS THERE WITH YOU!

When you know that He is with you and for you, and you put your problems in His mighty hands, you will begin to get a more accurate evaluation of just how "big" your problems are. When they were in your hands, the weight and burden of your problems may have crushed you. But when you involve Jesus, the once-monumental problems become microscopic in His hands!

God's Love For You Is Personal, Detailed And In-depth

Do you know why there are many believers today who don't cast their cares upon the Lord? It is because they don't have a revelation that He cares for them. Look at what His Word says: "casting all your care upon Him, for **He cares for you.**"[3] Unless you have absolute confidence that Jesus cares for you, you will not cast your cares upon Him. Just think, would you call upon the help of a relative or friend in your time of need if you were not confident that the person would respond to your call? Jesus cares for you. When you call upon Him, know that you have His fullest attention with all of heaven's resources backing you up!

Maybe you are thinking right now, "Well, I am sure that Jesus has more important things to do than to bother with my problem." Hang on. By saying that, you have just shown that you don't really believe that Jesus cares for you. Now, let's see what the Bible says: "But the very hairs of your head are all numbered. Do not fear therefore; you are of more value than many sparrows."[4]

I love and care for my sweet daughter, Jessica. But as much as I adore her and care for her well-being, I have never, not once, counted the number of strands of hair on her head! She does not know how great a blessing she has been to me. I love to kiss her, smell her hair and hug her tightly. Yet, in all my great love for her, I have never taken the time to count the number of strands of hair on her head in all these years!

But do you know that your heavenly Father numbers the very hairs on your head? I really hope that you are beginning to catch the heart of Jesus and not generalize His love for you. His love for you is all-encompassing. If He cares enough to keep track of the hairs on your head, is there anything too small for Him that you cannot talk to Him about?

God is vitally and intensely involved in the
day-to-day minute details of your life.

God's love for you is infinitely detailed. Jesus said that not one sparrow falls to the ground apart from the Father's will. Are you not of more value than a sparrow? Is God a God who winds the clock and leaves it alone to tick until Jesus comes back? Is He only involved with major events in the world? Is He only involved in significant events in our lives like our salvation, or is He vitally and intensely involved in the day-to-day minute details of your life? What do you think? The Bible says that He calls His own sheep by name.[5] My friend, His love for you is personal, detailed and in-depth!

See Jesus In The Midst Of Everything That You Do

When you study your Bible, knowing that the Lord is with you, you will be amazed at how God's Word comes alive. That is how I read the Word. I don't study just to prepare for messages to preach on Sundays. I come to the Word to drink of the living waters from Jesus. I am conscious that Jesus is by my side, teaching me, speaking to my heart, and I can tell you that we have the best conversations during these times and I always come away from such times feeling refreshed and energized.

Reading His Word has become a great personal time of intimacy between Jesus and me. I get completely lost and absorbed in His presence until I lose track of time. I can't tell you the number of times when I had looked up at my clock after digging into His Word and realized that it was already five in the morning! You know what it's like when you are enjoying a steaming cup of latte in a café with friends that you love, and you are having so much fun, laughing and sharing, that time just seems to disappear? Well, you can enjoy Jesus' presence in the same way!

Once you are conscious that Jesus is with you, reading the Bible no longer feels like a chore or duty. You won't catch yourself watching the clock going tick…tick…tick…tick…tick…and feeling as though an eternity has passed even though only five minutes has lapsed! That is what a chore feels like—as if time is standing still and you can't wait to get it over with. Bible study divorced from His presence is a dead work. But when it is like catching up with your best friend, there never seems to be enough time!

See the Lord in the midst of everything that you do and learn to bring Him into the picture. He makes everything beautiful in your life. When you look at your past, the scars of yesterday may still be throbbing in your memories. Perhaps you were sexually abused as a child or you were emotionally hurt by someone you trusted. As you look back now, you still feel angry, frustrated and disappointed all at the same time, and the hurt still pierces your heart. But in the midst of your pain, I want to challenge you to start involving Jesus. See the Lord holding you, gently healing your wounds. Jesus is right there restoring you, putting courage into your heart and taking away all the sense of shame and guilt.

Beloved, He wants you to know that your past will not determine the future that He has for you. Once you involve the Lord and put Him into your bitter waters, He will turn the bitterness into sweetness. That is what the Lord did for the children of Israel. When they came to a place called Marah, they could not drink its waters because they were bitter. Moses cried out to the Lord and the Lord showed him a tree, which Moses cast into the waters. When he did that, the Bible says that "the waters were made sweet."[6]

Your past will not determine the future that God has for you.

Why did the foul-tasting, undrinkable waters become refreshing and sweet? The answer lies in the tree that was cast in. The tree is a picture of the cross on which our Lord Jesus hung, bearing every broken heart and every sting of betrayal. When you bring Jesus into your situation, He can cause every bitter experience to become sweet! Talk to Him and allow His presence to restore you today!

When You Practice Jesus' Presence, His Glory, Beauty And Power Will Rub Off On You

David is a wonderful example of someone who talked to the Lord and practiced His presence all the time. Even as a young teenager taking care of his father's sheep in the fields, he would be singing psalms and hymns to the Lord and playing his harp.

In 1 Samuel 16, the Bible records that King Saul was very unsettled, and his servants told him that he was being troubled by a distressing spirit. They then advised him to bring David before him to play the harp for him, saying that evil spirits departed when David played the harp. One of the servants gave a glowing description of David as someone "…who is skillful in playing, a mighty man of valor, a man of war, prudent in speech, and a handsome person; and the Lord is with him."[7] Do you know why David could cause Saul to become refreshed just by playing his harp? Do you know why David could have such accolades heaped upon him? I believe that the key is in the last part of the verse: "the Lord is with him."

A few years after Wendy and I got married, an incident happened that I will never forget. I was on my way home one day and I had stepped into a cramped elevator. A group of ladies squeezed into the same elevator as it stopped on another floor and boy, their perfumes were so thick and overpowering they must have been wearing Chanel No. 1,000!

You cannot be in the presence of the Lord without His glory, His majesty, His beauty, His power, His love and His peace rubbing off on you.

Anyway, almost dizzy from near-suffocation, I got home and kissed Wendy with my usual "Hello darling, I'm back." Then, she looked at me and said, "That's a female fragrance. I know that fragrance." I told her, "Listen, darling, listen…honestly, just now…" And that's why it's so important to have trust in your marriage!

I am sure that you have experienced something similar before. Have you ever walked through a restaurant or some other place that is filled with smoke? You may not smoke, but your hair and clothes become infused with the smell of smoke by the time you get through the place. In the same way, you cannot be in the presence of the Lord without His glory, His majesty, His beauty, His power, His love and His peace rubbing off on you. You begin to "smell" like Jesus, be powerful like Him and be filled with peace like Him! No wonder Acts 4:13 records this about Peter and John: "Now when they [the rulers and elders of Israel] saw the boldness of Peter and John, and perceived that they were uneducated and untrained men, they marveled. And they realized that **they had been with Jesus**."

Practice The Presence Of Jesus In Your Career

Wherever you are, whatever it is that you do, with the Lord's presence and His unmerited favor covering you, there is no way you will not be a success. When I started working in my early twenties, I kept on practicing the presence of Jesus and in a short time, I became the top salesperson in my company. I not only closed the biggest deals for my company, but I also secured the greatest frequency of sales transactions.

I started as one of the lowest-paid employees in the company, but the Lord consistently promoted me, and gave me different income streams from within the same company until I became one of the highest-paid employees in that organization. Please understand that I am not sharing this with you to put a feather in my cap. I know beyond the shadow of a doubt that all the successes that I have experienced in my professional career are a result of Jesus' presence and unmerited favor in my life.

I shared with you about my professional career (before

I entered full-time ministry) so that you will not walk away thinking that I have personally experienced good success from the Lord only because I am a pastor. No. Like I mentioned earlier, whatever vocation you are in, you can experience the presence of Jesus and His unmerited favor, and **He** will make you a success!

Whether you are a chef, driver or consultant, it doesn't matter. God is on your side to bless and make you a success. Of course, you understand that I am referring to only morally upright professions. You cannot depend on God's unmerited favor if you are in an industry that requires you to compromise on your Christian morals. If you are involved in a morally corrupt industry or a job that expects you to lie, cheat or deceive, my advice to you is to get out! You do not have to depend on a job that puts you in a morally compromising position for your income. God loves you intimately and He has something so much better in store for you. Trust Him.

God is here to save you from destroying yourself. He wants to give you good success and He loves you too much to see you remain in a job that forces you to compromise. The Bible says, "A good name is to be chosen rather than great riches, loving favor rather than silver and gold."[8] God has a higher way and better plan for your life!

Practice Jesus' Presence By Thanking And Appreciating Him

There are Christians who know in theory that Jesus is with them, but they do not actively practice His presence. For me personally, one of the best ways to practice the presence of the Lord is to thank Him all the time. You can give thanks to Him for everything. Just say, "Lord, I thank You for this beautiful sunset. I thank You for Your love and for surrounding me with good things and good friends."

There is no limit to what you can thank Him for since every good and perfect gift that we enjoy today comes directly from Him.[9] Even if you have had a rough day at work and you are facing a seemingly impossible challenge, you can practice His presence. The moment you realize that your heart is heavy with worry and your mind is plagued by anxiety, share your challenge with Jesus and thank Him that this problem is not bigger than His hands. Begin to surrender it to Him and depend on Him for His strength, power and peace.

As you do that, you are already practicing the presence of the Lord. And as you honor His presence and behave like He is indeed with you, He sees it as faith in Him and intervenes on your behalf for your success in whatever situation you may be in.

It is sad when Christians behave like some husbands who bring their wives to a party, only to ignore them completely. Their wives could be right there with them physically, but these guys are so engaged with their own friends, talking about the stock market, economy or latest game on television, that their wives might as well not be with them.

Ladies, do you know men like that? Now, men who are reading this book, I know you are not like that, so don't get offended, all right? I know you cherish and love your wife. What I am trying to illustrate is that just because someone is with you physically, it does not mean that the person feels appreciated by you. Appreciation only occurs when you start acknowledging the presence of that person.

What I like to do is to look at Wendy across a room crowded with people, and when our eyes connect across the room, it is as if the rest of the people fade instantly into oblivion, and only Wendy remains. I want her to know that I appreciate her for coming along with me to that dinner event or meeting. I am not claiming that I am sensitive to Wendy all the time, but there are moments, and I do want to make it a point to make her feel special. She is special to me, but to actually appreciate her and to make her *feel* special is something else all together. Anyway, like all husbands, I am still growing in this aspect.

What you appreciate appreciates in value in your eyes.

Now, what does the word "appreciate" mean? It means "to increase in value." If you appreciate someone, the person increases in value in your eyes. My friend, the Lord is already with you, so start to practice His presence. Begin by thanking Him, appreciating Him and increasing His value in your eyes.

What did David mean when he said, "Oh, magnify the Lord with me..."?[10] Can we make God bigger? Of course not. The Lord is already very big. But the problem is that sometimes, our concept of Him is way too small. It reminds me of the story of a boy who was playing by the seaside. He was happily running back and forth between his sand castle and the sea, pouring pail after pail of water into the moat that he had dug around his sand castle. When it was time to leave, his little face clouded over and he tugged at his mother's sleeve worriedly. "Mummy," he said, "I think that the sea might be running out of water because I took so many pails of water from it."

Whether we are aware of it or not, that's how we see God sometimes. We are afraid to draw from Him, not knowing that His resources are endless. We become like that little boy who feared that he would dry up the ocean with his little plastic pail. So David said, "Hey brothers, come on, let us magnify the Lord. Let's make Him bigger in our hearts, in our minds, in our consciousness. Come on, magnify the Lord with me!" We cannot make the Lord bigger than He already is, but we sure can make Him bigger in our consciousness by being more and more aware of His presence with us.

Know Your Commander In Chief

It is interesting when you listen to how some Christians talk. You may hear them talking about what the devil did to them, how they got really mad at the devil and how they spent a whole night rebuking the devil. Such Christians may also go around town telling people what the devil has been telling them, but you will never hear them talking about what **the Lord** has been telling them. Guess what? They are tuned in to the wrong frequency!

Instead of magnifying Jesus and His presence and being conscious of Him, they are magnifying the devil and being more devil-conscious than Jesus-conscious. It's really sad! They are always talking about warfare and the devil. Do you know that the best warfare to engage in is to magnify the Lord Jesus in your life? The Bible declares, "Let God arise, let His enemies be scattered…"[11] Amen!

Recently, I had a conversation with a medical doctor about spiritual warfare. She said to me, "When there is a condition in your body, you must know what the correct medical name for it is so that you can pray against it accurately." Then, she told me somewhat smugly, "As someone who's been in the army, you should know this: The most important military strategy is to know your enemy."

I smiled at her and said, "Actually, I believe that the most important military strategy is not to know your enemy, but to know your commander in chief and his directives for you."

My friend, do you know your commander in chief, Jesus Christ? Do you know with full assurance that His presence and unmerited favor is with you? Start practicing the presence of Jesus in your life today, and see what a difference He will bring to your situation!

Chapter 6

Your Right To God's Unmerited Favor

T here is no doubt that all believers want to experience God's unmerited favor in their lives. All of us want to experience success in our marriages, families, careers as well as ministries. We all want to enjoy God's best and richest blessings. We want His provision, health and power flowing mightily in our lives, and we know that all these blessings are wrapped up in God's unmerited favor. When His unmerited favor is on your side, nothing can stand against you. But if His favor is unmerited, how can we qualify for it? If we cannot earn, deserve or merit it, how can we be confident that we have His unmerited favor?

Down through the corridors of church history, there have been many quality writings on how believers can experience the favor of God. We have been taught how to think big, be positive and to expect preferential treatment. I give thanks to God for Christian ministers and writers who are challenging believers to expect God's favor in their lives today. I have been very blessed by such ministries that bring tremendous hope and encouragement to the body of Christ.

We need more new covenant ministries like these all around the world, ministries that are full of the person of Jesus, exalting the cross and lifting up the finished work of Christ. We need ministries that remind believers that God is no longer angry with them because of their sins and that all their failings—past, present and even those in the future—have been perfectly nailed and judged at the cross. We have had enough of ministries that are based on the antiquated law, that represent God inaccurately as someone who is harsh and angry.

One of the key things that I desire to do in this book is to build upon the existing teachings on favor and to give believers a firm foundation on **why they have the right to God's unmerited favor** in their lives today. Do you know the answers to the following questions?

Why can you expect good to happen to you?

Why can you enjoy God's unmerited favor?

Why can you ask God for big things?

Your Righteousness In Christ Is Your Right To God's Unmerited Favor

Beloved, your answers are all found on the Mount of Golgotha, the place of the skull. It's the place where the sinless Man became sin, so that you and I can become the righteousness of God in Him. His righteousness is **your right** to God's unmerited favor.

You can expect good...

You can enjoy God's unmerited favor...

You can ask God for big things…

…because you have been made the righteousness of God through Jesus' sacrifice on the cross!

Don't just take my word for it. It is important that you read and know the Scriptures for yourself:

> For He [God] made Him [Jesus Christ] who knew no sin to be sin for us, that we might become the righteousness of God in Him [Jesus Christ].
>
> —2 CORINTHIANS 5:21

Your righteousness in Christ is the sure foundation on which you can build your expectations to receive God's unmerited favor. God sees you through the lens of the cross of His Son, and as Jesus is today deserving of blessings, peace, health and favor, so are you![1]

The Right Definition Of Righteousness

There is a lot of misunderstanding over the definition of "righteousness" today. Many believers associate righteousness with a list of things that they have to do, and if they fulfill this list, they feel "righteous." Conversely, when they fail in terms of their actions or behavior, they feel "unrighteous." But this is the wrong definition and understanding of righteousness.

Let's go back to what the Bible has to say. Look at 2 Corinthians 5:21 again. We are not righteous because **we** do right. We **became** righteous because of what **Jesus** did for us at the cross.

"Righteousness," therefore, is not based on **our** right doing. It is based entirely on Jesus' right doing. Christianity is not about **doing right** to become righteous. It is all about **believing right** in Jesus to become righteous.

Do you realize that all religions in the world are about doing right? All religions are based on a system of merit whereby you need to fulfill certain requirements—give to the poor, do good to others and care for the underprivileged—to attain a certain state of righteousness. It all sounds very noble, self-sacrificial and appealing to our flesh, which likes to feel that our good works have earned us our righteousness.

But God is not looking at your nobility, sacrifices or good works to justify you. He is only interested in Jesus' humility at the cross. He looks at His Son's perfect sacrifice at Calvary to justify you and make you righteous! Attempting to be justified by your good works and trying your best to keep the Ten Commandments to become righteous is to negate the cross of Jesus Christ. It is as good as saying, "The cross is not enough to justify me. I need to depend on my good works to make myself clean and righteous before God."

There is a beautiful verse in the New Testament where the apostle Paul says, "I do not frustrate the grace [unmerited favor] of God: for if righteousness come by the law, then Christ is dead in vain."[2]

My friend, let us not take this verse lightly. Consider carefully what Paul is saying here. He is effectively saying that if you are depending on **your** good works, **your** doing and **your** ability to keep perfectly the Ten Commandments to become righteous, then Jesus died for nothing! That's what **"in vain"** means—**for nothing!**

Your Righteousness Is Freely Given, Not Earned

If you have not watched *The Passion Of The Christ* directed by Mel Gibson, I encourage you to get the DVD and watch all that Jesus has done for you on His road to the cross. Observe the anguish that He endured in the garden of Gethsemane, where He prayed in preparation for the ordeal that He knew was to come.

See how your King was taken by ruthless Roman soldiers, who mocked Him and rammed a crude crown fashioned from thorns onto His head. Look at how your Savior suffered lash after lash from whips designed to inflict maximum pain—whips laced with broken glass and hooks, so that every stroke ripped off flesh from His already lacerated back.

In one scene, Jesus collapsed from the blows, and I screamed in my heart, willing Him to stay down so that His tormentors would relent. But He did not stay down. With you and me on His mind, He clung on to the beating post and dragged Himself up to receive the full measure of the scourging, knowing that it is by His stripes that we are healed.[3]

His agony did not end when the hardened soldiers grew tired of flogging Him. The soldiers shoved a heavy cross onto His completely bloodied back, forcing Him to carry the splintered planks toward Golgotha. After barely surviving such vicious treatment, it was no wonder that Jesus fell under the weight of the cross after staggering part of the way, and the soldiers had to force a passerby to help Him carry the cross. Our Lord was then stretched out over the cross and huge, long nails were hammered cruelly into His hands and feet.

Did Jesus endure all this for nothing? Was this all in vain?

That is precisely what Christians who insist on trying to earn their own righteousness through the law are saying.

Let me quote Paul again so that you can see for yourself what I mean:

> I do not frustrate the grace [unmerited favor] of God: for if righteousness come by the law, then Christ is dead in vain.
>
> —Galatians 2:21, kjv

My friend, do not frustrate the grace (unmerited favor) of God in your life by looking to yourself and trying by your own efforts to make yourself righteous before God. We cannot earn God's favor and acceptance. We can only receive righteousness as a free gift from God. God's righteousness is free for us, but it cost Him dearly. He paid for it with the blood of His only begotten Son, Jesus Christ. It is a gift that can only be given freely not because it is cheap, but truly, because it is priceless!

"But Pastor Prince, how can I, who did no right, be made righteous?"

Well, answer me this first: How could Jesus, who knew no sin, become sin on the cross for us?

Our righteousness is a result of Jesus' work and we can only receive His righteousness through His unmerited favor!

You see, Jesus had no sin of His own, but He took upon Himself all of humanity's sins. On the other hand, you and I had no righteousness of our own, but on that cross, Jesus took upon Himself all our sins, past, present and future, and in exchange, gave us His perfect, everlasting righteousness. Now, is this righteousness that we have received a result of our own works or His work? It is clear that our righteousness is a result of **His** work and we can only receive His righteousness through His unmerited favor!

Let me give you the clearest definition of grace (unmerited favor) in the Bible:

> And if by grace [unmerited favor], then it is no longer of works; otherwise grace [unmerited favor] is no longer grace [unmerited favor]. But if it is of works, it is no longer grace [unmerited favor]; otherwise work is no longer work.
>
> —ROMANS 11:6

Do you follow? There is no middle road. You are either righteous by God's unmerited favor or you are trying to merit righteousness with your own works. You are either depending on Jesus or you are depending on yourself.

The Voice Of Accusation

Perhaps you are wondering, "What's the big deal? Why is how I became righteous so important? Isn't this stuff for theologians and Bible school students to figure out?"

We are coming to the exciting part. This is important because while you are trying to believe God for big things and trusting Him that your prayers will be answered, you will be hounded by this voice of accusation:

"Who do you think you are?"

"Don't you remember how you yelled at your spouse this morning? Why should God give you favor for your important presentation at the office today?"

"Look at how easily you lose your cool on the road. How can you have the cheek to expect good things to happen to you?"

"You call yourself a Christian? When was the last time you read your Bible? What have you done for God? Why should God heal your child?"

Do these accusations sound awfully familiar? Now, how you respond to this voice of accusation will expose what you really believe. This is the litmus test of what you believe. This is where the rubber meets the road! A person could think, "Yeah, you are right. I don't deserve this. How can I expect God's favor to be on me for my presentation at the office when I was so harsh with my wife this morning?" Now, that's the response of someone who believes that he needs to earn his own righteousness and place of acceptance before God. This person believes that he can expect good from God only when his conduct is good and his own checklist of self-imposed requirements are met to the hilt.

He would probably storm into his office, still seething with anger at his wife. Worst of all, he feels cut off from the presence of Jesus because of his anger and thinks that he does not qualify to ask for God's favor for his presentation. He steps into the boardroom disheveled and disorganized. He forgets his points and fumbles, causing his company to lose that major account. His bosses are disappointed with him and give him a huge tongue-lashing. Frustrated and shamed, he drives home like a maniac, sounding his horn at every car that does not move the instant the traffic lights turn green. When he gets home, he is even more upset with his wife because he blames her for putting him in a foul mood in the morning, for his terrible presentation and for the loss of the major account! Now, it is all HER fault!

Now, see the difference if this person thinks, "Yeah, you are right. I don't deserve to have God's favor at all because I lost my temper with my wife this morning. But you know what? I am not looking at what I deserve. I am looking at what Jesus deserves. Even right now, Jesus, I thank You that You see me as perfectly righteous. Because of the cross and your perfect sacrifice, I can expect God's unmerited favor in my presentation. Every one of my shortcomings, even the tone I used this morning, is covered by Your righteousness. I can expect good not because I am good, but because You are good! Amen!"

See the amazing difference? This person is established upon Jesus' righteousness and not his own right doing or good behavior. He goes to work depending on the unmerited favor of Jesus, and he aces the presentation and clinches a major account for his company. His bosses are impressed by his performance and mark him for the next round of promotion. He drives home with peace and joy, feeling the Father's love and favor. Consequently, he is more patient with other drivers.

Right believing always leads to right living.

Now, does this mean that he sweeps all his failings under the carpet and pretends that they never happened? No way! This man, full of the consciousness that the Lord is with him, will find the strength in Christ to apologize to his wife for the tone he had used on her. You see, a heart that has been touched by unmerited favor cannot hold on to unforgiveness, anger and bitterness. Which of the above accounts demonstrate true holiness? Of course, it is the second account. Depending on God's favor results in a life of practical holiness. Right believing always leads to right living.

The Grace Of God Answers You In Your Most Undeserving Moment

The grace of God is the unearned, undeserved and unmerited favor of God. When God answers you in your most undeserving moment, **that** is grace. **That** is His amazing, unmerited favor! At your lowest point, your darkest hour, His light shines through for you and you become a recipient of His unmerited favor, and a recipient of favor can't help but want to extend grace to others.

My friend, in and of ourselves, we don't deserve anything good. But because we are in Christ and in His righteousness, God will not withhold any blessing from our lives today. Our part is not to struggle in our own works and be independent from God, but to focus on receiving all that we need from Him.

I believe that the more righteousness-conscious you are, the more of God's unmerited favor you will experience. When the voice of disqualification comes to remind you of all the areas that you have fallen short in, **that's** the time to turn to Jesus and hear His voice, which qualifies you. That is the true fight of faith! The fight of faith is to fight to believe that you are made righteous by faith and not by works. Paul, speaking of his own achievements under the law, said that he counts them all "as rubbish, that I may gain Christ and be found in Him, not having **my own righteousness, which is from the law**, but that which is through faith in Christ, **the righteousness which is from God by faith**."[4]

So there are clearly two types of righteousness in the Bible: (1) A righteousness that comes from **your** obedience and from **you** trying to earn your way to attain it. (2) A righteousness that comes from faith in **Jesus Christ**.

Only one of these has a solid, unshakable foundation. One is built upon **you** and **your** ability to keep the law, while the other is built upon the Rock of all ages—Jesus Christ. One can only give you the occasional confidence to ask for God's favor, depending on how well you perceive you have done. The other gives you confidence ALL THE TIME to access His unmerited favor, even when you feel that you are greatly undeserving.

What do you want to depend on when push comes to

shove—your wavering righteousness or the perfect, rock-solid righteousness of Jesus? It is your faith in the righteousness of Jesus that gives you the right to God's unmerited favor. Today, because of what Jesus did on the cross, you can expect good things to happen to you. You can ask God for big things and reach out to the blessed destiny that He has for you and your family.

His righteousness is your right to God's unmerited favor! Don't let any voice of accusation tell you otherwise!

Chapter 7

God's Peace For Your Success

eace is not the absence of trouble in your life. It is not the absence of turmoil, challenges or things that are not harmonious in your physical environment. It is possible to be in the midst of the biggest crisis in your life and still experience peace. That's the true kind of peace that you can experience with Jesus—peace that surpasses understanding. Naturally speaking, it does not make sense for you to feel completely at rest and at peace when you are in dire straits, but supernaturally, you can be filled with peace!

The world defines peace, harmony and tranquility based on what is happening in the sensory realm. The world's notion of peace would look something like this: A man lying in a hammock on a white sandy beach in Hawaii with luau music playing softly in the cabana, coconut trees swaying in perfect unison and warm, blue waves rolling languidly along the shoreline. The world calls that peace—until reality kicks in, and the transient peace that was experienced just moments ago dissipates into thin air!

You see, my friend, you cannot use your external surroundings to permanently influence the turmoil that you are feeling inside. Only Jesus can touch what you are feeling inside and turn that turmoil into His peace. With the Lord by your side, and from that abiding peace within, you can influence your external surroundings. It's not the other way round. With Jesus, transformation is always from inside out and not outside in.

Peace In The Midst Of A Storm

I remember reading about an art competition where the theme given was "peace." The artist who most effectively depicted peace in his artwork would win the competition. The artists gathered their paints, canvases and brushes and started working on creating their masterpieces. When the time came to judge the artworks, the judges were impressed by the various scenes of tranquility illustrated by the artists. There was a majestic piece capturing the brilliance of the sun setting over lush greenery, one that depicted a serene landscape of moonlit hills and another evocative piece that showed a lone man walking leisurely through rustic paddy fields.

Then, the judges came upon a peculiar piece that looked almost horrifying and perhaps even ugly to some. It was the very antithesis of every other piece that the judges had seen. It was a wild cacophony of violent colors and the aggression with which the artist had lashed his brush against the canvas was obvious. It depicted a raging storm where the ocean waves were swollen to menacing heights and slamming against the craggy edges of a cliff with thunderous force. Lightning zigzagged across the blackened sky and the branches of the single tree that was perched atop the cliff were all swept to the side by the force of the gale. Now, how could this picture be the epitome of peace?

Yet, the judges unanimously awarded the first prize to the artist who painted the turbulent storm. While the results initially appeared to be appalling, the judges' decision immediately became clear once you gave the winning canvas a closer look. Hidden in a crevice in the cliff is a family of eagles snug in their nest. The mother eagle faces the blustering winds, but her young chicks are oblivious to the storm and have dozed off under the shelter of her wings.

Now, *that's* the kind of peace that Jesus gives to you and me! He gives us peace, security, covering and protection even in the midst of a storm. The psalmist describes this beautifully: "He who dwells in the secret place of the Most High shall abide under the shadow of the Almighty…He shall cover you with His feathers, and under His wings you shall take refuge."[1]

Jesus gives us peace, security, covering and protection even in the midst of a storm.

There is no safer place than under the protective shelter of your Savior's wings. It does not matter what circumstances may be raging around you. You can cry to the Lord for His unmerited favor, as David did in Psalm 57:1—"Be gracious to me, O God, be gracious to me, for my soul takes refuge in You; and in the shadow of Your wings I will take refuge until destruction passes by." (NAS) The New King James Version says, "Be merciful to me, O God, be merciful to me! For my soul trusts in You; and in the shadow of Your wings I will make my refuge, until these calamities have passed by." What blessed assurance we can have today, knowing that even if destruction rages around us, we can take refuge in the Lord.

Start Your Day With Jesus

Do you know that your God has promised that no weapon formed against you shall prosper?[2] Now, He did not promise that weapons would not be formed against you. He promised that even if weapons were formed against you, they will not hurt or defeat you.

There are all kinds of weapons formed against humanity, especially in these last days. Just think of the many kinds of deadly viruses, sicknesses and diseases in the world. When you turn on the television and watch the news, all you seem to hear about are wars, unrest, disasters, financial collapses, violence, unemployment, famines, a global meltdown, the subprime crisis, mounting credit card debts, crashing stock markets and large organizations filing for bankruptcy. It is amazing how many people wake up in the morning, and the first thing that they do is grab the newspapers and read bad news before heading to work. Then, just before they go to bed, they watch the news!

Now, please understand that I am not against reading the newspapers or watching the news, or watching television for that matter. But I want to encourage you to start your day with Jesus instead, practicing His presence, acknowledging Him, committing your plans to Him and trusting Him for His unmerited favor, wisdom and strength for the day. Remember to be like Joseph in the Bible. The Lord was with Joseph and he was a successful man! Your success does not come as a result of you being updated about the latest virus or you being cued in to the latest disaster. No, your success will come as a result of your being tuned in to the presence of Jesus in your life!

There are many people in my church who start the day each morning by partaking of the Holy Communion, not as a ritual, but as a time to remember Jesus and the power of His cross. They look to Jesus for His strength, receiving His divine life for their physical bodies as they partake of the bread. They renew their consciousness of their free gift of righteousness purchased by the blood of Jesus on the cross as they partake of the cup. What a way to start the day!

I have also come to realize that the last thought before you go to sleep is very important. I have tried this before and you can try it too—go to bed thinking about Jesus, giving thanks to Him for the day. You can also meditate on one of His promises, such as the one found in Isaiah 54:17. Just say, "Thank You, Father. Your Word declares that no weapon formed against me shall prosper!" Most times, I wake up feeling rejuvenated, energized and refreshed even though I did not sleep for many hours.

Conversely, if I go to bed with what I have just heard on the news swirling in my mind, I could sleep many more hours than usual, but still wake up feeling fatigued. Sometimes I even get a headache. Have you been there before? Well, you don't have to experience that again. Sandwich your day with the presence of Jesus. Start the day with Him, enjoy Him during the day and end the day with Him on your mind!

You know, Psalm 127:2 aptly describes what we are talking

about. It says, "It is vain for you to rise up early, to sit up late, to eat the bread of sorrows; for so He gives His beloved sleep." The bread of the world is the bread of sorrows, but Jesus is our bread of life.[3] When you feed on Him, you will be nourished physically, emotionally and spiritually, whereas the bread of the world only depletes you physically and drains you emotionally by adding stress, anxiety and worry to your life.

Isn't it beautiful that quality sleep is a gift from God? If you are struggling to sleep at night, look to Jesus. Develop a knowing in your heart that you are His beloved and rest on the promise that "He gives His beloved sleep." Are you His beloved? Of course you are! So you qualify to enjoy the blessedness of sleep. Insomnia is not from God. Sleep is!

Guard What Comes Through Your Eye- And Ear-Gates

I was watching a popular program on television with the host of that program interviewing some so-called experts about the economy in America. One "expert" was very positive and gave his reasons for being so upbeat. Then, another "expert" interjected and gave his reasons for a bleak economic outlook. I watched this program for over an hour and none of these "experts" agreed on anything in the end.

The thing about such discussions, be it on television, the papers or the Internet, is that it's supposed to present two sides—one good and the other bad. No real solution or resolution is actually offered. Sometime after watching that program, I shared with my pastoral team that I realized that I had unknowingly been feeding on the tree of the knowledge of good and evil. That's all I got from watching such programs—more knowledge of what was good and what was evil, but this knowledge did nothing for me.

On the other hand, when we feed on the person of Jesus, who is the tree of life, we find that His wisdom, understanding, peace, joy and unmerited favor will flow in our lives! Again, I am not saying that you should not watch the news. I am just saying that it is important for you to watch your viewing diet. It is far more powerful to be full of Jesus than to be full of worldly knowledge.

When we partake of Jesus, wisdom, understanding, peace, joy and unmerited favor will flow in our lives!

I always encourage my church to be mindful of their eye- and ear-gates. Essentially, this means that we need to be conscious of what we watch and hear on a regular basis. The Book of Proverbs, which is chock-full of God's wisdom, tells us, "My son, **give attention to my words**; incline **your ear** to my sayings. Do not let them depart from **your eyes**; keep them in the midst of **your heart**; for they are **life** to those who find them, and **health** to all their flesh."[4]

God tells us to guard what we **hear**, what we **see** and what is **in our hearts**. He wants us to have our ears full of the gracious words of Jesus, our eyes full of the presence of Jesus and our hearts mediating on what we have heard and seen in Jesus. That's what "give attention to my words" means today in the new covenant, for Jesus is God's Word made flesh. John 1:14 says, "And the Word became flesh and dwelt among us, and we beheld His glory, the glory as of the only begotten of the Father, full of grace [unmerited favor] and truth."

The more we hear and see Jesus, the healthier and stronger we become! Our mortal bodies become infused with His resurrection life and power!

It is all about beholding Jesus, and as we behold Him, we are transformed more and more into His likeness, full of unmerited favor and truth! Don't miss this powerful promise my friend. The result of tuning our ear- and eye-gates to Jesus is that He will be **life** and **health** to us. The Bible shows us that there is a direct correlation between hearing and seeing Jesus, and the health of our physical bodies. The more we hear and see Jesus, the healthier and stronger we become! Our mortal bodies become infused with His resurrection life and power!

If we are constantly feeding on the news media, it is no wonder that we feel weak and tired. There is just no nourishment for us there. Please hear what I am saying. It is all right to keep yourself abreast of current world events and be in the know about what is happening in the Middle East, trends in the economy and developments in the political arena. Such information may even be necessary for the industry that you are in. I am not asking you to become an ignoramus or to live in a cave. I am just saying that you should not overdose yourself on world news and developments and let them consume you.

Receive Jesus' Shalom For Every Stress In Life

The best way to know if you are embroiled in the things of

this world is to be objective and ask yourself this: "Is my heart troubled?" I believe that the number one killer in the modern world is **stress**. Medical doctors in my church have told me that if a patient has high blood pressure, they can advise the patient to cut down on sodium. They can also advise their patients to cut down on other excesses such as sugar or cholesterol. But as doctors, there is one thing that they cannot control in their patients, and that is their patients' stress levels.

I personally believe that the physical root cause of many medical conditions today is stress. Stress can produce all kinds of imbalances in your body. It can cause you to age prematurely, give you rashes, cause gastric pains and even lead to abnormal growths in your body. To put it succinctly, stress kills! Doctors tell us that certain physical symptoms are "psychosomatic" in nature. That's because these symptoms are brought about by psychological problems such as stress. Stress is not from God. **Peace** is from Him!

I trust that you are beginning to understand why Jesus said, "Peace I leave with you, My peace I give to you; not as the world gives do I give to you. Let not your heart be troubled, neither let it be afraid."[5] Now, Jesus would not have used the word "peace." The Greek New Testament renders "peace" as *eirene*, but since Jesus spoke Aramaic-Hebrew, He would have used the word "shalom"—"**Shalom** I leave with you, My **shalom** I give to you; not as the world gives do I give to you."

In the Hebrew vernacular, "shalom" is a very rich and loaded word. There is no English word that can accurately encapsulate the fullness, richness and power contained in the word "shalom."

Hence, English Bible translators were only able to translate it as "peace." But while the word "shalom" includes peace, it means so **much** more. Let's look at the Brown Driver & Briggs Hebrew Lexicon to get a better idea of what Jesus meant when He said "Shalom I leave with you."

The Hebrew Lexicon describes "shalom" as **completeness, safety, soundness (in body), welfare, health, prosperity, peace, quiet, tranquility, contentment, peace used of human relationships, peace with God especially in covenant relationship and peace from war.**[6] Wow, what a powerful word! This is the shalom that Jesus has bequeathed you: His completeness, His safety, His soundness, His welfare, His health, His prosperity, His peace, His quietness, His tranquility, His contentment, His peace in human relationships, His peace with God through the covenant made at the cross and His peace from war. All these, my friend, are part of your inheritance in Christ today! I don't know about you, but I am jumping up and down in my heart and shouting praises to the Lord as I let this sink in!

Can you picture the full implications of what it means to experience Jesus' shalom in your life? Can you picture your life being free from regrets, anxieties and worries? How healthy, vibrant, energetic and strong you will be!

The Peace Jesus Gives Sets You Up For Success in Life

Jesus gives you His shalom to set you up for success in this life. You cannot be a success in your marriage, family and career when you are crippled and paralyzed with fear. Today, as you are reading this, I believe with all my heart that Jesus has already begun a work in your heart to liberate you from all your fears, whatever they may be. They may be the fear of failure, the fear of success, the fear of people's opinions of you or even the fear that God is not with you.

All the fears that you are experiencing in your life today began with an untruth, a lie that you have somehow believed. Perhaps you have believed that God is angry and displeased with you, and that His presence is far from you. That's why the Bible says, "There is no fear in love; but perfect love casts out fear, because fear involves torment. But he who fears has not been made perfect in love."[7]

This scripture tells us that when you begin to have a revelation that God loves you perfectly (not because of what you have accomplished, but because of what Jesus has accomplished for you), that revelation of the unmerited favor of Jesus will cast out every fear, every lie, every anxiety, every doubt and every worry that God is against you. The more you have a revelation of Jesus and how He has made you perfect, the more you will free yourself to receive His complete shalom and succeed in life!

The shalom of Jesus is on your side to make you a success in life.

My friend, know that as a believer in Jesus Christ, you have absolute peace with God. The new covenant of grace is also known as the covenant of peace. Today, you stand upon the righteousness of Jesus and not your own. Today, because of Jesus, God says this to you: "I would not be angry with you, nor rebuke [condemn] you. For the mountains shall depart and the hills be removed, but My kindness shall not depart from you, nor shall My **covenant of peace** be removed."[8]

God is on your side. The shalom of Jesus is on your side to make you a success in life. All of heaven's resources are on your side. Even if you are caught in the midst of a storm right now, just think of the picture of the eagle chicks nestled under the wings of their provider, sleeping soundly in spite of the storm. And may the shalom of God, which surpasses all understanding, guard your heart and mind through Christ Jesus.[9] Go in this peace, my friend, and rest upon His shalom!

Covenanted To Succeed In Life

This chapter could possibly be one of the most pivotal and crucial chapters in this book. I believe that if you take time to understand what the Lord has put in my heart for you today, He will lay a strong foundation in your life that will set you up for every success. My desire for you is that there will be no more compromises when it comes to understanding the gospel of God's unmerited favor in your life. God's grace and unmerited favor IS the new covenant that you can enjoy today. Compromise and confusion occur when believers start fighting to put themselves back under the old covenant of Moses.

Let me illustrate in essence what some believers are doing when they insist on remaining under the covenant of law. Imagine this: Your company has promoted you, giving you a substantial increment of several thousand dollars every month, plus a new car and a beautiful new home as additional benefits. To document this promotion, the human resource department prepares a new employment contract for you, stating all the new terms that your employers have agreed upon. Now, suppose you insist on being paid your old salary, driving your old car and living in your old apartment. Instead of rejoicing at the new employment terms being offered to you, you fight your bosses and demand that you be remunerated based entirely on your old employment agreement!

Sounds ridiculous?

Absolutely!

However, that is exactly what some believers are doing today. They have determined in their hearts that they will remain under the old covenant of law and depend on their own works to earn God's blessings, approval and favor. They have negated the cross and forgotten that God has enacted a new covenant of His **unmerited favor** through Jesus Christ's perfect sacrifice. Now, let me give you some scriptures that deal specifically with comparing and contrasting the new covenant and the old covenant, so you know that I am not making this up.

God Found Fault With The Old Covenant Of Law

You are under the new covenant of unmerited favor through Jesus' finished work. The old covenant based on your works is now redundant. Look at what Hebrews 8:13, says:

> By calling this covenant "new," He has made the first one obsolete; and what is obsolete and aging will soon disappear.
>
> —Hebrews 8:13, niv

Read this verse in your Bible carefully. It is not Joseph Prince who said that the old covenant is redundant. I am just reiterating what I read in my Bible. God's Word tells us in no uncertain terms that the covenant of Moses is antiquated and obsolete. It is no longer relevant for the new covenant believer who is in Christ today! So it is not me who found fault with the old covenant of the law. **God Himself** found fault with the old covenant of law.

Let's look at another verse:

> For if that first covenant had been faultless, then no place would have been sought for a second.
>
> —HEBREWS 8:7

The Living Bible captures the apostle Paul's exasperation with the old covenant of law: "The old agreement didn't even work. If it had, there would have been no need for another to replace it. But God himself found fault with the old one...".[1]

Think about this objectively for a moment. Just for a second, put aside all the traditional teachings that you have heard or read. Let's reason together, not based on what man says, but based completely on what God has said in His Word. His Word is our only unshakable premise. Based on this portion of the Scripture that we have just read together, if there was nothing wrong with the old covenant of law, why would God give up His one and only precious Son to be brutally crucified on the cross, so that He could cut a new covenant with us? Why would He be willing to pay such a heavy price, allowing Jesus to be publicly humiliated, and to suffer inhumane violence, if there wasn't something fundamentally wrong with the old covenant of law?

The cross demonstrated that God found fault with the old covenant and was determined to make it obsolete. He was determined to rescue us from our sins by cutting a new covenant with His Son Jesus. That's the amazing unconditional love that God has for you and me. He knew that no man could be justified and made righteous by the law. Only the blood of His Son would be able to justify us and make us righteous in Christ.

In all of Israel's 1,500 years under the covenant of law, not a single person was made righteous by the law. Even the best of them, such as David, failed. The Bible describes him as a man after God's own heart.[2] But even he failed—he committed adultery with Bathsheba and had her husband Uriah killed. What hope then do you and I have under the law?

Under the law, even the best failed. Under grace,
even the worst can be saved!

Thank God that under the new covenant of His unmerited favor, even the worst of us can call upon the name of Jesus and receive Him as our personal Lord and Savior. In an instant, we can be made righteous by faith in Jesus' mighty name! Under the law, even the best failed. Under grace, even the worst can be saved!

Know Your Covenant Rights In Christ

I cannot emphasize enough how vitally important it is for

a believer today to know that he is under the new covenant of God's unmerited favor and no longer under the law. Many good, well-meaning and sincere believers today are defeated by their lack of knowledge of the new covenant and all the benefits that Jesus has purchased for them at the cross.

"But Pastor Prince, we should not be looking at benefits when we believe in Jesus."

I am glad that you brought up this point. Let's look at what the psalmist thinks about this: "Bless the Lord, O my soul; and all that is within me, bless His holy name! Bless the Lord, O my soul, and **forget not all His benefits**: Who forgives all your iniquities, who heals all your diseases, who redeems your life from destruction, who crowns you with lovingkindness and tender mercies, who satisfies your mouth with good things, so that your youth is renewed like the eagle's."[3]

Beloved, this is the heart of God. He wants you to remember **all** the benefits that Jesus has purchased for you with His blood! It is His heart to see you enjoying every single benefit, every single blessing and every single favor from Him in the new covenant of His grace. Forgiveness of sin is yours. Health is yours. Divine protection is yours. Favor is yours. Good things and the renewal of youth are yours! These are all precious gifts from the Lord to you, and it brings Him unspeakable joy when He sees you enjoying these gifts and succeeding in life. But it is the **lack of knowledge** of what Jesus has accomplished at the cross that has robbed many believers of enjoying these good gifts and benefits.

This reminds me of a story I read of a man who visited an

impoverished old lady who was dying. As he sat next to her bed in the cramped confines of her dilapidated home, a single frame hanging on her spartan wall caught his attention.

Instead of a picture, the frame held a yellowed piece of paper with some writing on it. He asked the lady about that piece of paper and she replied, "Well, I can't read, so I don't know what it says. But a long time ago, I used to work for a very wealthy man who had no family. Just before he died, he gave me this piece of paper and I've kept it in remembrance of him for the past 40 or 50 years now." The man took a closer look at the framed contents, hesitated for a moment, then said, "Do you know that this is actually the will and testament of that man? It names you as the sole beneficiary of all his wealth and property!"

What we need is a greater revelation and appreciation of Jesus and everything that He has done for us!

For close to 50 years, that lady had lived in abject poverty, working day and night to eke out a meager existence for herself. During all this time, she was actually the owner of a sprawling estate and enviable riches. However, her own ignorance had utterly robbed her of a life of wealth and luxury that she could have enjoyed. It is a sad story, but what is even sadder is that this tragedy is played out every day in the lives of believers who do not realize the inheritance that Jesus bequeathed them when He gave up His life at the cross.

What we need today are not more laws to govern believers. What we need is a greater revelation and appreciation of Jesus and everything that He has done for us! In Hosea 4:6, God lamented,

"My people are destroyed for lack of knowledge…" Let's not be numbered among these people. Instead, let us be a people who are full of the knowledge of Jesus, His person, His love and His finished work. Don't allow your ignorance to rob you any more. Find out all about your covenant rights in Christ today!

Rightly Dividing The Old And New Covenants

To fully appreciate the new covenant of grace, we must first begin to understand what a "covenant" is. Down through the history of humanity, God has related to man through His covenants. A covenant is not merely a contract or legal agreement. It is much more than that. Also, in every covenant, blood is involved. That is why a marriage is not a contract. It is a covenant. In the act of consummating a marriage, there is supposed to be a shedding of blood. That shows you how serious a covenant is in God's eyes. It is blood-based and inaugurated by blood.

I am going to show you a very simple way for you to understand the entire Bible. Look at the portion in your Bible that's marked "Old Testament"; that deals essentially with the old covenant. When you look at the portion in your Bible that is marked "New Testament," **that** is essentially the new covenant. However, the new covenant does not actually begin with the four Gospels of Matthew, Mark, Luke and John as these books deal predominantly with the life of Jesus before the cross. In fact, the new covenant begins after the resurrection of Jesus Christ. Hence, the cross is our clearest marking point of where the new covenant begins.

"Pastor Prince, isn't this old and new covenants business just for Bible school students? How is this relevant to me?"

Hang on for a second here. Before you throw your hands up and give up, let me explain to you why understanding the division between the old and new covenants is of critical importance for every believer. It is critical because a whole lot of misunderstanding and misinterpretation of the Bible that exists in the church today is a result of people reading, studying, interpreting and teaching the Bible without a clear understanding of how to rightly divide the old and new covenants! They merrily quote Old Testament passages without appropriating the cross of Jesus in their interpretations. They make it seem as though the cross made no difference!

So before you quote an Old Testament verse to show how God is angry with believers for their sins, don't forget that it is in the context of the Old Testament, where Christ had not yet died on the cross. Am I saying that you should not read the Old Testament? No, you should read it, but with **Jesus as the key** to unlocking all the precious gems hidden in God's Word. While Jesus is in the Old Testament **concealed**, He is in the New Testament **revealed**. The stronger your foundation in the new covenant is, the more you will be able to see Jesus unveiled in the Old Testament.

If you are familiar with my ministry, you would know that I am a new covenant grace preacher who loves to teach from the Old Testament and unveil the hidden secrets of Jesus! All Scripture is God-inspired and beneficial—no questions about that. But all Scripture also needs to be studied and read in the light of the cross today. Consider this brilliant piece of wisdom that the apostle Paul wrote to his young apprentice, Timothy: **"Be diligent** to present yourself approved to God, a worker who **does not need to be ashamed, rightly dividing the word of truth."**[4] I believe with all of my heart that this advice from God's Word holds true today for all believers reading the Word and especially would-be Bible teachers.

Learn to rightly divide the covenants! God's personal promise to you when you do that is that you will not be ashamed. Nobody would be able to pull the wool over your eyes by quoting chapters and verses from the Old Testament out of context to convince you that God is out to punish you for your sins, when you know with certainty that Jesus died once and for all for the full payment of all your sins.[5] No one can hoodwink you into believing that sicknesses and diseases are sent by God to teach you character and humility, when you know beyond the shadow of a doubt that Jesus came to give you abundant life, and took upon His own body all your sicknesses, pains and infirmities at the cross.[6]

Today, all the righteous requirements of the law are fulfilled in your life through Jesus!

Don't let anyone tell you that if you don't keep all the requirements of the law, God will not make you a success, because what the law could not do, God did by sending His Son, Jesus.[7] Today, all the righteous requirements of the law are fulfilled in your life through Jesus!

Do you see how powerful this is? Don't let anyone fool you with obscure passages from the Bible when Jesus has given you so many clear, explicit portions of Scripture that declare His favor and blessings over your life in the new covenant! Just because someone calls himself a teacher, prophet or an apostle doesn't mean that he has the authority to teach God's Word. Stop disqualifying yourself with the lack of knowledge of Jesus and His new covenant. Don't let anyone tell you that you need the law to make you righteous when you know that you are righteous today because of Jesus Christ!

The Place Of The Law On This Side Of The Cross

So **who** is the law for? In 1 Timothy 1:8–10, Paul says, "But we know that the law is good if one uses it lawfully, knowing this: that **the law is not made for a righteous person**, but for the lawless and insubordinate, for the ungodly and for sinners, for the unholy and profane, for murderers of fathers and murderers of mothers, for manslayers, for fornicators, for sodomites, for kidnappers, for liars, for perjurers…"

My friend, are you getting this? The law is **not for you the believer**, who has been made righteous in Christ! The law is not applicable to someone who is under the new covenant of grace. The law is for unrighteous people—unbelievers who have not received Jesus as their Savior. Its purpose is to bring them to the end of themselves and to help them realize that they need the Lord.

Paul makes the purpose for the law very clear in the Book of Galatians when he says, "Therefore the law was our tutor to bring us to Christ, that we might be justified by faith. But after faith has come, we are no longer under a tutor."[8] That's the role of the law—to show us that in and of ourselves, we will never be able to reach God's perfect standards. Therefore, the law leads us to depend on Jesus, who justifies and makes us righteous through His finished work! I am **for** the law, but only for the reason God gave the law. He gave the law to point us to Jesus. The law was never designed for man to keep and no man has, or will ever be able to keep it.

The law is designed to expose all your deficiencies, but grace (unmerited favor) points you to your sufficiency in Christ.

You see, my friend, the law **demands** from man, but grace (unmerited favor) **imparts** to man. The law condemns the sinner, but grace (unmerited favor) makes the sinner righteous. The law brings death, but grace (unmerited favor) brings abundant life. The law is designed to expose all your deficiencies, but grace (unmerited favor) points you to your sufficiency in Christ. Under the law, God will leave when man fails. But under grace (unmerited favor), God will never leave you nor forsake you even when you fail.[9]

The law makes you sin-conscious, while grace (unmerited favor) makes you righteousness-conscious. The law tells you that you have failed, but grace (unmerited favor) shows you how you are more than a conqueror in Christ. The law is about what **you** must do, but grace (unmerited favor) is all about what **Jesus** has done. The law puts the burden on you to perform, while grace (unmerited favor) puts the burden on Christ's performance. The law makes you self-conscious, but grace (unmerited favor) makes you Christ-conscious. I trust that you are beginning to see that the new covenant of God's unmerited favor, which God says is "established on better promises,"[10] is far more superior to the old covenant of law.

There was a time in church history during the dark ages where God's Word was kept from man. Interpretation of the Scriptures was limited to an exclusive group of people, and they used this to control and manipulate the masses. All kinds of heresies and superstitions that were based on man's traditions and not God's Word, were used to keep people in fear. This shows us that without God's Word, the Church has no light. Thanks be to God that today, His Word is available in many languages. God's people no longer have to be subject to the interpretation of the Word based on the traditions of man, but they can read the Word and search out the heart of God for themselves. In addition, God has raised up the fivefold ministry of new covenant pastors, teachers, apostles, prophets and evangelists to equip the body of Christ.

Sit Under New Covenant Ministries

Be sure that you are receiving from a ministry that is established on the new covenant of grace, and not from a ministry that slips in and out of the two covenants. Failure to rightly divide God's Word leads to confusion and God calls this "mixture." He cannot bless mixture, which portrays Him as being angry with us sometimes because of our failure to keep the law, but wanting to bless us at other times because of His grace. Mixture teaches that God is happy with us sometimes, but at other times, our fellowship with God is broken because of our failures.

A believer can find no peace, no assurance and no confidence in mixture. You cannot put new wine into an old wineskin because you will lose both.[11] The law will lose its convicting power to lead you to Christ if it is balanced with grace. Grace will lose its essence of being unmerited, unearned and undeserved when people are told that they still need to depend on themselves and their works to deserve God's presence and favor. It is an outright contradiction. What man calls "**balance**," God calls "**mixture**."

Test Everything You Hear With God's Word

I encourage you to test everything you hear with God's Word. I always tell my church to read the Bible for themselves instead of simply swallowing all that any preacher, including myself, says. Be wise and don't just swallow everything—hook, line, sinker, fisherman and even his boots! Be discerning when you hear something that does not sit well in your spirit, such as when a preacher tells you that "God gives you sicknesses to teach you a lesson." Ask yourself, "Is this in line with the new covenant of God's unmerited favor? Are there new covenant scriptures to back this teaching up?"

The answer is obvious once you align it with Jesus and what He has done on the cross for you! Why would God give you sicknesses when Jesus has taken every sickness and disease upon His own body at the cross? With full assurance in your heart that sickness is not from God, you can have faith to be healed! But what assurance can you have if you believe the lie that the condition is from God? Now, instead of thinking that God is against you, you realize that He is on your side! Your confidence is restored, faith is renewed and His healing can flow unabated through every cell, tissue and organ in your body!

To end this chapter, let me just share with you the words of Miles Coverdale, who said, "It shall greatly help thee to understand scripture, if thou mark not only what is spoken or written, but of whom, and unto whom, with what words, at what time, where, to what intent, with what circumstance, considering what goeth before, and what followeth after."[12]

Essentially, he was saying that to understand the Bible, we need to read everything in its context. What powerful advice from the man who translated and produced the first English Bible in the 16th century.

My friend, rightly divide the covenants whenever you read the Bible and you will never be ashamed. Now that you have received Jesus into your life, you are under the new covenant and it is your new covenant right to enjoy Jesus' unmerited favor to succeed in life!

Chapter 9

God's Covenant Of Unmerited Favor With Us

My friend, as we talk about God's unmerited favor in your life, there is something I want you to know: God's unmerited favor is not just something that you pray for at certain moments, such as when you are preparing for a job interview or about to deliver an important presentation. Of course, you can ask the Lord for His favor in such situations, but the reality is that His unmerited favor in your life is so much more! God's unmerited favor is a covenant. Why settle for just having momentary experiences of His favor in your life when you have full, constant access to the everlasting covenant of His favor?

When you understand this covenant that you have through Jesus Christ, you will go beyond merely catching glimpses of His unmerited favor here and there, and become conscious of how His unmerited favor permeates every aspect of your life, beginning with your relationship with Jesus. You will begin to see His undeserved favor manifest in your family life, career and relationships. Get ready to see God's favor becoming more and more evident in your life and be astounded by its results.

Guys, get ready to be given the best seats in the house when you bring your date out for a romantic dinner. Get ready to receive special discounts "for no apparent reason." Ladies, begin to see how relatively empty boutiques fill up with customers after you step in because you carry God's unmerited favor everywhere you go. And when the presence of the Lord is with you, everything you touch becomes blessed. You are a blessing waiting to happen!

God's unmerited favor is a covenant you have with Him.

This unmerited favor that you can enjoy is a covenant you have with God. Earlier in this book, you saw how a covenant is much more than just a legal contract. To help you establish yourself in the covenant of God's unmerited favor, let's dive deeper into the study of covenants in the Bible. I want you to have a better understanding of the covenant that we are under today.

Throughout history, God has cut several covenants with man. These include the Adamic, Noahic and Abrahamic covenants, just to name a few. But the two central covenants are the old covenant of Moses and the new covenant of Jesus. If you understand these two major covenants and know how they are distinctively different, I believe that you will have an unshakable foundation for your faith and confidence in God's unmerited favor.

Various terms have been used to describe these two covenants. As discussed in the previous chapter, the old covenant is so called because it is old and has become obsolete. It is also known as the Mosaic covenant (because it was given through Moses), the

Sinaitic covenant (because the Ten Commandments were given at Mount Sinai) and the covenant of law (because it is based on man's keeping of the law). On the other hand, the new covenant of Jesus, which is the covenant that we live by today, is also known as the covenant of grace (because it is based on God's undeserved, unearned and unmerited favor) and the covenant of peace (because it expresses the shalom of Jesus).

The Major Difference Between The Old And New Covenants

Let me give you a scripture that shows clearly the difference between the old and new covenants:

> For the law was given through Moses, but grace [unmerited favor] and truth came through Jesus Christ.
> —JOHN 1:17

Notice that truth is on the same side as God's unmerited favor and both grace (unmerited favor) and truth came through Jesus Christ. When I did a study of this verse in its original Greek, I found out that "grace and truth" are actually referred to as a singular unit, since they are followed by the singular verb "came." In other words, in God's eyes, grace and truth are synonymous—unmerited favor is truth and truth is unmerited favor.

Sometimes, people tell me things like, "Well, it's good that you preach grace, but we also have to tell people about truth." This makes it seem as though grace and truth are two different things when in fact, they are one and the same. You cannot separate truth from grace and grace from truth as they are both embodied in the person of Jesus Christ. In fact, just a few verses before this, John 1:14, referring to the person of Jesus, says, "And the Word became flesh and dwelt among us, and we beheld His glory, the glory as of the only begotten of the Father, **full of grace [unmerited favor] and truth**." Grace and truth **came** together through the person and ministry of Jesus. Grace is not a doctrine or teaching. Grace is a Person.

You cannot separate truth from grace and grace from truth as they are both embodied in the person of Jesus Christ.

This is contrasted with the old covenant of law that was **given** through Moses on Mount Sinai. We can see that God is very precise in dealing with the two covenants and does not mix them together. Grace is grace and law is law. Grace came by Jesus whereas the law was given through Moses. Jesus didn't come to give us more laws. He came to give us His unmerited favor, which is His truth! It would be of immense profit to you to keep in mind that every time you read the word "grace" in the Bible, you translate it mentally as "unmerited favor," because that is what it is.

The Abrahamic Covenant Of Grace

Many years ago, when I was studying God's Word, the Lord spoke to me, saying, "Before the law was given, none of the children of Israel died when they came out of Egypt. Even though they murmured and complained against God's appointed leadership, not a single one of them died. This is a picture of pure grace." I had never heard anyone teach this before or read it in any book, so I quickly went through that portion in my Bible and indeed, I could not find anyone who died before the law was given!

God had delivered the children of Israel from a lifetime of slavery by performing great signs and wonders. But when they found themselves caught between the Red Sea and the advancing Egyptian army, they complained to Moses, saying, "Because there were no graves in Egypt, have you taken us away to die in the wilderness? Why have you so dealt with us, to bring us up out of Egypt?"[1] What audacity! And yet, did God punish those who murmured? No, in fact, He saved the Israelites spectacularly, opening up the Red Sea for them to escape from their pursuers who were closing in on them.

Before the law was given, none of the children of Israel died even though they murmured and complained against God's appointed leadership. This is a picture of pure grace.

After they had crossed over to the other side of the Red Sea, they continued to murmur over and over again, in spite of God's miraculous provisions and gracious protection. At a place called Marah, they complained that the waters were bitter and God made the waters sweet and refreshing for them.[2] Then, when they had no food, they grumbled to Moses again, saying, "Oh, that we had died by the hand of the Lord in the land of Egypt, when we sat by the pots of meat and when we ate bread to the full! For you have brought us out into this wilderness to kill this whole assembly with hunger."[3]

Their ungrateful diatribes were directed not only at Moses, but also at God. So did God rain fire and brimstone on them? No! He rained bread from heaven to feed them! It was as if every fresh murmuring brought forth fresh demonstrations of God's goodness!

Do you know why?

It is because all these events occurred before the Ten Commandments were given. You see, before the law was given, the children of Israel lived under grace (unmerited favor), and all the blessings and provisions that they received were dependent on God's goodness and not their obedience. The Lord delivered them out of Egypt not because of their goodness or good behavior. He brought them out by the blood of the lamb (a picture of the blood of the Lamb of God) that was applied on their doorposts on the night of the first Passover.

The children of Israel were dependent upon God's faithfulness to the Abrahamic covenant, which was a covenant based on His grace (unmerited favor). Abraham lived more than 400 years before the law was given, long before there were the Ten Commandments. God had related to Abraham based on Abraham's faith in His grace and not based on Abraham's obedience to the law. God's Word makes it clear that Abraham was not justified by the law: "For if Abraham was justified by works, he has something to boast about, but not before God. For what does the Scripture say? 'Abraham **believed God**, and it was **accounted to him for righteousness**.'"[4] How was Abraham made righteous? He believed God and it was accounted to him for righteousness!

The good news for you and me is this: Today, we are under the new covenant of grace (unmerited favor), and God's unmerited favor is upon us. His blessings and His provisions for us are based entirely on HIS GOODNESS and HIS FAITHFULNESS. Hallelujah! When the Israelites journeyed from Egypt to Mount Sinai, they were under the Abrahamic covenant of grace. Therefore, in spite of their sins, God delivered them out of Egypt and provided for them supernaturally, **not based on their goodness and faithfulness, but based on His goodness and faithfulness.** How cool is that?

The Exchange Of Covenants

God's desire was to have a relationship with the children of Israel. When they arrived at Mount Sinai, God told Moses to tell them this: "You have seen what I did to the Egyptians, and how **I bore you on eagles' wings and brought you to Myself.** Now therefore, if you will indeed obey My voice and keep My covenant, then **you shall be a special treasure to Me above all people**…And **you shall be to Me a kingdom of priests and a holy nation.**"⁵ When God said this, it was with tenderness in His voice as He recounted how He had brought them to Himself so that He could forge a special relationship with them.

However, the tragedy of all tragedies occurred for the children of Israel when they responded to God after hearing this at the foot of Mount Sinai. They were proud and did not want the relationship God had envisioned. They wanted to deal with God at arm's length, through impersonal commandments. They seemed to have forgotten that it was God's unmerited favor that had brought them out of Egypt, that it was His unmerited favor that had opened a way for them when there was no way, and that it was His unmerited favor that had given them manna from heaven.

Now, they wanted to exchange the covenant of grace that they had been under for a different kind of covenant. When Moses told them what God had said, they responded arrogantly (which can be seen from the Hebrew syntax), saying in essence, "All that God commands us, we are well able to perform!"[6] In other words, this is what they said to God, "God, don't judge us and bless us anymore based on Your goodness and faithfulness. Assess us based on our merits. Bless us based on our obedience because we are well able to perform whatever You demand of us!"

From that moment onwards, God immediately changed His tone with the children of Israel. He distanced Himself from them and told Moses to command the people not to go near Mount Sinai for the mountain was holy. What happened? Once God's grace was rejected, and the people presumed upon their own righteousness and obedience to respond to Him, God drew back from them. Look at the tone that He used on the Israelites after they chose to come under the covenant of law: "Behold, I come to you in the thick cloud…Whoever touches the mountain shall surely be put to death. Not a hand shall touch him, but he shall surely be stoned or shot with an arrow…"[7]

What a change! The Lord's presence had been with them every step of the way in the pillar of cloud by day and pillar of fire by night. He had brought them through the Red Sea and provided for their every need. He was good to them because of His faithfulness to the Abrahamic covenant based on His grace (unmerited favor). But now, He warned the children of Israel to keep away from His presence! He could no longer deal with them in the same way after they had elected to come under a different covenant in their dealings with Him—one that was based on their performance and obedience, not on His goodness as before.

In fact, in the beginning of the very next chapter after the Israelites had told God to judge them based on their performance, God gave them the Ten Commandments and the covenant of law was introduced. But were the Israelites able to live up to their boasting that they could perform all that God commanded them to do? Absolutely not! Right at the foot of Mount Sinai, they created a golden calf out of the very gold that God had given them and worshipped it as the god who had brought them out of the land of Egypt!

The more you try to keep the law by your efforts, the more it will bring forth what it was designed to bring forth—your failings and sins.

Immediately, once they presumed upon their ability to keep God's commandments, they broke the very first commandment: "You shall have no other gods before Me."[8] **Why did they commit such a terrible act?** The apostle Paul tells us that "the strength of sin is the law."[9] The more you try to keep the law by your efforts, the more it will bring forth what it was designed to bring forth—your failings and sins. And this will happen until it brings you to the end of yourself, until you realize that you cannot meet God's perfect standards on your own and you cast yourself totally upon His grace (unmerited favor) and goodness.

After they had exchanged covenants, God's response to the children of Israel when they murmured changed. In Numbers 21:5, the Bible records that they complained, "Why have you brought us up out of Egypt to die in the wilderness? For there is no food and no water, and our soul loathes this worthless bread." This sounds like one of the complaints that they made earlier, doesn't it? But look what happened this time: "So the Lord sent fiery serpents among the people, and they bit the people; and **many of the people of Israel died**."[10]

Now, I want to point out that God did not create the serpents to bite the people after they had murmured—the serpents were there in the wilderness all the time. God simply lifted His hand of protection over them and allowed the serpents to move in on them. We see that now, when the Israelites murmured, they died! Why did God respond so differently to the same sin of murmuring? It was because He was now operating under a different covenant with them. The Israelites had exchanged the Abrahamic covenant, which was based on God's grace (undeserved favor), for the Mosiac covenant, which was based on their performance. Protection was contingent on their ability to keep the law perfectly. But thank God we are no longer under the old covenant. Because of the cross, God will not lift His hand of protection over us.

The Terms Of The Old Covenant

In Deuteronomy 28, there is a beautiful passage that records the wonderful blessings from God that affect every area of our lives, including our families, careers and finances. Let's look at some of these blessings:

> Blessed shall you be in the city, and blessed shall you be in the country. Blessed shall be the fruit of your body, the produce of your ground and the increase of your herds, the increase of your cattle and the offspring of your flocks…The Lord will open to you His good treasure, the heavens, to give the rain to your land in its season, and to bless all the work of your hand. You shall lend to many nations, but you shall not borrow.
>
> —DEUTERONOMY 28:3–4, 12

These were blessings that were promised under the old covenant of law. But how would these blessings come upon you if you were under the old covenant?

God answered this question when He said, "And the Lord will make you the head and not the tail…**if you heed the commandments of the Lord your God,** which I command you today, and are careful to observe them. So **you shall not turn aside from any of the words which I command you** this day, to the right or the left, to go after other gods to serve them."[11] The key operative word to access God's blessings under the old covenant is one big "IF"—**IF** you can keep God's commandments perfectly, then you can enjoy His blessings! Is this a good deal? This basically means that the old covenant of law was entirely contingent on your works and ability to keep

God's commandments impeccably. Only then could you be blessed!

But what happens **IF** you fail to keep God's commandments perfectly? Under this old covenant of law, the Lord said:

> But it shall come to pass, **if** you do not obey the voice of the Lord your God, to observe carefully all His commandments and His statutes which I command you today, that all these curses will come upon you and overtake you: Cursed shall you be in the city, and cursed shall you be in the country…Cursed shall be the fruit of your body and the produce of your land, the increase of your cattle and the offspring of your flocks…The Lord will send on you cursing, confusion, and rebuke in all that you set your hand to do, until you are destroyed and until you perish quickly, because of the wickedness of your doings in which you have forsaken Me.
>
> —Deuteronomy 28:15–16, 18, 20

Wow, this is heavy stuff! If you were offered the choice to go back under the old covenant of law today, would you?

Under the old covenant, you would be blessed if you kept God's law perfectly, but you would also attract horrific curses when you failed! Why do you think that God found fault with this covenant? The old covenant of law was not His best for the children of Israel. They asked for it when they boasted in their ability to be blessed based on their own works. They rejected

His unmerited favor. They rejected the Abrahamic covenant and declared that they wanted to be evaluated based on their own goodness rather than His goodness.

God wanted to bless His people based on His unmerited favor, but because they wanted to be blessed based on their own law-keeping, He had to humble their self-consuming arrogance. He showed them His perfect standards that no man could ever maintain—He gave them the old covenant of law.

The Law As A Shadow Of Good Things To Come

How do we know that the covenant of law was not God's best? Well, if that covenant was good enough, God would not have had to send Jesus to die on the cross for us. But look at what God did—He sent His only Son, Jesus Christ, to fulfill the law perfectly on our behalf at the cross. Jesus, who knew no sin, took upon His own body all the curses and the full payment for all the sins of humanity, so that under this new covenant through Him we can completely depend on His unmerited favor for every blessing in our lives. My friend, the unmerited favor that we enjoy today through Jesus under the new covenant is God's best for us!

To prove to you that Jesus (and not the law) is God's best, do you know that God had already concealed shadows pointing to Jesus' sacrifice on the cross in the very same chapter that the Ten Commandments were given?

Let me show you something about reading and understanding the Old Testament. The Old Testament is full of shadows, types and pictures that point to the person of Jesus and His death on the cross. Paul explains this in the Book of Hebrews when he speaks of the law as "having a **shadow** of the good things to come."[12]

When you see the shadow of an object, you know that the object is nearby. Knowing that the law is a shadow of "good things to come," we need to find out what "the good things to come" refers to. Paul answers this question for us when he talks about how the rituals under the law "are a **shadow** of things to come, but **the substance is of Christ.**"[13] The shadows hidden in the Old Testament point to the **substance** in the New Testament, which is Jesus Christ! Would eating the shadow of a hamburger satisfy you? No, you need to partake of the actual substance to be filled!

Jesus is in the old covenant concealed and in the new covenant revealed. He is the key to unlocking the Old Testament.

Now, let's get back to what we were talking about earlier. Do you know that even as God gave the Ten Commandments, Jesus was on His mind? God was already preparing to send His Son to die for you and me! Jesus is in the old covenant concealed and in the new covenant revealed. He is the key to unlocking the Old Testament, and that makes unveiling every detail that is recorded in the Bible so exciting. My ministry is all about unveiling the person of Jesus and what I am about to share with you really gets my spiritual hormones bubbling.

Are you ready? Let's look at Exodus 20 again, where the Ten Commandments were given. We can see that even when God was giving the law, Jesus' death on the cross was already on His mind. He knew that the people could not keep the law, so He made provision for the cross as the answer to the people's failure. God's immediate instruction to Moses after the law was given was to build Him an altar. What is an altar? An altar is a place where offerings were sacrificed. Right here you see a shadow of the cross of Calvary, where Jesus was sacrificed. But God didn't stop there. He gave some instructions about building the altar, which reveal even more about the cross.

In the last two verses of Exodus 20, God told Moses, "And if you make Me an altar of stone, you shall not build it of **hewn stone**; for if you use your tool on it, you have profaned it."[14] What this instruction tells us about the cross is that there can be no human effort (no hewn stone) involved. It tells us that man's works cannot be added to the finished work of Jesus, for that would profane it. God also said, "Nor shall you **go up by steps to My altar**, that your nakedness may not be exposed on it."[15]

You cannot add to Jesus' sacrifice nor can you deserve His favor by depending on your obedience to the law.

My friend, man cannot gain access to God's unmerited favor **by his own steps**. Man's self-efforts to deserve God's favor will only expose his own weaknesses. Favor comes only from Jesus' work on the cross. You cannot add to His work nor can you deserve His favor by depending on your obedience to the law. Jesus did a complete work on the cross and declared that "It is finished!"[16] Now, isn't it exhilarating to see Jesus unveiled in the Old Testament?

But I am not done yet. I have only mentioned the altar. What about the offerings? I am not going to go into every detail about the offerings in this book. However, suffice it to say that God told the children of Israel to sacrifice offerings to Him. These offerings are found in the Book of Leviticus, which gives a detailed account of the burnt offering, peace offering, meal offering, sin offering, and trespass offering.

"Pastor Prince, why are there so many types of offerings and why is this important to me?"

Because, all five offerings are **shadows** that point to our one perfect offering—Jesus Christ on the cross. That one sacrifice of Jesus is so rich with truths that it takes five offerings to depict His one offering on the cross.

So you see, my friend, even as God gave the Ten Commandments, His heart was already set on sending Jesus as the final sacrifice to redeem man from his failings. He knew from the very beginning of the covenant of law that man would fail him and that no man could ever keep the law fully and be blessed. And that is why in His love for man, He made a provision for the offerings even as He gave the law. God wanted to ensure that there was a way out for His people so that when they failed to keep His laws, they could bring their offerings to Him before the curses could come upon them. Hallelujah! How can we not love Him?

Beloved, you will find that even the **process** that the Israelites followed when they made their offerings is full of truths. God doesn't tell us everything plainly, for "It is the glory of God to conceal a matter, but the glory of kings is to search out a

The priest examines the lamb to see if it is perfect.

matter."[17] However, because you are reading this book today, you are about to see more beautiful shadows of what happened at Calvary. For example, when a sinner brings his offering to the priest, the lamb that he brings must be without spot, wrinkle or blemish. After the priest has examined the lamb, the sinner must lay his hands upon the lamb's head. The sinner then kills the lamb and offers it upon the altar as a sacrifice.

"Why can't the sinner just bring any lamb to the priest?"

The lamb must be perfect because it is a picture of Jesus' perfection—He is our perfect sacrifice, without any spot, wrinkle or blemish of sin!

"What has a sinner laying his hands on a lamb got to do with us today?"

This act has dual significance: The sinner is transferring his sins to the innocent lamb, while the lamb's innocence is transferred to the sinner. The sinner is now made righteous and

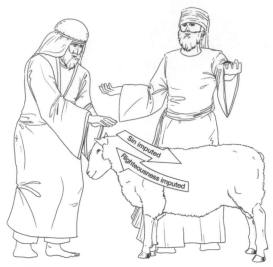

*The sinner transfers his sins to the innocent lamb,
while the lamb's innocence is transferred to the sinner.*

walks away free from any curse. It has everything to do with us because this is an amazing picture of the divine exchange that took place on the cross. At the cross, **all** our sins were put upon Jesus, the Lamb of God who took away the sins of the world. But Jesus did not only take away our sins. He also **transferred His righteousness to us,** so that today, you and I can be forever redeemed from the curse of the law!

"Why did the lamb have to be killed?"

For the sacrifice to be complete, the lamb has to be killed. Now, the man who brought the offering can walk away with the righteousness of the lamb. Instead of the curses that he deserves, he can now expect God's blessings.

Jesus' one perfect payment cleared your lifetime of sins and now you walk in newness of life with the righteousness of the Lamb of God! You can now live life with a confident expectation

The lamb suffers the judgment of God. The offerer
walks away under the blessings of God.

of God's blessings coming upon you. What a life!

Beloved, Jesus had to die an agonizing death because "the wages of sin is death."[18] He did not just take away your sins and give you His righteousness. He also took upon His own body the **punishment** for your sins. Once you accept Jesus as your personal Lord and Savior, you are no longer a sinner. All your sins—past, present and future—have been punished at the cross once and for all. Jesus does not need to be crucified ever again. His one perfect payment cleared your lifetime of sins! Today, you can enjoy all the blessings of the new covenant because of what Jesus has done for you. You are now under the covenant of His unmerited favor and all the terms to be met for you to be blessed have been met by Jesus!

Chapter 10

Perfected By Unmerited Favor

*I*n the last chapter, we talked about how you can enjoy all the blessings of the new covenant because you are now under the covenant of His unmerited favor, and all the terms of this covenant you have with God have been fulfilled by Jesus. God found fault with the old covenant—where man could only be blessed by his goodness and obedience to the law—and replaced it with the new covenant of His unmerited favor where you can be continually blessed because of Jesus' obedience.

I trust that you are beginning to understand that no man can be perfected by the Ten Commandments. No man can keep the law perfectly, and be perfected and blessed based on the law. Our dependence today for God's blessings in our lives has to be on Jesus and Him alone. Only Jesus can meet the full righteous requirements of the law on our behalf. If you review the Old Testament, you will find that not a single person under the old covenant was blessed, justified or sanctified by the law. They all failed to meet the perfect standard of the law. Even King Solomon, who ushered in the golden age of ancient Israel, failed despite all his wisdom and understanding.

Under the old covenant, God knew that it was impossible for the children of Israel to be blessed by their perfect adherence to the law, so He provided a way out for them. They were not annihilated by the curse of the law despite their sins because they offered burnt offerings to God every morning and evening.[1] In the previous chapter, we learned that shadows that pointed to Jesus were hidden in the Old Testament. I am about to reveal another shadow to you. Jesus, our perfect offering, hung on the cross from 9am to 3pm,[2] thus fulfilling the type of the morning and evening offerings!

There are no insignificant details in the Bible. God did not record all the details of the offerings in the Bible just so that we can carry a big and impressive Bible to church on Sundays. No, the details all point beautifully to the one sacrifice of Jesus on the cross such that even the **timings** at which God told the Israelites to make their offerings point to our Savior. Hence, even under the old covenant of law, the children of Israel could be blessed even when they failed because of JESUS. Every offering that God taught them to make pointed to Jesus' work on the cross!

If you fail in just one law, you are guilty of breaking all the laws!

Think about this for a moment. If it were possible for the Israelites to keep God's law perfectly, why would there have been a need for animal sacrifices and offerings under the covenant of law? They may have attempted to keep the laws outwardly. Physically, they may not have worshiped idols, committed adultery or murdered anyone. But the standard of the law is immaculate and they would have failed in God's eyes because they would have sinned inwardly.

For instance, if any man looked at any woman apart from his wife with lust or if anyone got angry with his neighbor, God judged them as having committed the sins of adultery and murder. And if they failed in just **one** law, they were guilty of breaking **all** the laws![3] God's standards are much higher than man's standards. Man may judge based on outward appearances, but God was not interested merely in **outward** adherence to His laws. He demanded adherence to the law in their hearts and thoughts as well!

*"But Pastor Prince, isn't that a little bit harsh? Who can keep the Ten Commandments completely both inwardly **and** outwardly?"*

That is exactly right, my friend. No man could or can! The law is an impossible standard and it was designed to silence all human efforts to earn God's blessings. That is why the children of Israel needed the right offerings and sacrifices to cover them. They could never have kept the law perfectly the way God demanded it. By the way, I did not make up the standard of the law. It was Jesus who taught that the law had to be kept inwardly as well as outwardly. He said that "whoever is angry with his brother without a cause shall be in danger of the judgment [for murder],"[4] and that "whoever looks at a woman to lust for her has already committed adultery with her in his heart."[5]

Jesus came to show man the pristine standard of God's law. The Pharisees had brought God's law down to a level that could be upheld through their own efforts, so that they could boast of their ability to keep the law. But Jesus came to expose their utter failure and showed them that God's law was an impossible standard for man. It was Jesus who said, "If your right eye causes you to sin, pluck it out and cast it from you…And if your right hand causes you to sin, cut it off and cast it from you…"[6] Clearly, He did not mean for man to take His words literally, otherwise, the church would look like a huge amputation ward! No, Jesus merely brought the law to its purest form so that every man would come to the end of himself and see his need for the Savior!

No Man Can Be Justified By The Law

Let me elucidate this further. Turn with me to the Book of Romans, where God's Word says this about being under the old covenant of law:

> There is none righteous, no, not one…Now we know that whatever the law says, it says to those who are under the law, **that every mouth may be stopped**, and all the world may become guilty before God. Therefore by the deeds of the law **no flesh will be justified in His sight**, for by **the law is the knowledge of sin**.
> —ROMANS 3:10, 19–20

These verses are loaded with several truths. First, it tells us that the law was designed to show "all the world" that they are guilty of sin before God. NO flesh can be justified by the deeds of the law. All humanity needs the Savior to rescue them! This passage also explains why the law was given. God gave the law to **expose** man's sin, "for by the law is the knowledge of sin."

Listen carefully to what I am saying. **The Ten Commandments were never given to stop sin.** They have no power to stop sin. God gave the law to **expose** man's sin! If you can understand this last statement, you will understand one of the greatest misunderstandings occurring in the church today.

Today, we hear all kinds of teachings about the Ten Commandments in the church. There are people who think that some believers are struggling with sin because there is not enough teaching on the Ten Commandments. These people are under the impression that if you preach strong and hard about the law, and about all the "Thou shalt nots," believers would be free from sin! In all the 1,500 years that the children of Israel were under the old covenant of law, did the law stop sin from occurring? Is there any scriptural basis that a strong emphasis on teaching the Ten Commandments will bring about holiness and stop sin? Absolutely not.

The Law Stirs Up Sin

I know that I may be stepping on some toes here, but let's go by what God's Word says and not by what man says. I have not found any scripture in the New Testament that tells me I should teach more about the law so that sin will stop. On the contrary, it says in 1 Corinthians 15:56 that "the strength of sin is the law." The apostle Paul explains this further in Romans 7 when he shares, "…I would not have known sin except through the law. **For I would not have known covetousness unless the law had said, 'You shall not covet.' But sin, taking opportunity by the commandment, produced in me all manner of evil desire. For**

apart from the law sin was dead."[7] Read the verses again. The law does not stop sin. It stirs up sin and produces "all manner of evil desire"!

To help you understand this, you need to realize that our human propensity to sin is aroused when a law is given. For example, imagine a group of boys walking down a street that is flanked by rows of greenhouses. None of the greenhouses pique their interest and the boys barely pay attention to them. Then, they come to one particular greenhouse that is plastered with signs that say, "Fragile glass. Do not throw stones. Trespassers will be prosecuted." Suddenly, they stop in their tracks and start daring each other to do exactly what the signs say **not** to do.

Our human propensity to sin is aroused when a law is given.

The next thing you hear is the sound of glass shattering and the boys hooting with laughter as they run away. Notice that this same group of boys had passed by the same type of greenhouses earlier without any incident. But once a law is introduced, their human propensity to sin is awakened. That is what the law does. It stirs up the flesh and in Paul's words, produces "all manner of evil desire."

Paul goes on to say:

> **I was alive once without the law, but when the commandment came, sin revived and I died**. And the commandment, which was to bring life, I found to bring death.
>
> —ROMANS 7:9–10

Wow, Paul said some powerful things here. C S Lewis wrote a brilliant book entitled *The Screwtape Letters*. It tells the story of a senior demon teaching a junior demon how to exploit man's weaknesses and frailties. Along the same lines, I would *imagine* that Romans 7:9 is probably the most studied and memorized verse in hell. All junior demons would be taught this verse and the lecture would be titled, "How to bring about a revival of sin"! According to Paul, when you introduce the law, there will be a REVIVAL OF SIN! And that's not all. Apart from reviving sin, the law also kills and brings death! Isn't it amazing then, that there are well-meaning ministers who preach strongly on the Ten Commandments, thinking that imposing the law would cause sin to be removed?

Earlier on, we saw that according to Romans 3:20, **"by the law is the knowledge of sin."** In other words, without the law, there would be no knowledge of sin. For instance, you can drive at any speed that you like on a road that doesn't have a speed limit and nobody can accuse you of speeding. But once the authorities put a speed limit on the same road, you now have the knowledge that if you drive beyond say, 70 miles an hour on this road, you would be breaking the law.

The enemy uses the law to heap condemnation upon you and give you a sense of guilt and distance from God.

In the same way, Paul said, "For I would not have known covetousness unless the law had said, 'You shall not covet.'" That is why the enemy always pours accusations on you using the voice of a legalist. He uses the law and the commandments to show up your failures, to put a spotlight on how your behavior has disqualified you from fellowship with God, and to constantly point out how you are undeserving of His acceptance, love and blessings! The enemy uses the law to heap condemnation upon you and give you a sense of guilt and distance from God. He knows that the more condemnation and guilt you experience, the more likely you are to feel alienated from God and to continue in that sin.

The Law Has Been Nailed To The Cross

But beloved, I pray that today, you will know the TRUTH that Jesus has already nailed the law to the cross:

> …having **wiped out the handwriting of requirements** that was against us, which was contrary to us. And He has taken it out of the way, having **nailed it to the cross**. Having disarmed principalities and powers, He made a public spectacle of them, triumphing over them in it.
>
> —COLOSSIANS 2:14–15

What does this mean for believers today? When all the laws of the old covenant were nailed to the cross of Jesus, the enemy and all his minions were DISARMED! The devil had armed himself with the law to accuse and condemn man, but we have good news for you, my friend. The devil can no longer use the law as a weapon to condemn the believer and stir up sin because under the new covenant, the believer in Christ is free from the law! Our Savior has already wiped out the handwriting of requirements that was against us! Unfortunately, many new covenant believers do not know that they are no longer under the law. They are defeated by their lack of knowledge, and the enemy takes advantage of their ignorance and continues to wield the old covenant of the law to condemn them and revive sin in their lives.

"Pastor Prince, since Jesus had to nail the law to the cross, does this mean that the law is bad?"

No! A thousand times no! Paul himself answers this question in Romans 7:12 when he states that "the law is holy, and the commandment holy and just and good." But, while the law is holy, just and good, it has **no power** to make you holy, just and good. The law is like a mirror. All that a mirror can do is tell you the truth and point out your deficiencies. If you look in the mirror and the person looking back at you is ugly, dirty or imperfect, is it the mirror's fault? Of course not. The mirror is just doing its job. Likewise, that's what the law does. It shows you God's perfect holiness, justice and goodness, but at the same time, it also exposes your imperfections and your inability to meet God's standards. And in the same way that you can't use a mirror to clean the dirt that it has exposed off your face, you cannot use the law to remove the sins that it has exposed and make you holy.

In the same chapter, Paul explains further why the law had to be nailed to the cross:

> For we know that the law is spiritual, but I am carnal, sold under sin. For what I am doing, I do

not understand. For what I will to do, that I do not practice; but what I hate, that I do.

—ROMANS 7:14–15

There is no doubt that the law from God is pure and spiritual, but Paul shows us clearly that the law did not stop him from wanting to sin when his flesh was stirred up by it. Notice his anguish when he says in verse 19, "For the good that I will to do, I do not do; but the evil I will not to do, that I practice."

If you fully subject yourself to the law, it will drive you to the end of yourself and you will come to a place where you have a crystal clear revelation that in and of yourself, you can't save yourself!

So what was Paul's solution? In his exasperation, he cried, "O wretched man that I am! Who will deliver me from this body of death?"[8] Those who **fully** subject themselves to the law instead of lowering it to such a standard that they can delude themselves into thinking that they can fulfill the law will truly experience what Paul experienced. The law will drive you to the end of yourself and you will come to a place where you have a crystal clear revelation that in and of yourself, you can't save yourself!

Notice that Paul's cry is for a person. He asked, "...**Who** will deliver me from this body of death?" His answer? "I thank God—through Jesus Christ our Lord!"[9] The solution is not found in objects—the two cold and impersonal pieces of stone on which the commandments were written. It is found in the person of Jesus! You can't have a relationship with cold pieces of stone, but you can have a relationship with the person of Jesus! Your answer is found in Christ and Christ alone! Even when you fail, His blood makes you righteous, just and good. You are perfected by His grace (unmerited favor) in your life.

My friend, when Jesus died on the cross, He paid the full price for your sins. He took upon Himself the full penalty for **all** your sins. But He did not remove your ability to be tempted, to have sinful desires or to have sinful thoughts. As long as you are in your present body, you will experience what Paul himself experienced. You will experience temptations, sinful desires and sinful thoughts. That is the truth and Paul was not afraid or ashamed to talk about it. If Christ died to remove sinful actions, thoughts and deeds from us, then with all due respect, He failed because we all know that we can still be tempted to sin today. The law can't stop sin. Only a revelation of His grace can.

The Power To Sin No More

The solution to these temptations, sinful desires and thoughts is found in the very first verse of the next chapter: "Therefore there is now no condemnation for those who are in Christ Jesus."[10] (By the way, some Bible translations, like the New King James Version, goes on to say "who do not walk according to the flesh, but according to the Spirit." This was added by the later Bible translators. In the oldest manuscripts of the New Testament available today, the Greek simply states, **"There is therefore now no condemnation for those who are in Christ Jesus."**)

You may experience temptations and sinful thoughts from

time to time, but right in the midst of that temptation, you need to know this: There **is** therefore **now** no condemnation for those who are in Christ Jesus. Notice that this verse is in the present tense. Right now, even if at this very moment, sinful thoughts are going through your mind, there is no condemnation because you are IN CHRIST JESUS! Are we then to sit still and entertain those sinful thoughts? Of course not.

Sin cannot take root in a person who is full of the consciousness that he is righteous in Christ. You cannot stop birds from flying over your head, but you can certainly stop a bird from building a nest on your head. In the same way, you cannot stop temptations, sinful thoughts and desires from passing through your mind, but you can certainly stop yourself from **acting** on these temptations, sinful thoughts and desires. How? By confessing at the very moment of temptation that you are the righteousness of God in Christ Jesus!

You now have the power of Christ to rise above your temptation and to rest in your righteous identity in Christ apart from your works.

The power of Jesus to overcome every temptation kicks in when you remain conscious that even at the point of temptation, Jesus is **still** with you and that you are righteous in Him apart from your works![11] When you do that, you reject the condemnation for the temptation that you faced. You now have the power of Christ to rise above your temptation and to rest in your righteous identity in Christ apart from your works. That, beloved, is the overcoming life in Christ!

I have received so many testimonies from people who have

been set free from destructive habits. These are sincere and precious people who desired to experience breakthroughs but did not know how to. However, once they learned about righteousness that comes from Christ apart from their works, they began to confess that they were still the righteousness of God every time they felt tempted. And bit by bit, the more they started to believe that they were righteous in Christ, and the more they refused to accept the condemnation for their past mistakes and for their present temptation, the more they became set free from the very addictions that bound them!

A brother from the US, who has been listening to my messages for some time, wrote to share that he had been addicted to pornography and had lived a lifestyle of sexual immorality since he was 14 years old. Although he had accepted Jesus when he was 18 years old, he continued to struggle with this aspect of his life. This is what he wrote:

As a result of some bad influences and some of my own bad choices, I became a pornography addict and began to lead a sexually immoral life at the age of 14. I got saved when I was 18 years old, but I still struggled with those kinds of thoughts and some old, bad habits. I tried everything to break free from immorality and lustful thoughts.

Then, I heard Pastor Prince's message titled, "Good Things Happen To People Who Believe God Loves Them." I listened to it over and over again, and for the first time, God's love became consistently real to me. I was able to receive God's unconditional love over and over again, and it healed my heart.

God's love has set me free! *Thank you so much for the message that your church sends out to the world. It is truly changing lives!*

The revelation that God loves him **unconditionally** despite his failures and imperfections was what helped this brother break free from habits that had gripped him for many years. God does **not** want you to sin because sin will destroy you. But even if you have failed, you must know this: There is no condemnation because you are IN CHRIST JESUS and your sins are washed away by His blood! When God looks at you, He does not see you in your failures. From the moment you accepted Jesus as your personal Lord and Savior, God sees you **in** the risen Christ, seated at His right hand! As Jesus is spotless and without blame, so are you! God sent His Son to die on the cross for you **while** you were still a sinner. Obviously, He does not love you only when you are perfect in your behavior and thoughts. His love for you is unconditional!

Another dear sister from my church wrote to share about how the Lord had thoroughly transformed her life. She used to frequent nightclubs and pubs regularly, spout vulgarities, take drugs, stay away from home, and get involved in illegal activities such as theft and peddling pirated software. During this time, she was often depressed and even entertained thoughts of suicide. Finally, she hit rock bottom and she felt that everything in her life had gone wrong. She could hardly convince herself to live on. It was during this period that her sister brought her to New Creation Church and she was impacted by the gospel of grace. This is her testimony:

*I was introduced to grace for the first time and **learned that God does not despise or condemn delinquents like myself**...I was amazed as I began to see Christianity from a new light for the first time.*

To cut a long story short, I challenged the Lord one day to prove His existence and love for me and He did just that. Within a span of two weeks, I was completely won over by Jesus and gladly accepted Him into my life. As what people always say, the rest is history.

*I would like to testify that it was GRACE and not the LAW that drew a great sinner like me to God. Over time, the Lord transformed me from a delinquent into a lady who is so in love with Jesus! He did not modify my outward behavior immediately when I was still a baby Christian. Instead, **He poured His love and grace abundantly into my life, which eventually transformed me from the inside out.** Grace may not produce immediate results, but the fruits are sure and permanent!*

Just when family members had given up their hopes on me, my Daddy God did a miracle by changing me radically into a new person! Everyone around me marveled at the change when they saw the works of God in my life. I am a walking testimony of God's existence and grace! Hallelujah!

It is vital for you to receive the gift of no condemnation because that is what will give you the power to overcome your weaknesses, destructive habits and addictions.

Praise the Lord, isn't this an awesome testimony? This sister was rescued at the lowest point in her life because she realized one powerful truth—God does not despise or condemn her. He LOVES her and it was this revelation of His love and grace (unmerited favor) that turned her life around completely!

Beloved, it is vital for you to receive the gift of no condemnation because that is what will give you the power to overcome your weaknesses, destructive habits and addictions. If you believe that God condemns you for your failures, would you run to Him for help?

Look at how Jesus gave a sinner the power to sin no more. He defended the woman who was caught in adultery. He looked tenderly into her eyes and asked her, "Woman, where are those accusers of yours? Has no one condemned you?" She said, "No one, Lord." And Jesus said to her, "Neither do I condemn you; go and sin no more."[12]

You see, the Ten Commandments, in all their pristine holiness, cannot make you holy and cannot put an end to sin. The power to stop sin from destroying your life comes from receiving the gift of **no condemnation** from Jesus. Your Savior, who has fulfilled the law on your behalf, says to you, "Where are those who condemn you? NEITHER DO I CONDEMN YOU. Now, go and sin no more." This is grace, my friend. This is His unmerited favor! Religion says that God will not condemn you only **if** you stop sinning. However, Grace says, "I have taken your condemnation on the cross. **Now**, you can go and sin no more."

Romans 6:14 says that **"sin shall not have dominion over you, for you are not under law but under grace [unmerited favor]."** If you are still struggling with sin, it is time to stop depending on the law. Fall upon His unmerited favor like Paul did. When you know that Christ has made you righteous apart from your works, and that He has perfected you by His unmerited favor, that will give you the ability to overcome every sinful temptation, habit and addiction in your life!

Right now, when you reach out to your Savior Jesus, God sees you as perfect in Him. He does not condemn you for your past, present and even future mistakes because all the mistakes that you will make in this life have already been nailed to the cross. You are now free to sin no more, and experience victory and success over every sin and bondage in your life!

Chapter 11

Transforming The Next Generation

When I was the president of my youth ministry, I used to preach hard and strong messages, telling my youths, "You've got to love God! You've got to love the Lord with all your heart, all your mind and all your soul!" All that time, when I was preaching this to the young people, I was wondering to myself, "How in the world do I do that?" I would look at myself and check my heart, mind and soul—did I really love the Lord that perfectly? How could I expect my youths to love the Lord that way when I knew that I myself had failed? At that time, I was not established in the new covenant of grace yet. I did not know that by preaching that way, I was actually placing all my youths under the law because the sum total of the law is to love God with all your heart, all your soul, all your mind and all your strength.[1]

Let me ask you this: Has anybody ever been able to love the Lord with all his heart, mind and soul? No one. Not a single person has been able to do that. God knew all the while that under the law, no one could love Him that perfectly. So do you know what He did? The Bible says, "For God **so** loved the world that He gave His only begotten Son…"[2] I love that little word "so." It speaks of the intensity with which God loves us.

When God sent Jesus, He was effectively saying this to us: "I know that you can't love Me perfectly, so watch Me now. **I** will love you with all My heart, all My soul, all My mind and all My strength." And He stretched His arms wide and died for us. This is what the Bible says about what Jesus did on the cross: "For scarcely for a righteous man will one die; yet perhaps for a good man someone would even dare to die. But God **demonstrates His own love toward us**, in that while we were still sinners, Christ died for us. Much more then, having now been justified by His blood, we shall be saved from wrath through Him."[3]

When you are overflowing with God's love, you will fulfill the law effortlessly without even trying.

My friend, the cross is not a demonstration of our perfect love and devotion to God. The cross is God's demonstration of **His** perfect love and **His** perfect grace (unmerited favor) toward us, for it was while we were **still** sinners that Jesus died for us. He did not die for you and me because of our perfect love for God. He died for you and me because of HIS perfect love for us! Let me give you the Bible's definition of love to make this even clearer for you: "In this is love, **not that we loved God, but that He loved us** and sent His Son to be the propitiation for our sins."[4] Beloved, that's the emphasis of the new covenant of grace (unmerited favor)—HIS love for us, not our love for Him!

As we raise up a new generation of believers, let us raise up a generation that is impacted by God's unmerited favor and that boasts in His love for us. When we receive His love for us and start believing that we are His beloved, look at the result that 1 John 4:11 spells out: "Beloved, if God so loved us, we also ought to love one another." Notice that the love for one another comes after our experience of His love for us! It stems from an overflow. You cannot love others when you have not first been filled by His love. And when you are overflowing with His love, you will fulfill the law effortlessly without even trying because God's Word tells us, "Love does no harm to a neighbor; therefore **love is the fulfillment of the law.**"[5]

Flee Temptation With The Knowledge Of God's Grace

We do not need to impose the law on our young people, thinking that without the law, they would go out and sin. Joseph was only a young man when at 17 years old, he was sold as a slave in Egypt. He lived many years **before the Ten Commandments were given**, yet look at his response when Potiphar's wife tried to seduce him. Referring to God's unmerited favor in his life and how the Lord had promoted him, Joseph said, "There is no one greater in this house than I…How then can I do this great wickedness, and sin against God?"[6]

Joseph was not governed by the Ten Commandments. He acted based on God's unmerited favor in his life. He had a living relationship with the Lord. Do you know what Joseph did after he said what he said to Potiphar's wife? He ran away from the woman. Similarly, I believe that young people who are full of Jesus will have the courage to run away from temptation! There is nothing wrong with running away from temptation. Joseph ran away from Potiphar's wife because he did not put confidence in his own flesh to resist temptation. He ran away before he could change his mind!

In fact, the apostle Paul's instructions in the new covenant are to FLEE from youthful lusts and to pursue God's righteousness instead. He tells Timothy, "Flee also youthful lusts; but pursue righteousness, faith, love, peace…"[7] If Internet pornography is a temptation, then let's teach our young people not to put confidence in their own flesh to resist temptation, and to flee from it instead. Parents, at the same time, you can make pragmatic changes by placing your home computers in the living rooms and not in your son's or daughter's room. This is parenting with grace: You can trust your teenagers, but you can also teach them not to trust their flesh, and to flee from temptations!

Teenagers and young adults who are dating, learn to flee from temptations like Joseph did. Don't go to dark, quiet places or lock yourselves alone in your rooms where raging hormones can bring you further than where you want to go. God designed sex to be enjoyed within the marriage covenant. He is not robbing you of fun. He loves you too much to see you go from one broken sexual relationship to another, and end up feeling used, cheated, manipulated, cheap and empty. He loves you too much to see you at risk of or suffering from sexually transmitted diseases. He loves you too much to see you go through an unwanted pregnancy and become a parent before you are ready.

You are precious in His sight and I want you to picture His destiny for your life. His destiny for you is to enjoy a blessed marriage with someone you can give yourself totally to, and with whom you can have a blessed family with beautiful children in due season. Trust Him—don't rush into having sex before marriage. He will make all things beautiful in His time. Also, know this: No matter what your past is like, there is therefore now no condemnation. His blood washes you whiter than snow and you have a new beginning in Him!

Encountering Jesus Leads To Fulfilling The Law

Youth leaders, parents and fellow ministers, it is vital to give our young people a picture of what God's heart for them is in the new covenant. When our young people have an encounter with the person of Jesus and receive His love, His love will lead them to fulfill the law. They will learn to love themselves and not inflict harm on themselves by experimenting with sex, drugs, alcohol, cigarettes and other destructive activities. Grace brings about a restraint that is supernatural. Grace is our hope for transforming the next generation.

We need a whole new generation of youth leaders who have a revelation of God's unmerited favor burning in their hearts. Only grace can transform our young people. Throwing laws at them will only stir up their flesh to rebel. But just one encounter with Jesus, just one drop of His unmerited favor, and I can guarantee you, our young people will never be the same again. Think about your own life. How were you first impacted by Jesus? Was it through the law or was it His grace in your life that touched your heart? We all began our relationship with the Lord because we were impacted by His love and grace. Let us then continue in that grace.

Paul warned the Galatians against turning back to the law

after beginning in grace. He said, "I marvel that you are turning away so soon from Him who called you in the grace [unmerited favor] of Christ, to a different gospel, which is not another; but there are some who trouble you and want to **pervert the gospel of Christ**."[8] Paul takes this very seriously. He calls any gospel apart from the gospel of grace (God's unmerited favor) a **perversion.** Attempting to be **justified** by the works of the Ten Commandments is a perversion of the gospel of Christ.

Don't start with grace and end up with the law. Don't start with the new covenant, only to turn back to the old covenant!

Paul asked the church in Galatia point-blank, "…Did you receive the Spirit by the works of the law, or by the hearing of faith? Are you so foolish? Having begun in the Spirit, are you now being made perfect by the flesh [self-effort]?"[9] Paul was saying to them, "You began by believing in His grace, why are you now depending on your works? That is foolishness! You should be continuing in His unmerited favor!" These are strong words by Paul. Don't start with grace and end up with the law. Don't start with the new covenant, only to turn back to the old covenant! There are those who say that they are not justified by the law, but believe that they should keep the law for sanctification. My friend, both justification and sanctification come by our faith in Jesus' finished work alone.

"Pastor Prince, how would I know if I have gone back to the old covenant?"

It is actually very easy to identify the difference between old and new covenant teachings. Just ask yourself if the teaching is putting the emphasis on what **you** have to do or what **Jesus has done**. Does it make you introspective, always looking to **yourself** and how you fared or failed? Or does it make you turn your eyes **away from yourself** to look upon Jesus?

When you are established in the new covenant of grace, you will experience a tremendous sense of confidence and security in Christ. When your confidence is in His unmerited favor and not your performance, you will not feel as if you are constantly jumping in and out of His favor and acceptance.

It is unfortunate that some believers have put themselves back under the old covenant without realizing it. Sometimes, they feel that God is on their side, but at other times, they feel that God is far away from them. Sometimes, they feel that God is satisfied with them, but at other times, they feel that God is angry with them. All these feelings are based predominantly on their own evaluation of how **they** have performed, how **they feel** about themselves, and not how God sees them. Because there is no new covenant scriptural basis for such evaluations, they end up arbitrarily deciding if they are deserving of God's blessings and favor in their lives or not, when in fact, they actually have access to His blessings all the time, simply because of Jesus and His finished work at the cross.

Defeated By Our Lack Of Knowledge

When I was a teenager, I used to belong to a Christian fellowship group. We would sing this song which you may be familiar with. It went like this: "Is He satisfied, is He satisfied, is He satisfied with me? Have I done my best? Have I stood the test?

Is He satisfied with me?"[10] Let me just say that 10 out of the 10 times that we sang this song, I would always believe that God was **not** satisfied with me. When we look to ourselves, all there is to see is the inadequacy and futility of our ability and performance. In and of ourselves, we will never meet God's standard for Him to be satisfied with us. We will always fall short!

When we look to ourselves, all there is to see is the inadequacy and futility of our ability and performance.

You can imagine how condemned we felt each time we sang this song. After all, we had never been taught that God was satisfied with His Son's sacrifice at the cross, and we did not understand what the new covenant of grace was all about. We were young and zealous for God, but defeated by our lack of knowledge. How I wish we could have read a book like the one you are holding during those times. It would have saved us from our constant sense of inadequacy and failure!

With all due respect to the songwriter, whom I believe had the best intentions when he wrote the song, this song is not based on the new covenant of God's unmerited favor. It negates the cross, instills fear and places the emphasis back on you—what **you** must do, what **you** must perform and what **you** must achieve for God to be satisfied with you. But the question to ask today is not if God is satisfied with you. The question that we need to ask is this: Is God satisfied with the cross of Jesus? And the answer is this: He is completely satisfied!

> *God will not punish the believer again, not because He has gone soft on sin, but because all our sins have already been punished in the body of Jesus.*

At the cross, our acceptance is found. There, Jesus cried out with His last breath "It is finished!"[11] The work is complete. The full punishment for all our sins was exacted on Jesus at the cross. God will not punish the believer again, not because He has gone soft on sin, but because all our sins **have already been** punished in the body of Jesus. God's holiness and His justice are now on your side! Today, God is not assessing you based on what you have or have not done. He is assessing you based on what Jesus has done. Is God satisfied with Jesus today? Yes, of course He is! Then, to the same extent that God is satisfied with Jesus, He is satisfied with you.

Sounds too good to be true? Not when you realize that this new covenant reality came at a heavy price. God's own Son had to be crushed at Calvary for this blessing to become a reality in your life. The gift of His unmerited favor and His righteousness is only a free gift for you today because the full payment for this gift was exacted upon Jesus' body. The cross made all the difference! Don't let anyone hoodwink you into thinking that you need to pay for your own sins. Don't let anyone deceive you with the lie that your eternal salvation in Christ is uncertain and shakable!

Transformation By Revelation

In the previous chapter, we learned that under the old

covenant of law, you could be blessed by God only if you obeyed His commandments perfectly, both inwardly and outwardly. Conversely, if you failed, you would be cursed. We also saw how God knew from the beginning that it was impossible for anyone to be blessed under the old covenant as no man could keep the Ten Commandments perfectly. Therefore, He made a provision for man's failings to be paid for through the blood sacrifice of innocent animals. But we know today that the animal sacrifices were only a shadow of the blood that Jesus, our perfect Lamb of God, would shed on the cross for us. Remember that we are no longer under the **old** covenant of law as we have the new covenant of grace![12]

Yet, would you agree with me that more Christians today know about the Ten Commandments than about the new covenant of God's unmerited favor? For that matter, if you walked down Times Square in New York City and started to interview random people, most would probably have heard about the Ten Commandments, but know nothing about the new covenant of grace that came by Jesus Christ. In fact, the world identifies Christianity with the Ten Commandments. Isn't it sad that the world knows us by the laws that are obsolete and not by the unmerited favor that Christ died to give us?

When young people catch a revelation of Jesus and
just how precious they are in His sight,
their lives will be supernaturally transformed.

It is no wonder we are losing a whole new generation of young people to the world! The law holds no appeal or attraction and the Bible itself calls the law obsolete.[13] If we keep on shoving the Ten Commandments down the throats of our young people, don't be surprised when they are turned off by legalistic forms of Christianity. More importantly, don't forget that the strength of sin is the law. The law has no power to stop sin. The law will not impart to them their precious identity in Christ, which will give them the strength to abstain from premarital sex, prevent them from getting into drug abuse and stop them from losing their sexual identity. Only God's own sacrifice on the cross can give them their new identity as a new creation in Christ Jesus!

When young people catch a revelation of Jesus and just how precious they are in His sight, their lives will be supernaturally transformed. They will stop being harassed by suicidal thoughts. They will stop wanting to put themselves at risk to "fit in" or to get the attention that they crave. The self-esteem of our young ladies will dramatically improve as they learn to value themselves in the same way Jesus values them. Overflowing with Jesus' perfect love for and acceptance of them, they will not be under the illusion that they need to give their bodies away to find acceptance and love from some guy. They will love themselves as Jesus loves them!

As for our young men, I believe that they will develop supernatural self-control to manage their raging hormones. They will do it not by their own willpower, but through Jesus' power flowing through them. They will learn how to flee youthful lusts. They will know that being "cool" means respecting the opposite sex, and not putting themselves and their girlfriends at risk of contracting sexually transmitted diseases and having unwanted pregnancies.

We will have a generation of teenagers who know that Jesus has an awesome destiny laid out for each of them, and the desire to be involved in gangs and destructive activities such as alcohol and drug abuse and promiscuity will dissipate in Jesus' unmerited favor and love for them. Supernaturally, their desires for the things of the world will disappear as they get replaced with the desire for Jesus! That's the power of God's grace (unmerited favor) and His unconditional acceptance of us through the cross. What the law could not do, God did by sending His own Son Jesus Christ!

Youth leaders, parents and fellow ministers, this is the solution for our young people. It is not too late to reach out to our young people with arms of grace and to embrace them with the true gospel of Jesus. Let's stop knocking our youths with the Ten Commandments and start giving them a revelation of Jesus. Let's start unveiling the Father's love for them!

We need a new generation of preachers who are full of grace and mercy, full of unadulterated new covenant teachings, and full of the person of Jesus, His beauty, His love and His perfect work at the cross. We cannot have the world associating Christianity with the law anymore. If we really want to impact the world and a whole new generation for Jesus, then they need to know the church for the cross and for the unmerited favor that flows from the pierced hands of our Savior!

Saved By Jesus' Love

Let me share with you a precious testimony of a teenager whom the Lord rescued from the brink of suicide. This teenager was a school athlete who was used to excelling in sports. However, she developed some serious health problems and was told that she may never be able to compete athletically ever again.

Devastated by the prospect of being crippled by her debilitating condition, she plunged into a deep depression. When she found herself alone in her room one day, she decided to gather some Panadol tablets and a bottle of vodka, and considered taking her own life. That night, she was looking through the music files that she had in her computer, wanting to play herself a final song before swallowing the lethal combination she had prepared.

After randomly selecting from her playlist, she "happened" to play "I'm Held by Your Love," a song that was penned by our church keyboardist and sung by one of our worship leaders. As the lyrics washed over her, she began to weep uncontrollably as the love of Jesus filled her heart:

I'm held by Your love
Upheld by Your strength
On Your shoulders You bore me
By Your faith I stand
Cherished by You, Lord
Treasured in Your sight
So close to Your heart
Held firm in Your hands...[14]

Overwhelmed by the tangible presence of the Lord, her resolve to kill herself melted, and she began to cry out to God instead. She wrote to the church and the female worship leader who sang this song met with her and ministered Jesus to her. Today, this girl has completely recovered and is no longer on medication. Hallelujah! All glory to our Lord Jesus!

Let me share with you another testimony of a youth whose life has been radically transformed by the unmerited favor of God. This young man smoked his first cigarette when he was only nine years old. By the time he was 14, he was already a seasoned gangster, peddling as well as taking drugs, and selling pirated movies. With the money earned, he would treat his gang members to fancy clothes or meals, and even cover transport expenses for them to congregate for gang fights! At 15, the law caught up with him and he was sent to a boys' reformatory home where he realized that his life needed to be turned around. And that was when God came into the picture. He said:

The home was where I first encountered God, even though I did not know it was Him then. One of my counselors, a Christian lady, prayed for me and for the first time in my life, I felt that there was "someone" looking or talking with me. I did not think much about it then, but that's when my heart and my perspective on life began to change.

I started attending New Creation Church (NCC) in September 2005. A friend had invited me to NCC earlier, but I declined. However, one day I happened to oversleep on the train and missed my stop. The platform I got off on was completely deserted, but I noticed a plastic bag left on one of the benches. I looked at its contents to see if I could tell who it belonged to and realized that inside it were actually sermon CDs from NCC!

So even when I didn't want to attend NCC, God sent the church to me! It was no coincidence. It was God-directed! When I played the CDs at home out of curiosity, the presence of God was so real. I experienced such intimacy with God. As I listened to Pastor Prince's

*teachings, I knew that this was the God I had always believed in, **a
God who loves me regardless of who I am or what I do!***

*Pastor Prince's teachings have set me free, and given me a
supernatural strength and passion to do His work. I don't feel any
more bondage when it comes to communicating with God, knowing
that He can lead me in every single situation.*

*The most significant change I have experienced has been my inward
transformation. I used to have a very bad temper, which got me into
a lot of fights **because I was easily provoked. Being conscious of
His love for me** has delivered me from that. I also went from failing
in high school to doing well enough in the polytechnic to qualify for a
place in a university.*

This young man is now a confident, cheerful person with
a bright future. He gives talks at schools and at the boys'
reformatory home that he was in to share his journey with the
youths and to encourage them. His life has been so radically
transformed that even a government agency has enlisted him to
speak to troubled youths. He says that ever since Jesus entered
His life, he has seen His grace and favor superabound in his life.
Many doors have opened for him and his life has really been
enriched, with breakthroughs in areas such as his work, studies,
family and relationships. Let's give Jesus all the glory!

That's what our young people need—a revelation of Jesus'
perfect love for them! There is a lost and dying world out there.
My friend, the Ten Commandments **cannot** be the only thing
that youths know about Christianity anymore! How can they
help but think that Christianity is just another religion that
is full of rules, laws and regulations on what they should or

should not be doing? How can they help but imagine God to be someone who is angry with them and looking for opportunities to punish them? They have no idea that Christianity is actually an intimate **relationship** with a loving God. If they knew, they would be banging down the doors of churches every Sunday to get in to hear Jesus and His grace preached!

We need a gospel revolution to reach and impact the next generation with the true gospel of Jesus.

Clearly, the world has not heard the unadulterated gospel of grace. They have not heard the good news of God's unmerited favor. However, this can change when we, the church, start to understand and preach the new covenant of grace! It's a sad reality when more Christians know about the Ten Commandments under the old covenant than they do about the new covenant of grace. We need to change that! We need a gospel revolution to reach and impact the next generation with the true gospel of Jesus. Only a revelation of God's unmerited favor will transform the next generation for Jesus. Let's not lose our precious young people to the world.

Right now, if you are a young person reading this, I want you to know that all your answers are found in the person of Jesus. He suffered, bled and died for you. Whatever confusion you may be experiencing right now, there is hope. It is not over, so don't give up. Jesus will **never** give up on you! Find your identity in Him and He will give you a new beginning, a fresh start and a new page to begin an exciting life with Him!

Like Joseph in the Bible, His presence will be with you and you will be a success in this life. Jesus will cause everything that your hands touch to yield prosperous results. Your relationships will be blessed. Jesus will give you good friends who won't judge or despise you. He will also give you a loving relationship with your parents. Your studies will be blessed. Your future in Jesus will get brighter and more glorious each day!

Jesus is with you, my precious friend, and you know what? He will never leave you nor forsake you no matter what mistakes you may have made.[15] He forgives you completely and all your mistakes have been forever forgotten, washed away by His blood. Now, with Jesus by your side, you can start afresh and begin your new life of unmerited favor and success!

Chapter 12

Our Part In The New Covenant

W hile we are on the subject of covenants, it's important to know that in every covenant, there are certain terms and conditions detailing how we can experience God's blessings. In the Edenic covenant, all Adam and Eve had to do was to not partake from the tree of the knowledge of good and evil. Under the old covenant of law, we know that to enjoy God's blessings, one had to obey perfectly the Ten Commandments.

What about the new covenant? Since it is based entirely on God's unmerited favor and not our ability to keep the law or what we need to do, what exactly is our part in this covenant? How can we enjoy God's blessings in the new covenant when it is based on the finished work of the cross of Jesus? Do we have a part to play in the new covenant of grace? These are important questions, so let's explore this issue of "our part" in the new covenant.

To begin, let's establish the fact that when there is a new covenant, it does not make sense to try to experience God's blessings by going back under the old covenant. Imagine this: Your company has just been awarded a new contract with a major multinational company, and it is worth millions of dollars more than the old contract. Would you be reviewing the payment terms of the agreement based on the old contract or the new one? The answer is obvious. Yet, there are believers today who are trying to go back to the terms of the old covenant. They don't realize that the old covenant is no longer valid and that today, we don't even have the only provision that made being under the old covenant work for the children of Israel—the animal offerings to cover their sins.

The Terms Of The New Covenant

Since we have a new covenant, what are its terms? Turn with me to Hebrews 8:10–13 and see for yourself:

> For this is the covenant that **I will** make with the house of Israel after those days, says the Lord: **I will** put My laws in their mind and write them on their hearts; and **I will** be their God, and they shall be My people. None of them shall teach his neighbor, and none his brother, saying, 'Know the Lord,' for all shall know Me, from the least of them to the greatest of them. For **I will** be merciful to their unrighteousness, and their sins and their lawless deeds **I will** remember no more." In that He says, "A new covenant," He has made the first obsolete...
>
> —Hebrews 8:10–13

The old covenant of law is all about what **you** must do. However, the new covenant is full of what **God** will do. Notice the number of times "I will" appears in this passage? Instead of having laws written on cold pieces of stone, God, under the new covenant, has declared that He Himself will put His laws in your mind and write them on your heart. God is very clear that He is done with the old covenant, so make no mistake about this—the laws that He will write on your heart are **not** the Ten Commandments. So what are the laws that He will put in you?

In John 13:34, God said that He has given us a new commandment—to love one another as He has loved us. In Romans 3:27, the apostle Paul mentions the law of faith. So the laws that God will put in your heart are His royal law of love and the law of faith.

Love Is The Fulfillment Of The Law

What does it mean to have God's law of love put in our minds and inscribed on our hearts? This brings about such powerful ripple effects that I don't even know where to start! When you begin to experience God's love and unmerited favor in your life, knowing that you don't deserve His grace, you will fall head over heels in love with Jesus. When you are full of the love of Jesus, that love overflows into all your relationships, first with God, then with your spouse, family members, friends, co-workers and with everyone whom you meet.

Without any commands from God, you will start falling in love with your spouse all over again. Romance blossoms and the grace of Jesus refreshes your marriage. You won't want to entertain thoughts of adultery because you are in love with your spouse. In fact, it is only when you are filled with Jesus' love for you that you can fulfill Paul's commandment in Ephesians 5:25—"Husbands, love your wives, just as **Christ also loved the church** and gave Himself for her." Men, do you realize that the focus is not on what we have to do or on our love for our wives? The truth is that we first need to be filled with the love of Christ for us. We can love only because He first loved us!

Similarly, when you are consumed by Jesus' love, you will not be consumed by murderous anger even when you have been wronged, but would instead, have the supernatural ability to forgive others. That is why Paul said:

> For the commandments, "You shall not commit adultery," "You shall not murder," "You shall not steal," "You shall not bear false witness," "You shall not covet," and if there is any other commandment, **are all summed up** in this saying, namely, "You shall love your neighbor as yourself." Love does no harm to a neighbor; **therefore love is the fulfillment of the law.**
>
> —Romans 13:9–10

In fact, when you receive God's love, you will not just fulfill the law effortlessly, but you will also exceed it. The new covenant is all about having a living, dynamic and intimate relationship with Jesus. The law is inferior—**it can only command you not to commit adultery, but it cannot make you love your spouse.** Under the law, a person can stay home and not commit adultery physically with someone else, but his heart can be cold toward his spouse and he can be fantasizing about what he sees on the television and Internet. Under the law, you can have a **form** of law-keeping. But under grace, you will experience the true substance.

The law deals purely with the superficial, but grace goes much deeper. The law will not tell you how to save your marriage. But today, when God puts His laws into your heart, you can run to Him saying, "Lord, I can feel my wife growing further away from me. Teach me how to love her," and God will lead you because He has promised that "all shall know Me, from the least of them to the greatest of them."[1] If you feel the prompting to say some words of encouragement and affirmation to her, do it. If you feel the prompting to give her a hug, do it! Follow those promptings in your heart because the Lord will lead you to love your spouse!

Today, God speaks to you directly through His promptings and He has made it easy for you to know His will.

God made it so easy for us in the new covenant. We no longer have to run to prophets to find out His will for us. He Himself leads us! For those of you who want to serve the Lord, but don't know where to start, just ask yourself what is in your heart. If you have a desire to work among children, then do so. As a new covenant believer, that's how your Father leads you. He puts His laws in your mind and writes them on your heart!

Perhaps you feel a prompting to bless someone financially, even though the person looks prosperous. Follow that prompting because today, God speaks to you directly and He has made it easy for you to know His will. We all know how looks can be deceiving. For example, many con artists feel that church folks are gullible. Therefore, they dress down with a well-rehearsed sob story so as to move you to give to them. On the other hand, there are noble people who dress up on Sundays to honor the occasion, but they are in dire straits financially. Hence, we need to follow the promptings of our hearts and not the sight of our eyes. So when you feel a desire to do something good for someone, do it, knowing that you have a brand-new heart that hears God, and that it is God who works in you both the willingness and the performance of it![2]

The Clause That Makes The New Covenant Work

Now, you know that the old covenant was contingent on the works and obedience of the Israelites to the law. So what does the new covenant hinge on? Beloved, God is so good. The new covenant that **God** has made is not dependent on anything that you and I must do because He knows that we will always fail. Listen carefully. The new covenant works because of one thing only, and it is the last clause of the new covenant—Hebrews 8:12. To the measure that you have a revelation of this clause and all its blessings, to that measure you will walk in it. Are you ready to look at this clause?

> **For** I will be merciful to their unrighteousness, and their sins and their lawless deeds I will remember no more."
>
> —HEBREWS 8:12

Note the word "For." It means "because." The new covenant works **because** God says that He will be merciful to our unrighteousness, and our sins and lawless deeds He will remember no more! "No more" means that there was a time God remembered our sins, even to punish them to the third and fourth generations.[3] This is found in the Ten Commandments. However, today, God says emphatically, "No more!" (Double negative in the Greek.) "No more" means that God will never again remember our sins against us because He remembered (to punish) all our sins in the body of His Son. Jesus bore God's punishment of our sins on the cross. Now, we can walk in the new covenant and hear God say, "Your sins and lawless deeds I remember no more."

My friend, the new covenant works because of the last clause. In other words, because of Hebrews 8:12, God can put His laws in our minds and write them on our hearts, and all of us can know Him and be led by Him!

Our Part In The New Covenant Of Grace

So here comes the million-dollar question: What is our part in the new covenant of grace? Our part in the new covenant of grace is to simply **believe**!

Next question: What should we believe? The answer is simple. We are to believe in Jesus! But follow me closely now, this answer may not be as straightforward as it seems. If you were to ask people on the streets if they believed in Jesus, you would probably get all kinds of answers. There would be those who believe that Jesus existed as a historical figure, moral philosopher, charismatic leader or prophet. Sadly, the truth is that believing all these things about Jesus will not save them.

Your part in the new covenant of God's unmerited favor is to believe that you are completely forgiven of all your sins, and that the blood of Jesus cleanses you from all your unrighteousness and lawlessness.

Today, we have bookstores filled with fictional literature such as *The Da Vinci Code*. Such books are based on the occult teachings of the Gnostics, who do not believe that Jesus is the Son of God. These writings attempt to devalue and naturalize Jesus to make Him a mere mortal, a historical figure and nothing more. Just because you see the word "Jesus" mentioned in books or on their covers does not mean that their authors believe in Jesus. These occult, new age writings are actually anti-Christ.

What It Means To Believe In Jesus

So let's establish what it means to believe in Jesus. To believe in Jesus is to first and foremost, believe and receive Him as your personal Lord and Savior who died on the cross for all your sins. To believe in Jesus is to believe that Jesus is the only way to salvation and that once you receive Him, you receive the gift of eternal life. Furthermore, to believe in Jesus is to believe beyond the shadow of a doubt that all your sins—past, present and future—were all punished on the cross and that today, (this is where the last clause of the new covenant applies) all your sins and lawless deeds He remembers NO MORE!

Based on the new covenant of grace, what does God want you to believe? He wants you to believe with all your heart that He meant every word when He said, "…I will be merciful to their unrighteousness, and their sins and their lawless deeds I will remember no more." You see, in the new covenant, there is nothing for us to do but to believe! Your part in the new covenant of God's unmerited favor is to believe that you are completely forgiven of all your sins, and that the blood of Jesus cleanses you from all your unrighteousness and lawlessness.

In God's eyes today, you are made perfectly righteous by Jesus' finished work. The emphasis of the new covenant is to know and believe that you are forgiven of all your sins and that God has literally erased them from His memory. If you don't believe this, it will be impossible for you to depend on and expect God to protect, provide and prosper you. If you don't believe this, it will rob you of the ability to receive His goodness, His blessings, His unmerited favor and His success in your life.

The Power Of The Blood Of Jesus

"But…but…but…Pastor Prince, God is all-knowing. How can He possibly forget my sins?"

Under the new covenant, God can declare that He will no longer remember your sins because your sins were already remembered in the body of Jesus at the cross. My friend, there is only one thing that God cannot do—He cannot lie. So He **means** it when He says that He will remember your sins no more. Our part in the new covenant of God's unmerited favor is to **believe** that God indeed remembers our sins no more!

There is power in the blood of Jesus to forgive you from all your sins! The enemy fears this truth the most and that is why he attacks this teaching on the forgiveness of sins so vehemently. If the enemy can get you to believe the lie that you are not completely forgiven and keep you sin-conscious, he will be able to keep you defeated, condemned, fearful of God and caught in a vicious circle of failure.

> *If the enemy can get you to believe the lie that you are not*
> *completely forgiven, and keep you sin-conscious,*
> *he will be able to keep you defeated, condemned,*
> *fearful of God and caught in a vicious circle of failure.*

Gnostic writings are malevolent because they propagate the lie that Jesus was a mere mortal, which means that His blood has no power to cleanse us from all our sins. This is a lie from the pit of hell! Jesus is the Son of God and His blood is untainted by any sin. That is why the shedding of His pure and innocent blood is able to cleanse us from all unrighteousness. His blood does not cover sins temporarily like the blood of bulls and goats in the old covenant. His blood blots out and **completely erases** all our sins. This is the blood of God Himself, shed for the forgiveness of all our sins! We need to start to realize that this is not a "basic teaching." This **is** the gospel of Jesus Christ.

In the end times, people will not be anti-God, but they will be anti-Christ. The anti-Christ movement in the end times will attempt to devalue Jesus' deity, the cross and His power to forgive all our sins. That is why, in these last days, we need more preaching about Jesus, His finished work and the new covenant of His unmerited favor. We need more new covenant, Christ-centered preachers who will put the cross of Jesus as the focus of all their preaching. The only way to stem this deception from creeping into the church is to focus on exalting the person of Jesus and the central tenet of the new covenant, which is the complete forgiveness of sins! This is the gospel and when the gospel truth is preached, people will be set free.

Believe that all your sins are forgiven—
that is your part in the new covenant.

There should be no compromise when it comes to the gospel of Jesus. Forgiveness of sins is based on His grace (unmerited favor) alone and we have access into this grace by **faith**. Our part is to only believe! This is what makes the gospel the good news. Take away the complete forgiveness of sins and it is no longer the "gospel," which means "good news." Believe that all your sins are forgiven. That is your part in the new covenant.

Be Free From A Judgment Mentality

In the new covenant of grace, God is effectively saying, "I want you to believe that you are forgiven. I want you to believe that you are a person enjoying My mercy. I want you to believe that I remember your sins no more." I am not the one saying this. Read Hebrews 8:12 for yourself again.

Sadly, some Christians believe the complete opposite. They don't believe that their sins are totally forgiven. They don't believe Hebrews 8:12, that God does not remember their sins. This affects their relationship with God. Instead of seeing that their sin debt has been completely cleared and settled by Jesus on their behalf, they expect God to deal with them according to their sins. When something negative happens in their life, their first thought is, "I knew it—the rooster has come home to roost. God is coming after me for what I did in the past!" Instead of taking God at His Word, these believers believe that negative things happen to them because God is punishing them for some sin in their life.

Perhaps someone had told them that God punishes them when they fail. Perhaps they were taught that you reap what you have sown. Beloved, today, we do not reap what we have sown. That is old covenant talk. In the new covenant, we are enjoying the benefits of the heavy price that Jesus paid on the cross. We sowed nothing, but through Jesus, we have reaped every blessing. That's called unmerited favor!

There are passages in the Bible that have been erroneously used to justify and perpetuate a judgment mentality among believers, like Galatians 6:7–8, which says, "Do not be deceived, God is not mocked; for whatever a man sows, that he will also reap. For he who sows to his flesh will of the flesh reap corruption, but he who sows to the Spirit will of the Spirit reap everlasting life."

Sowing And Reaping In The New Testament

My friend, when reading the Bible, it is important to rightly divide the Word, and more importantly, study the scripture in its full context. The context of Galatians 6:7–8 is about sowing **money**. It has nothing to do with sowing **sin**. However, some ministers have used the principal of sowing and reaping to intimidate believers into thinking that if they sowed sin, they should expect to reap judgment, condemnation and punishment from God.

Conversely, if they sowed righteous deeds, does that mean that they should expect to reap eternal life? If that is so, where is the cross of Jesus in this equation? Such a religious interpretation of this passage negates the cross and places our eternal salvation on a fragile balance. In this man-made equation, our "salvation" hangs on what we do and are careful not to do, instead of being rooted in what Jesus has done.

Jesus reaped all the punishment of the sins that we sowed and we reaped all the blessings that He sowed.

Don't allow anyone to confuse you with faulty interpretations of the Word. The context of Galatians 6:7–8 is about sowing and reaping money. The verses before and after (verse 6 and verses 9 and 10) clearly show that the context is talking about blessing the teachers of God's Word with all good things, and blessing the household of faith. Hence, sowing to the flesh here refers to using money for self-indulgence instead of being generous for the kingdom of God. The verse is saying that sowing money to indulge oneself leads to results that can decay, whereas sowing money into the kingdom of God leads to results that are eternal.

While it is true that in the old covenant, he who sows to the wind shall reap the whirlwind[4] (in the context of sin), it is no longer true. Jesus, at the cross, changed EVERYTHING! He reaped all the punishment of the sins that we sowed and we reaped all the blessings that He sowed. Hallelujah!

In the new covenant, there is no verse on sowing and reaping that is used in the context of sin! The principle of sowing and reaping is only used in the context of sowing and reaping money, and sowing and reaping God's Word.[5] It is never used in reference to sin! So don't let inferior interpretations of Bible passages rob you of the certainty that ALL your sins have been forgiven. Your total forgiveness of sins is clearly spelled out in scriptures like Ephesians 1:7, which declares that in Christ "we have redemption through His blood, the forgiveness of sins, **according** to the riches of His grace [unmerited favor]"!

Your Forgiveness Is Based On His Perfect Sacrifice

You are forgiven not according to the riches of your good works, but according to the riches of God's grace (unmerited favor). All your sins—past, present and future—have been forgiven. Don't draw a timeline of God's forgiveness of your sins. There are some Christians who believe that the forgiveness they received spans only from the day they were born to the day they became Christians. From that point onwards, they think that they need to tread very carefully in case they lose their salvation. Did you know that this belief is not scriptural? Colossians 2:13 states clearly that we have been forgiven of all our sins:

> And you, being dead in your trespasses and the uncircumcision of your flesh, He has made alive together with Him, having forgiven you **all** trespasses.
>
> —Colossians 2:13

Does "all" mean the same thing to you as it does to me? My Bible says that all our sins have been forgiven by Jesus' one sacrifice on the cross. We have been forgiven once and for all! The high priests in the old covenant had to offer sacrifices for sins daily. Jesus, our perfect new covenant High Priest, "did once for all when He offered up Himself."[6] On the cross, He took upon Himself all the sins that you will commit in your lifetime, and once for all paid the full, complete and perfect price for all your sins. Christ does not need to be crucified again for your future sins. In fact, all your sins were in the future when He died on the cross. So when you received Jesus into your heart, ALL your sins were completely forgiven!

Why A Revelation Of Your Forgiveness Is So Important

"But…Pastor Prince, why is an understanding of the complete forgiveness of my sins so important for me to walk in God's unmerited favor?"

That is a great question. Let me share with you some of the implications involved. First, if you have no confidence that all your sins have been forgiven, then your eternal security and salvation will always hang in the balance.

Second, if you think that your sins were not fully dealt with at the cross, then you can never have the confidence to enjoy the Lord's presence because you can never be sure if He is on your side, or if He is waiting to punish you for your failures. You will constantly feel unworthy because of your assessment of your conduct, and you can never really have the boldness to ask God for big things, or believe that He will give you success in your life.

Third, if you do not believe that Jesus has already forgiven all your sins, it means that when you fail, you will believe that you are not "right" with God and that fellowship with Him has been cut off. And instead of depending on His unmerited favor to overcome your failure, you will feel that you need to confess your sin, be remorseful and make amends with God before you can restore fellowship with God and depend on Him again.

Once you don't have a clear sense of your complete forgiveness, you will constantly be on an emotional seesaw.

It comes down to this: Once you don't have a clear sense of your complete forgiveness, you will constantly be on an emotional seesaw. Sometimes, you feel that things between you and God are all right, but at other times, you don't think that it is so. Sometimes, you feel confident that the Lord is with you to make you a success, but at other times, you feel like you blew it and the Lord will not help you until you confess your sin and make amends.

You will be in a constant cycle of feeling insecure, where you are always hopping in and out of God's favor. All these feelings depend on how well you think you have performed, and ignore the cross of Jesus altogether. My friend, God does not evaluate you based on your behavior. He sees only Jesus' perfect work. But because you do not believe that Jesus has indeed forgiven you of all your sins, you end up feeling like a total and complete hypocrite and failure.

I hope that you are beginning to see that understanding the complete forgiveness of your sins is not just for theologians. Thinking that your sins are not completely forgiven will fundamentally affect your relationship with Jesus. While He is all ready to bless you, give you favor and make you a success, unbelief in His finished work robs you of the ability to receive His goodness, His blessings, His unmerited favor and His success in your life.

While Jesus is all ready to bless you, give you favor and make you a success, unbelief in His finished work robs you of the ability to receive His goodness, His blessings, His unmerited favor and His success in your life.

The cross of Jesus qualified you, but unbelief in the main clause of the new covenant disqualifies you. Meditate on what God says about your sins in the new covenant and free yourself to receive from Him today. The new covenant is based entirely on His unmerited favor. There is nothing for you to do, nothing for you to perform, nothing for you to accomplish. Look at the table on the next page. It encapsulates the essential differences between the old and new covenants. Your part in the new covenant is just to have faith in Jesus and to believe that you are totally forgiven and free to enjoy the new covenant blessings through His finished work!

The Differences Between The Old Covenant Of Law And New Covenant Of Grace

Under the old covenant of law...	Under the new covenant of grace...
God demanded righteousness from man.	God imparts righteousness to man through the finished work of Jesus (Romans 4:5–7).
God will visit your sins to the third and fourth generations (Exodus 20:5).	God will by no means remember your sins (Hebrews 8:12; 10:17).
The children of Israel were blessed only if they obeyed God's commandments perfectly—inwardly and outwardly (Deuteronomy 28:13–14).	Believers don't have to depend on their self-efforts to receive God's blessings, because Jesus fulfilled every one of the requirements of the law on their behalf (Colossians 2:14).
The children of Israel were cursed if they did not obey God's commandments perfectly (Deuteronomy 28:15–16, 18, 20).	Believers can enjoy God's blessings and undeserved favor because Christ became a curse for them on the cross (Galatians 3:13).
Depending on self-effort produces behavior modification without heart transformation.	Beholding the loveliness of Jesus and His finished work brings about inner transformation, which produces good works that are motivated by God's love (2 Corinthians 3:18).
The blood sacrifices of animals covered the sins of the children of Israel for only one year, and the process had to be repeated every year (Hebrews 10:3).	The blood of Jesus has removed the sins—past, present and future—of believers, completely and perfectly, once and for all (Hebrews 10:11–12).
Obeying the law could not and did not give the children of Israel the power to stop sin in their lives. The law has no power to make anyone holy, just and good.	Sin has no dominion over believers (Romans 6:14), as the power of Jesus to overcome temptation kicks in when they are conscious that they are righteous in Christ apart from their works (Romans 4:6).

Under the old covenant of law ...	Under the new covenant of grace ...
The children of Israel were robbed of their confidence in the goodness of God because they were always looking at themselves to see how well or poorly they performed (i.e. self-conscious).	Believers can have a tremendous sense of confidence and security in Christ because they are now looking to Jesus and not themselves (i.e. Christ-conscious).
The children of Israel could not have an intimate relationship with God because their unrighteousness put distance between them and God.	Believers can enjoy a close, intimate relationship with God as their Father because they are made righteous by faith in Jesus (2 Corinthians 5:17; Romans 5:7–9; Hebrews 10:10).
The children of Israel could not enter the holy of holies (where the presence of God was). Only the high priest could, and that only once a year, on the Day of Atonement (Leviticus 16:2, 14).	Not only can believers enter God's holy presence, they can also come boldly to His throne of grace to find mercy and grace in their time of need because of Jesus' perfect atonement (Hebrews 4:16).
The children of Israel were under the ministry of death (2 Corinthians 3:7).	Believers are under the ministry of Jesus' abundant life (2 Corinthians 3:6; John 10:10).

Chapter 13

How Unmerited Favor Is Cheapened

everal years ago, when I was in my study reading the Word and just enjoying the Lord's presence, He asked me this question: "Do you know how grace (unmerited favor) is cheapened?" With that one simple question, He began to reveal to me how believers today are cheapening His grace (unmerited favor).

Let me just make this clear from the onset: The grace (unmerited favor) that you and I enjoy today is NOT cheap. To call grace "cheap" is to directly insult the cross of Jesus Christ! Grace, God's undeserved, unearned and unmerited favor, is so valuable that it is priceless. You cannot buy it, achieve it or earn it. Something that is priceless can only be given. And that is exactly what God did—He gave you His grace (unmerited favor), His righteousness, His goodness and all the benefits and blessings of the cross as gifts to be freely received when you received Jesus as your personal Lord and Savior.

If you ever feel unsure if God really loves you or if He sees any value in you, just look at the cross. Look at the price that God paid to redeem you and the sacrifice that He made to save you. At the cross is where you will find your assurance of His love and desire to bless you! My friend, you must know this so that you don't disqualify yourself from receiving all that He has for you.

Wrong Believing Cheapens God's Grace

Unfortunately, there are some believers who are cheapening grace and the finished work of Jesus because of their wrong beliefs. Wrong believing always leads to wrong behavior. If you believe wrong, you will inevitably live wrong. Conversely, when you start believing right, you will live right. For example, when you start believing that you are righteous in Christ, you will start to live righteously. Everything you do will stem from the revelation of your righteous identity in Christ. This is a powerful truth. There is no point in merely addressing wrong behavior—we want to go after its root cause and address the wrong beliefs that have led to the cheapening of God's unmerited favor.

When you believe that you need to do something to earn God's forgiveness so that He will bless you, that's cheapening the grace of God.

When you believe that **you** need to do something to earn God's forgiveness so that He will bless you, **that's** cheapening the grace of God. And the problem with that is that it will rob you of a strong sense of security in the goodness of God toward you. In the previous chapter, we saw how the Bible clearly states that **all** your sins—past, present and future—have been forgiven at the cross. If instead of accepting Jesus' work on the cross as complete and final, you think that it is not enough and insist that YOU need to play a part in securing your forgiveness, you are undermining what Jesus accomplished at the cross. And once it involves **your** doing, once it is not based completely on God's unmerited favor, your forgiveness can never be secure. In turn, you will find it hard to expect God to be gracious to you. You are likely to live life with an expectation of God's judgment coming on you instead of His unmerited favor operating in your life.

Do We Need To Confess Our Sins To Receive Forgiveness?

Depending on your religious background, you may have been taught different things about what you need to do to receive God's forgiveness. For example, when I was an earnest young adult, I was taught that I had to confess all my sins in order to be forgiven. I loved the Lord and wanted to be pleasing to Him in every way, so I ran as hard as I could with this teaching. I was told that you had to keep "short accounts" with the Lord, which meant that once you sinned in thought or deed, you had to confess your sin as soon as possible, so that you could always be "right with God." I did not want to spend even one minute not being "right with God," so whenever I had a wrong thought, I would confess that sin immediately. I would cover my mouth and whisper my confession **every time** I felt that I had failed.

I took this teaching very seriously and ended up confessing my sins **all the time**. When I was talking to my friends, I would stop mid-sentence to confess my sin if I realized that I had said something I shouldn't have. During meal times, I would confess my sin when a bad thought slipped into my mind. Even when I was playing soccer, I would stop to whisper my confession when I caught myself shouting angry words at my opponents! Can you imagine how weird I appeared to the people around me? They had no idea why I was always whispering into my hand. I was trying my best to keep short accounts with the Lord, but I was actually being a bad testimony to my friends, who thought that Christians were strange.

The constant, unceasing confession of my sins made me so sin-conscious and so aware of every thought that I believed that there was no more forgiveness for my sins, and that I had lost my salvation. The enemy took advantage of my sin-consciousness and constantly put me under condemnation. The oppression was so heavy that it came to a point where I felt that my mind was about to snap! I went to the elders of the church that I was attending then but they offered no relief. Some encouraged me to keep on confessing my sins, while one elder actually told me that I **had** lost my salvation! Can you believe that? It was a dark and terrible time for me, and even though I was confessing my sins out of a sincere heart, I was sincerely wrong. Confession of sins did not liberate me. It just made me so conscious of sin that I almost went over the edge.

This teaching on the confession of sins has caused so much bondage and oppression in the church. Sincere, well-meaning believers live in fear that they have not searched their hearts diligently enough to discover and confess every sin that they have committed. As such, they believe that they must forfeit their fellowship with God and His blessings. But in reality, there is no scriptural basis for this teaching! Ephesians 1:7 explicitly states that the forgiveness of sins is "**according** to the riches of His grace [unmerited favor]." Nowhere in the Bible does it say that the forgiveness of sins is according to the confession of our sins. Nowhere! My friend, here is the truth of the matter: The forgiveness of your sins is established on unmerited favor. You cannot earn it with your confessions.

The forgiveness of your sins is established on unmerited favor. You cannot earn it with your confessions.

Instead of receiving forgiveness by grace, some Christians have made it into a law that no man can ever keep perfectly. If you believe that you are not right with God unless you confess all your sins, then let me ask you this: Have you confessed **all** your sins today? Have you confessed your worries? Have you confessed "whatever is not from faith" since the Bible considers anything that falls into that category a sin?[1] Have you confessed every wrong thought that you had in the last five minutes? When was the last time you made a confession? How short are the accounts you are keeping with the Lord?

You see, once you make the forgiveness of your sins **your** responsibility and maintaining it a law you need to abide by, you will surely fail. There is no way any person can confess all their sins perfectly. You will just drive yourself crazy. If you really believe in the confession of sins for your forgiveness, you cannot just randomly pick and choose which sins you want to confess and ignore the rest. The law works in totality and the Bible states clearly that "whoever shall keep the whole law, and yet stumble in one point, he is guilty of all."[2] If you really need to confess your sins to be forgiven, you need to confess **every** point of failing **all** the time. Otherwise, you are still "guilty of all" for "judgment is without mercy."[3]

Are you beginning to see just how absurd the teaching about confession of sins is, and the bondage and oppression that comes with it? This is not God's heart for you and this is certainly not based on the new covenant of His unmerited favor, which declares that all your sins and your lawless deeds, He remembers no more! And if He remembers them no more, then sin can no longer prevent you from being separated from Him and from receiving the blessings that He wants you to enjoy. So let's have clarity on this issue: Are you right with God because you have confessed all your sins perfectly, or because of the one sacrifice of Jesus for sins forever? Which is it? You cannot believe both at the same time. You either believe in Jesus and Jesus alone for your forgiveness, or you believe in your own confession of sins for forgiveness.

Paul Did Not Write About Confession Of Sins

"But Pastor Prince, what about 1 John 1:9, which says, 'If we confess our sins, He is faithful and just to forgive us our sins and to cleanse us from all unrighteousness'?"

Good question. I was just about to address this verse. Every time the teaching on the confession of sins is brought up, someone quotes 1 John 1:9. Before I go into the context of 1 John 1:9, let me establish first that you cannot build a doctrine based on one verse in the Bible. The teaching needs to be confirmed and established by various verses in the Bible before it can be sound.

Now, have you ever wondered why Paul, the apostle of God's unmerited favor, the man who wrote over two-thirds of the new covenant epistles, did not make the slightest mention of "confession of sins" to all the churches he wrote to? Don't take my word for it. Review all the letters that Paul wrote: Romans, Corinthians, Galatians, Ephesians, Philippians, Colossians, Thessalonians, Timothy, Titus, Philemon and Hebrews (the author of the Book of Hebrews is not clear, but many prominent Bible scholars believe that Paul was the author, as do I). Paul wrote extensively to all these churches, and yet there was not one mention of the confession of sins in all his Spirit-inspired letters. Why was this so?

Paul had the perfect opportunity to teach the Corinthians to confess their sins of fornication when he wrote to them as they had clearly sinned. But what did Paul do instead? He said, "…do you not know that your body **is** the temple of the Holy Spirit who **is** in you…?"[4] He did not say, "Do you not know that your body **was** the temple of the Holy Spirit? Now, go confess your sins and restore your fellowship with God and perhaps He will put His Spirit back in you." There was not even one mention that they had to confess their sins. Instead, Paul reminded them of their identity in Christ, and even in their failures, he maintained that their body **is** (present tense) still the temple of the Holy Spirit. Paul apparently believed that to remind believers to be conscious of who they are and what they have in Christ continually is the key to victory over their sins.

If confession of sins is so important for the church, how could Paul have left it out in every one of his letters to the churches? If our forgiveness of sins is indeed contingent on our confession of sins, hasn't he done us a great injustice by not including this teaching in any of his letters? Don't you think that Paul, who loved the church, would have written about the confession of sins in every one of his letters, and given us detailed instructions on how to confess our sins, if the confession of sins was truly necessary for us to experience forgiveness of our sins?

Now, all Scripture was written by the inspiration of the Holy Spirit. Would God Himself have forgotten to include this teaching in all of Paul's letters if the forgiveness of our sins was based on the effectiveness of our confession of sins? Of course not! Instead, we have clear and certain passages in all of Paul's letters that state beyond the shadow of a doubt that **all** our sins are forgiven, and that our forgiveness of sins is "according to the riches of His grace [unmerited favor]," and not by our works!

1 John 1:9 Was Written To The Gnostics

Since Paul did not mention the confession of sins in his letters, we are left with only one verse—1 John 1:9—that people have used for years to justify this teaching. Now, before we carry on, remember what Miles Coverdale, who translated and produced the first English Bible, said: "it shall greatly help thee to understand scripture, if thou mark not only what is spoken or written, but of whom, and unto whom, with what words, at what time, where, to what intent, with what circumstance, considering what goeth before, and what followeth after." When reading the Bible, always look at the context of the verses. When you take the "text" and interpret it out of its "context," all you are left with is a "con"! So don't be conned. Read everything in its context.

When you are reading chapter 1 of 1 John, one of the things that you need to be clear about is **whom** it was written to. Notice that in the first part of 1 John, there are no greetings to believers. If you look at Paul's letters, you will see that it was common during those days for the author to greet believers when writing to them. For instance, Paul would write "To the saints who are in Ephesus"[5] or "To the church of God which is at Corinth, to those who are sanctified in Christ Jesus, called to be saints."[6]

When you compare 1 John with the greetings found in 2 John and 3 John, you can see that John greets believers directly in the other two letters. In 2 John, he writes, "…To the elect lady and her children, whom I love in truth…Grace, mercy, and peace will be with you from God…,"[7] and in 3 John, he writes, "…To the beloved Gaius, whom I love in truth: Beloved, I pray that you may prosper in all things and be in health, just as your soul prospers."[8] In stark contrast, there are no greetings to believers in 1 John 1. Why is that? It is because John was not writing to believers in that chapter. He was addressing the Gnostics who had infiltrated the early church. Gnostics are heretics who do not believe in the existence of sin. That is why John wrote:

> If we say that we have no sin, we deceive ourselves, and the truth is not in us. If we confess our sins, He is faithful and just to forgive us our sins and to cleanse us from all unrighteousness. If we say that we have not sinned, we make Him a liar, and His word is not in us.
>
> —1 John 1:8–10

John used the editorial "we" in his writing, but we know that this does not mean that he did not believe in the existence of sin. This passage was clearly written to the unbelieving Gnostics to encourage them to stop their denial of sin, acknowledge the truth that sin exists and acknowledge that **they** have sinned. It was written to bring them to the realization that "**all** have sinned and fall short of the glory of God."[9]

Essentially, John was preaching the gospel to the Gnostics and telling them that if they confessed their sins, God would be faithful and just to forgive them their sins and cleanse them from all unrighteousness. That is why at the beginning of 1 John, John said, "…that which we have seen and heard we declare to you, **that you also may have fellowship with us**; and truly our fellowship is with the Father and with His Son Jesus Christ."[10] John was clearly preaching to non-believers (in this case, the Gnostics) about Jesus and His finished work, and inviting them to fellowship in Christ with the other believers in the early church.

In that very instance when you prayed the prayer of salvation, all the sins that you would commit for your entire life were forgiven once and for all, and all God's blessings, His favor, His health and His success became yours!

With this context in mind, it becomes clear that **1 John 1:9 was not written to believers**. The verse is a reference to the prayer that a sinner prays to accept Jesus as his personal Lord and Savior. You may know this as the "prayer of salvation" or "the sinner's prayer." If you are a believer today, it means that you have already prayed that prayer. Now, let me ask you this: How often do you have to pray the prayer of salvation? Only once! You are "born again" only once! You cannot be born again and again.

In the same way, how often do you have to confess your sins for Jesus to forgive you and cleanse you from all unrighteousness? Only once! In that very instance when you prayed the prayer of salvation, **all** the sins that you would commit for your entire life were forgiven once and for all. You received the full redemptive work of Jesus on the cross into your life, and all His blessings, His favor, His health and His success became yours! Let me say this plainly: You do not need to confess your sins again and again to be forgiven. You **are already** forgiven! Today, you can be honest with your Father about your mistakes and failures, knowing that He loves you and has already forgiven you. You don't confess your sins to Him in order to be forgiven.

While chapter 1 of 1 John was written to the Gnostics, John directs his attention to believers when it comes to chapter 2. It becomes immediately clear that he is talking to believers once the chapter begins because he writes, "My **little children**, these things I write to you, so that you may not sin. And **if anyone sins, we have an Advocate with the Father**, Jesus Christ the righteous. And He Himself is the propitiation for our sins, and not for ours only but also for the whole world."[11]

Right after John addresses the believers, he states clearly that if any one of us sins, we have an Advocate with the Father! Notice that there is no mention of confession of sins at all. Hey, this is the same John who wrote 1 John 1:9, which has been wrongly used to teach believers that they have to confess all their sins and to keep short accounts with the Lord to have fellowship with Him. No, when we as believers fail today, our Advocate fights for us. Our Advocate shows any accuser His nailed-pierced hands as a receipt for the payment that He made for our sins at the cross. Whenever we fail today, there is no power in confessing our sins, but there is power in confessing our righteousness in Christ, our identity in Christ and our unmerited favor in Christ!

Instead of being sin-conscious, become righteousness-conscious and receive the power of God to step out of that sin that seems to have a grip on you. Receive the power and wisdom of God to turn around any failure in your life.

Furthermore, in verse 12 of the same chapter, John states, "I write to you, little children, because your sins are forgiven you for His name's sake." Here, John takes it for granted your forgiveness of sins without confessions. It would be a strange double-talk for John to write 1 John 1:9 and 1 John 2:12 **both** to believers.

Beloved, instead of being sin-conscious, become righteousness-conscious, and receive the power of God to step out of that sin that seems to have a grip on you. Receive the power and wisdom of God to turn around any failure in your life. Sin-consciousness will make you depressed and keep you in a cycle of sin even when the unmerited favor of God is on your side. Every time you search your heart for sin and failings, guess what? You **will** find something! Instead of looking at your own failures, turn away from yourself and look at Jesus. Look at His heart of love and His forgiveness toward you. When you know that you do not deserve His grace (unmerited favor), and yet receive it, how can you help but be transformed? How can you help but want to worship Him?

Jesus wants you to have no more consciousness of your sins. Instead, He wants you to have a consciousness of your righteousness in Him. The more you are conscious of your righteous identity in Him, the more you are transformed by His unmerited favor, the more the desire to sin dissipates and the more you become a true worshiper. My friend, believers who know that their entire life of sins is forgiven by the blood of Jesus won't want to run out there and sin like the devil. Instead, they become true worshipers of Jesus with hearts purified by His blood and having no more consciousness of sins![12]

Would Complete Forgiveness Produce License To Sin?

Let's look at Luke 7:36–50 to see what Jesus said about the forgiveness of sins. Simon, a Pharisee, had invited Jesus to his house. While Jesus was seated at the table in Simon's house, a woman came to Him. She began to weep and she washed His feet with her tears. Then, she wiped His feet with her hair, kissed them and anointed them with fragrant oil.

When Simon saw this, he said to himself, "This Man, if He were a prophet, would know who and what manner of woman this is who is touching Him, for she is a sinner." Even though Simon did not speak aloud, it is interesting that Jesus answered him by posing this question to him: "There was a certain creditor who had two debtors. One owed five hundred denarii, and the other fifty. And when they had nothing with which to repay, he **freely forgave them** both. Tell Me, therefore, which of them will love him more?" Simon answered, "I suppose the one whom he forgave more." Jesus said to him, "You have rightly judged."

Then, Jesus turned to the woman and said to Simon, "Do you see this woman? I entered your house; you gave Me no water for My feet, but she has washed My feet with her tears and wiped them with the hair of her head. You gave Me no kiss, but this woman has not ceased to kiss My feet since the time I came in. You did not anoint My head with oil, but this woman has anointed My feet with fragrant oil. Therefore I say to you, her sins, which are many, are forgiven, for she loved much. But to whom little is forgiven, the same loves little."

You will only love Jesus much when you experience His lavish grace and unmerited favor in forgiving you of all your sins—past, present and future.

The woman loved Jesus **much** because she **knew** that she was forgiven **much**. In actuality, no one has been forgiven little. We have all been forgiven much. As for this woman, she knew it. So the most "dangerous" thing about this doctrine of complete forgiveness of sins is that you will fall in love with Jesus and end up effortlessly fulfilling the greatest commandment: "You shall love the Lord your God with all your heart, with all your soul, and with all your mind."[13] Hallelujah!

If you **think** that you have been forgiven little, then you will love little. But when you know the truth of how much you have been forgiven, you will love Jesus much! Knowing how much you have been forgiven is the secret to loving Jesus! In other words, you will only love Jesus much when you experience His lavish grace and unmerited favor in forgiving you of all your sins—past, present and future. But His grace is cheapened when you think that He has only forgiven you of your sins up to the time you got saved, and after that point, you have to depend on **your confession of sins** to be forgiven.

God's forgiveness is not given in installments. Don't go around thinking that when you confess a sin, He forgives you only for that sin. Then, the next time you sin, you need to confess your sin again for Him to forgive you again. Such is the kind of belief that cheapens His grace. And the result of this is that because you think that He has forgiven you little, you will end up loving Him little, and deprive yourself of running to Him and seeing Him help, deliver and prosper you.

Beloved, with one sacrifice on the cross, Jesus blotted out all the sins of your entire life! Don't cheapen His unmerited favor with your own imperfect efforts to confess all your sins. Accord this gift that Jesus has given you the value that it deserves by fully receiving and experiencing His unmerited favor today!

Chapter 14

The Secret To Good Success

God does not simply want you to experience success in your life. He wants you to have **good success**. Is there such a thing as "bad success"? Yes there is and I am sure you have seen it yourself. There are people who are high achievers according to the world's definition. Perhaps they are movers and shakers of the economy, famous celebrities who live in fabulous pads or sports stars who make millions of dollars a week hitting or kicking a ball around. However, for some of these people, what they have is only success in amassing wealth.

But, my friend, having financial success alone does not equate to good success. Good success is holistic and permeates every spectrum of your life. If you were to take a closer look at individuals who only have financial success, you would find that other areas of their lives are suffering. For instance, while they may have plenty of money, their lives could be scarred by one broken marriage after another. Beloved, being a public success but a private failure is not good success at all!

There are people who get promoted through the ranks so quickly and take on so many work responsibilities that they no longer have time to put their own kids to bed or read their little ones a bedtime story. They become victims of their own career success, and to hang on to the "success" they have created in the cutthroat corporate world, they allow their lives to zip past them. They may have earned more money than they will ever need, but they can't enjoy their spouses and their children grow up without really knowing them.

Realize this: Even if you do win the rat race after scampering around all day, all you would have achieved is the status of number one rat! Is it really worth sacrificing your marriage and your children for that? Don't just bury yourself in climbing the corporate ladder. Make sure your ladder is placed against the right building, and don't wait till you reach the top before you realize that it's not what you really want out of life.

Not Every Promotion Is Necessarily God's Best For You

I often tell my congregation that they should believe God not just for a job, but depend on His favor for a **position of influence**. However, I also remind them to be careful not to get promoted *out* of their place of blessings, because not every promotion is necessarily God's best for them.

Do you know that you can be promoted out of the good success that you are currently enjoying into a place where you enjoy only partial success? That promotion that you receive may also come with new responsibilities that will cause you to compromise your time with your family and draw you away from being in the house of God. All of a sudden, instead of being in God's house on Sunday morning and bringing your kids for a picnic after church, you find yourself in the office every weekend. Perhaps you need to respond to urgent emails, resolve major crises, attend pressing board meetings or have yet another critical business trip to go for. You see, it can all sound very legitimate, but is this the "good success" that God wants for you?

Listen carefully to what I am saying. I am all for you being promoted in your workplace. In fact, I believe that God can promote you way beyond your educational qualifications and work experience! Just look at what God did for Joseph. He was promoted from a slave (the lowest possible position) to an overseer in Potiphar's house. And even when he was thrown into prison, the Lord's favor caused him to be promoted again and he became the overseer of all the prisoners.

Joseph experienced one promotion after another until he became the prime minister of Egypt (the highest possible position)! There is no doubt that God wants to promote and increase you. But note that Joseph's eyes were not fixed on any of the promotions that he received. His eyes were fixed on the Lord each step of the way. **That** made him safe for the next round of promotion and he grew in the **good success** that the Lord had for him.

Fear Robs You Of Your Inheritance In Christ

Let's look at Joshua 1, which records a critical point in Israel's history, to see what we can learn about having the "good success" that God promised Joshua. Joshua was appointed as the new leader of Israel after Moses died and he was to bring God's people into the Promised Land. This was a mammoth responsibility. Forty years before that, the children of Israel were on the brink of entering their Promised Land. But because they had refused to believe God's promises to them, that generation spent 40 years wandering in the wilderness.

That was not God's will for them. God wanted to bring them into a land that was **flowing** with milk and honey. He wanted to give them a land filled with large and beautiful cities they did not build, houses full of good things they did not fill, hewn-out wells they did not dig, and vineyards and olive trees they did not plant.[1] In other words, He wanted them to enjoy the fruits and labor of another.

We do not have to strive and strain to be blessed.

Beloved, *that* is good success. That's the kind of success where you enjoy abundance of provision in every area of your life. That's the kind of success that is characterized by rest because today, the Bible says that our promised land is God's rest.[2] We are enjoying the fruits and labor of Another. And that's the kind of success Christ has given us today. We do not have to strive and strain to be blessed.

What caused the entire generation to be robbed of their promised inheritance? To answer this question, we need to ask another: Who were the leaders over that generation? The Lord showed me that Moses had followed his father-in-law's advice to appoint "able men, such as fear God, men of truth, hating covetousness"[3] as his leaders to help him rule over the children of Israel.

The 12 spies who were sent to spy on Canaan must have been picked from this pool of leaders. This means that they were all able men who **feared God**, men of truth, hating covetousness. (By the way, when Jesus was tempted by the devil in the wilderness, He said, "Away with you, Satan! For it is written, 'You shall **worship** the Lord your God, and Him only you shall serve.'"[4] Jesus was quoting from Deuteronomy 6:13, which actually reads, "You shall **fear** the Lord your God and serve Him…" Jesus substituted the word "fear" with the word "worship." So according to Jesus, to fear God is to **worship** God.) But despite having all these leadership attributes, **none** of these spies or leaders whom Moses appointed entered the Promised Land apart from Joshua and Caleb. None! Why was this so?

The answer is this: They lacked courage! We can read an account of this story in Numbers 13:17–14:9. Moses sent 12 spies into the Promised Land. Only Joshua and Caleb came back with a good report of the land, saying, "The land we passed through to spy out is an exceedingly good land. If the Lord delights in us, then He will bring us into this land and give it to us, 'a land which flows with milk and honey.' Only do not rebel against the Lord, nor fear the people of the land, for they are our bread; their protection has departed from them, and the Lord is with us. Do not fear them."[5] The other 10 spies gave a bad report, saying, "We are not able to go up against the people, for they are stronger than we…all the people whom we saw in it are men of great stature. There we saw the giants…and we were like grasshoppers in our own sight, and so we were in their sight."[6]

They all saw the same land, the same giants, but what a stark contrast in the reports that they brought back! Joshua and Caleb had a different spirit[7] (a spirit of faith) and focused on the promises and goodness of God. But the rest cowered in fear and saw only the giants and challenges in the land. **They had good leadership qualities, but it was all negated because they were fearful.** Fear paralyzed them! The nation of Israel could only go as far as their leaders could bring them. Because their leaders were fearful, the entire generation was robbed of God's promises for their lives!

Don't Be Fearful Of Man's Opinion Of You

Let's get back to Joshua 1. In that one chapter, Joshua was exhorted to be strong and courageous four times.[8] This is a powerful leadership lesson. God's appointed leadership needs to be full of His strength and courage. Every believer is a leader in some capacity, so that exhortation applies to YOU. It means that you need to dare to be different. You need to stand up for what you believe, instead of compromising on your Christian morals and values. It also means that you do not act out of fear of man's opinion of you, or allow your decisions to be shaped by the need for man's approval.

Fellow pastors and ministers, be strong and of good courage. Your people can only go as far as their leadership leads them. They need you to lead them into the promised land. They need you to bring them to a place where they can enjoy the good success that Christ has purchased for them! Stop compromising on God's new covenant promises. Don't back away from the gospel of grace just because there is a small minority of people who abuse the gospel of grace and claim it as their license to sin.

Whether you preach grace or not, this handful of people will still exercise their free choice and continue to live in sin. In fact, the only way to help them is to preach grace radically, since only grace (unmerited favor) has the power to transform a sinner and remove the dominion of sin over him.[9]

> *The gospel of grace is not the license to sin. On the contrary,*
> *it is the power for people to sin no more!*

My leaders have no qualms about confronting people who attend our church but insist on living in sin. They do not back down from the gospel of grace even if these people argue that they have the right to continue living as they please because they are "under grace." In fact, my leaders would tell them outright that they are **not** under grace, because according to Romans 6:14, if they are under grace, then sin shall not have dominion over them! (Thank God that it has only been a few folks down through the years and that itself is a testament to the power of the gospel of grace being preached in our church.) The gospel of grace is not the license to sin. On the contrary, it is the power for them to sin no more!

A pastor once told me that after he had got hold of my teachings on the complete forgiveness of sins, he searched the Scriptures and studied all the verses that I had used in my teachings. He confirmed that **all** our sins—past, present and future—were indeed forgiven when Jesus died on our behalf. But despite knowing that God's Word declares that all our sins have been forgiven and telling me that "it's in the Bible and I see that," he actually told me that he would not preach it to his congregation because "there's no telling what they would do." I was flabbergasted and deeply saddened. This pastor had more faith in the flesh of his people than in the Holy Spirit who indwells them.

What we need is a whole new generation of grace preachers who can be very strong and courageous in preaching the unadulterated gospel of Jesus, His person and His perfect work on the cross. We need leaders who are established in the new covenant of grace (unmerited favor), and who will not be satisfied with putting new wine into old wineskins by compromising with a mixture of law and grace! Be bold and preach the gospel as it is without adding to it by magnifying man's works, or subtracting from it by trying to remove God's unmerited favor from the equation. It is the gospel of Jesus and His unmerited favor that produce good success. It's time for us to bring the people into their promised inheritance!

Meditate On The Word Of God

Coming back to Joshua's appointment as Moses' successor, look at the instructions that God gave Joshua: "This Book of the Law shall not depart from your mouth, but you shall meditate in it day and night, that you may observe to do according to all that is written in it. For then you will make your way **prosperous**, and then you will have **good success**."[10] God told Joshua that to have good success, he had to meditate on the law day and night. Joshua lived under the old covenant, so how should we, who live under the new covenant, benefit from this scripture?

We need to read this portion of scripture in view of Jesus'

finished work. That is why it was essential for me to spend the last couple of chapters establishing you firmly on the rock-solid foundation of the new covenant of grace. Now that you know that we are no longer under the law, what is the new covenant way to be blessed and to experience good success? Joshua only had the law to meditate upon because the New Testament had not been written yet. For us, the secret to good success is found in meditating on God's Word in the light of the **new covenant of grace**.

The secret to good success is found in meditating on God's Word in the light of the new covenant of grace.

Before we can go into what it means to meditate on God's Word, what exactly does it mean to "meditate"? Well, it definitely does not mean mumbling some chants while seated in a cross-legged "lotus" position—that's a new age practice and it certainly does not bring God's blessings into your life. Let me just say that new age practices like transcendental meditation and the attempt to "become one with the universe" are dangerous as they open up your mind to the realm of darkness.

When the Bible talks about meditation, it's not telling you to "empty your mind." The Hebrew word for meditation in the Old Testament is the word *hagah*, which means to utter or mutter.[11] So to *hagah* is to speak under your breath. Notice that the Lord told Joshua, "This Book of the Law shall not depart from your **mouth**..." He did not say that it "shall not depart from your mind." The key to meditating on God's Word is not mental contemplation. It is in speaking God's promises with your mouth!

"Pastor Prince, does this mean that I should keep repeating God's Word? For instance, should I keep saying 'by His stripes I am healed' when I need healing?"

Meditating on God's Word does not mean making vain repetitions of scriptures. Meditating on the Word is much more and is something that first occurs deep in your heart. The psalmist David captured the essence of meditation most aptly when he said, "My heart was hot within me; while I was musing, the fire burned. Then I spoke with my tongue..."[12] As you are meditating on God's Word, ask the Holy Spirit to give you a fresh revelation of Jesus. Let that scripture burn with revelation in your heart. And as you speak out of that burning revelation, God anoints the words that you speak. When you declare, "By His stripes I am healed," and that declaration is uttered with a sense of revelation and faith in Jesus, there will be power in your declaration.

Meditate On Jesus, The Word Made Flesh, And Experience Good Success

Under the new covenant, we get to meditate on the **person of Jesus** when we meditate on the Word. Jesus is the Word made flesh, and as you meditate on His love for you, on His finished work, on His forgiveness and on His grace, God guarantees that you will have good success.

You can just take one verse and meditate on Jesus' love for you. For example, you can begin to mutter Psalm 23:1 under your breath: "The Lord is my shepherd, I shall not want." As you meditate on this simple verse, you begin to realize that the

Lord **is** (present tense) your shepherd. A shepherd provides for his sheep, feeds them and protects them. Because Jesus is your shepherd, you shall not be in want for anything. You shall not lack wisdom, direction, provision—anything. You begin to see that Jesus is present with you, providing for you, watching out for you, and making sure that you and your family will have more than enough. Now, right at that moment, in that short period of meditating on Jesus, faith is imparted and your heart is encouraged with the reality that Jesus **is** with you, even when you are facing some challenges.

Whether you are a homemaker, salesperson or business owner, your soul will be nourished and strengthened when you meditate on Jesus. In fact, every time you meditate on God's Word, Jesus will propel you into success without you even realizing it! Without you having to scheme, devise or make all sorts of plans, Jesus will direct your steps, lead you to the place that you are supposed to be and cause doors of opportunity to supernaturally open wide for you. When you meditate on Jesus, your ways always become prosperous. Now, don't be afraid to use the word "prosperous." It's God's promise in the Bible. When you meditate (mutter) on Jesus day and night, the Bible says that "you will make your way prosperous, and then you will have good success"!

Some people think that they are prosperous once they have made their first million. But when you examine their lives, you find that somewhere along the way in their struggle to make more and more money, they have lost the very things that are really important. They may have built up an impressive investment portfolio, but their children want nothing to do with them anymore and they have hurt the people who once loved them. That is not true prosperity or good success.

When God blesses you with prosperity, financial blessings are included, but only as a small part of the whole. Good success from Jesus will never take you away from your church. It will never take you away from your loved ones. Most of all, it will never take you away from yourself. You will not wake up one day in the midst of your pursuit of success and find that you no longer know the person looking back at you in the mirror.

My friend, learn to meditate on the person of Jesus. **He** is your good success. When you have Him, you have everything. The Bible tells us that "faith comes by hearing, and hearing by the word of God."[13] The word for "God" here in the original Greek text is *Christos*,[14] referring to Christ. In other words, faith comes by hearing and hearing the Word of **Christ**.

Jesus is your good success. When you have Him,
you have everything.

Faith does not come just by hearing the Word of God. Faith comes by hearing the Word of **Jesus** and His finished work. In the same way, meditating on God's Word is about meditating, muttering and hearing about Jesus. This does not mean that you read only the four Gospels of Matthew, Mark, Luke and John. No, every page of the entire Bible from cover to cover points to the person of Jesus!

If you desire to experience good success in your life, then I encourage you to meditate on messages preached by ministries that are all about exalting the person of Jesus, His beauty, His unmerited favor and His perfect work for you on the cross. Listen to new covenant ministries that do not mix law and grace, but which rightly divide the Word of God and preach the unadulterated gospel of Jesus. The more you hear of Jesus and the cross, the more faith will be imparted to you and you will experience good success in your life!

Chapter 15

The Blessed Man Versus The Cursed Man

When learning anything, there are always foundations that need to be established before you can continue further. In Mathematics, you must learn addition before you can move on to learning multiplication. In learning the English language, you must first be established in recognizing letters in the alphabet before you can move on to the basics of spelling, sentence structure and punctuation.

Similarly, if you want to delve deeper into God's Word, you must first be established in the truth that you are now under the new covenant of grace. Every revelation in God's Word is built upon the revelation of Jesus Christ and His finished work. My desire is that as you continue to walk through the pages of this book with me, you will come to a place of maturity in your understanding of the new covenant of grace.

The Book of Hebrews tells us that "everyone who partakes only of milk is unskilled in the **word of righteousness**, for he is a babe."[1] This means that if you are established in your righteousness (the word of righteousness) through Christ, you are no longer a spiritual baby. Once you have the revelation that your righteousness is not dependent on your own right **doing**, but on your right **believing** in Jesus, you have matured and become skillful in the word of righteousness.

You see, it does not take the Holy Spirit to understand the law. If you were to walk down any street and interview passers-by to find out how a person can get to heaven, most of them will probably tell you that you can get to heaven if you behaved well and did good deeds. This emphasis on one's own behavior, efforts and merits is actually *works* based on the system of the law.

In fact, *all* religion is based on the system of the law. Simply put, if you do good, you get good. If you do bad, you get beat! The world calls it karma and has no problems understanding concepts like retribution and judgment under the system of the law. You may have seen the sitcom *My Name Is Earl*. Well, the people of the world are generally like Earl. When Earl does something good, he expects something good to happen to him. Conversely, when he does something bad, he expects some form of punishment.

Jesus did everything on our behalf and He qualified us for heaven and for every blessing of good success!

But you know what? You and I we have something that the world *cannot* understand, and it is called grace (unmerited favor)! We did not do anything—Jesus did everything on our behalf and He qualified us for heaven and for every blessing of good success! Even when we fail, we can have a confident expectation of good instead of a fearful expectation of punishment. This is not because we have stored up enough merits or good deeds. It is purely because the blood of Jesus has washed us whiter than snow. What we have as new covenant believers is so good that we need the Holy Spirit to be able to understand the exceeding richness of Jesus' unmerited favor toward us.

Cursed Is The Man Who Trusts In Man

I want to show you the difference between a blessed man and a cursed man. The Bible is amazingly clear on how you can be a cursed man. But just in case you are interested, I thought I should mention that the Bible also shows you how you can be a blessed man. Are you interested to learn more about this? Turn with me to Jeremiah 17:5–8:

> "Cursed is the man who trusts in man and makes flesh his strength, whose heart departs from the Lord. For he shall be like a shrub in the desert, and shall not see when good comes, but shall inhabit the parched places in the wilderness, in a salt land which is not inhabited. Blessed is the man who trusts in the Lord, and whose hope is the Lord. For he shall be like a tree planted by the waters, which spreads out its roots by the river, and will not fear when heat comes; but its leaf will be green, and will not be anxious in the year of drought, nor will cease from yielding fruit.
>
> —JEREMIAH 17:5–8

Let's start with how one can become a cursed man. From verse five, we see that when a man "trusts in man" and not in the Lord, he becomes a cursed man. To trust in man also refers to someone putting confidence in his own good works and efforts, claiming to be "self-made," choosing to depend on himself and rejecting God's unmerited favor.

A man who "makes flesh his strength" is also cursed. When you see the word "flesh" in your Bible, it does not always refer to your physical body. You have to look at the context of the verse. In this context, "flesh" can be paraphrased as "self-effort." In other words, we can read verse five as "Cursed is the man who trusts in man and makes **self-effort** his strength."

Don't use all your health to chase after wealth, only to spend all your wealth later to get back your health!

My friend, there are essentially two ways to live this life. The first is for us to depend and trust entirely in the Lord's unmerited favor, while the other is to depend on our efforts, and strive and struggle for success. We can never bring about good success that comes from God by depending on our self-efforts. No matter how we strive and struggle, we cannot work for our own righteousness or attain our own forgiveness. Any success that we may achieve is only partial success.

On the other hand, God's kind of success is complete, whole and permeates into every facet of our lives—spirit, soul and body. God's Word says, "The blessing of the Lord makes one rich, and He adds no sorrow with it."[2] God never gives us success at the expense of our marriage, families or health. Like I always say to the business people in my church, don't use all your health to chase after wealth, only to spend all your wealth later to get back your health! Which is a prosperous man? A man who has a fat bank account but is flat on his back with sickness, or one who may not have much in his bank account but is enjoying divine health?

Look around you. It is clear that true prosperity and good success cannot be measured in terms of how much money we have in our bank accounts. With the unmerited favor of God, the man who may not have much at this point in his life **will** experience good success.

Health and wholeness in your physical body are part of God's blessings. If you are constantly under tremendous stress and have regular panic attacks because of the nature of your work, then I would encourage you to take a step back and seek the Lord's counsel. Stress robs you of health, whereas good success from the Lord causes your youth to be renewed.

When you depend on your efforts, you can struggle for many years and get a certain measure of success. But God's ways are higher. With just one moment of His favor, you can experience accelerated blessings and promotion that years of striving and struggling can never achieve.

Look at Joseph's life. He was nothing but a lowly prisoner. Yet, within an hour of meeting Pharaoh, he was promoted to the highest office in the entire Egyptian empire. Beloved, even if you are down and out (like Joseph was) at this point in your life, the Lord can promote you supernaturally in an instance when you choose to put your eyes on Him!

Let's continue reading the passage in Jeremiah 17, which goes on to describe the cursed man: "For he shall be like a shrub in the desert, and **shall not see when good comes**." Now, this is amazing! Let me ask you a question. According to this passage, does good come along the way of the cursed man? Yes, it does! But the sad reality is that he cannot see it.

As a pastor, I have seen, down through the years, people who don't put their trust in the Lord when it comes to their marriages, finances and other areas of weaknesses. They are determined to trust in their own efforts, and tend to be rather arrogant and frustrated with the people around them. Many a time, when you observe people like that, you realize that they cannot see the good things that are right under their noses. They don't appreciate their spouses, neglect their children and even when other blessings come their way, **they miss them**!

People living under grace can truly enjoy the blessings around them because they know that these blessings are undeserved.

Why is it that they can't see good when it comes? It is because people who trust in their own efforts have **no ability** to see and receive blessings from the Lord. They only believe in the "good" that can come from their own efforts. That is why they are proud. You would probably notice that such people don't say "thank you" very often to the people around them. They feel like they are entitled to and deserve whatever they receive. They are rarely grateful or appreciative, and that is why they take their spouses for granted instead of seeing them as a blessing from the Lord.

In contrast, people who are living under grace and who trust in the Lord's unmerited favor are constantly thankful, praising God and giving thanks to Jesus. They are grateful and appreciative of the people around them.

When I was still a bachelor, I had an idea of the kind of wife I wanted and brought my request to the Lord. But you know what? He over-answered my prayer and gave me Wendy! I am truly grateful to the Lord for Wendy and I know that it is the unmerited favor of Jesus. When I look at my daughter Jessica, I know that I don't deserve such a beautiful daughter, and yet the Lord gave this precious girl to me. You see my friend, I did nothing to deserve it, but the Lord blessed me with an amazing family. People living under grace can truly enjoy the blessings around them because they know that these blessings are undeserved.

A Picture Of The Blessed Man

Let's look at some of the pictures that the Bible paints for us in Jeremiah 17. God's Word is amazing. He speaks to us through word pictures and imagery in the Bible. It says that the cursed man "shall be like a shrub in the desert." What a dismal image of a man! A person who is always trusting in himself is like a dried-up shrub, looking old, tired and haggard.

But thank God the Bible didn't just stop with the description of the cursed man. It goes on to paint a beautiful picture of the blessed man. Jeremiah 17:7–8 tells us: "Blessed is the man who trusts in the Lord, and whose hope is the Lord. For he shall be like a tree planted by the waters, which spreads out its roots by the river, and will not fear when heat comes; but its leaf will be green, and will not be anxious in the year of drought, nor will cease from yielding fruit." Wow! I know which man I would rather be. Truly, a picture is worth more than a thousand words! I want you to see yourself as this tree planted by the waters today!

When I was on vacation with Wendy in the breathtaking Canadian Rockies, we spent a lot of time just roaming around and soaking in the splendor of our heavenly Father's creation. As we wandered along the bank of a tranquil river that we chanced upon, we found a majestic tree anchored by the water's edge. Its trunk was sturdy and strong, and its branches stretched out to form a perfect canopy above it. In contrast to the other trees that were further away from the river, its leaves were refreshingly green and luscious. This was because the tree was constantly nourished by the river.

Looking at that impressive, beautiful tree, I couldn't help but recall the blessed man described in Jeremiah 17, and I remember saying to myself then, "I am like this tree in Jesus' name!" When you depend on and trust in the Lord, you are like this tree too. Jesus will cause you to be a picture of robust strength, vitality and good success. See yourself like a beautiful tree planted by the waters. God's Word says that even when heat comes, you will not fear it!

Did you notice a crucial difference between the blessed man and the cursed man? While the cursed man cannot see good when it comes, the blessed man will not fear even when heat comes! The King James Version says that the blessed man "shall **not see** when heat cometh." This is amazing. It means that heat comes even to the blessed man, but he is not conscious of seasons of heat, but continues to be strong and to flourish. He will be like a tree whose leaf continues to be green. When you are like the blessed man, you will be evergreen! This means that you will enjoy divine health, youthfulness, vibrancy and dynamism.

The blessed man is not conscious of seasons of heat,
but continues to be strong and to flourish.

When you are blessed, your body will be full of life as the Lord renews your youth and vigor. Your health will not fail you, nor will you lose your youth. There will be no stress, fear and panic attacks because the blessed man "will not be anxious in the year of drought." A year of drought speaks of a severe famine, and in our modern vernacular, it would be no different from the global financial meltdown, the subprime crisis, the collapse of global investment banks, the volatile stock markets and rising inflation. While it may be bad news for the world, the blessed man can remain at rest and not be anxious because God has promised that even in the midst of a crisis, he will not "cease from yielding fruit." How will this happen? It will happen because he puts his trust in the Lord!

During the late 1990s, I stood up in my church one day and told my congregation that the Lord had given me a word of wisdom. He said that a dearth, a financial famine, was coming to Asia. But at the same time, He also said that even when the famine hits, we would not have to worry because He would take care of us and our church would have more than enough to help those in need.

A few months later, the Thai baht fell suddenly and dramatically. This produced a domino effect on all the regional currencies, plunging us into the Asian financial crisis. During that time, our church, by the grace of God, had the privilege of financially blessing other churches in our nation as well as in the region. God was able to use us to help keep some of these ministries afloat and from retrenching staff. We were also able to help the precious lives under their care who were going through difficult financial setbacks.

God's word came to pass and we went through the crisis not seeing the heat. In fact, there were people in my church who even benefited from the crisis, buying new houses and cars at greatly reduced prices. Even in the season of famine, their businesses, careers and financial health continued to flourish and they did not "cease from yielding fruit."

We don't take any credit for these blessings. We know that they came entirely because of the Lord's unmerited favor. Our part was simply to continue trusting Jesus and to keep our hope in Him. The Greek word for "hope" in the New Testament is *elpis*, which means an "expectation of good."[3] Keep on hoping in the Lord!

Our church experienced the same blessings during the 2008 to 2009 global financial meltdown. **Before** the subprime crisis took center stage, the Lord was already preparing our people. As I was preaching one Sunday, I exhorted the church not to get into any new debt. I urged them to hold off buying new houses, cars or any major expense and to keep their debt to a minimum. Many people in our church began to position themselves, and they were prepared and ready when the severe famine started.

On a separate occasion, when the stock market in my nation was at its **all time high** before its collapse, I prophesied to my church and encouraged them to get **out** of the stock market even though everyone was scrambling to get onto the bandwagon. Then, in just a couple of months, Bears Sterns collapsed, followed by the Lehman Brothers. We all know that this led to a massive frenzy in the global financial markets and billions of dollars were completely wiped out during the panic selling that ensued.

Some time later, one of the key leaders in my church, who works in a major American bank, told me that he had brought a friend to church on the Sunday that I had told my congregation to get out of the stock market, and I had used the word "volatile" to describe the situation ahead. His friend, who was financially trained and savvy, began to take defensive actions on his investment based on the expectation of volatile conditions, and instead of losing money from his investments, he made substantial gains from them.

Now, for those of you who don't know me, I don't monitor the stock market and I don't know much about investments. In fact, not too long ago, when I was preaching at a conference overseas, I visited a bookstore and flipped through a book titled *Investing For Dummies*. Now, this is slightly embarrassing for me, but I am going to tell you this anyway—I did not understand it! What docs that say about me and investments? Don't laugh so hard. I am a pastor, not a stockbroker. But that's just me. Ask any of my leaders, and they will tell you that I don't read business publications and have no interest in the ebb and flow of the stock market. ALL glory goes to the Lord for preparing the church and protecting our people from the financial onslaught that was ahead!

By the Lord's unmerited favor, our church has been supporting churches, ministries, and missionaries worldwide throughout the crisis. We have given generously to the needy and to the down-and-out in our own nation, helping to feed the hungry and clothe the poor. Our entire church, comprising more than 19,000 people then, was part of a national initiative to help the poor with truckloads of groceries. Many also bought brand-new household necessities such as beds, refrigerators and washing machines for families who could not afford them. We are humbled that during that period, the Lord continued to bless us to be a blessing to others. But our boast is not in our good works. Our boast is in the Lord and His love for us.

The Only Way A Believer Can Fall Under The Curse

"Pastor Prince, is it possible to be a Christian and still trust in your self-efforts?"

Yes, absolutely. There are believers today who would rather depend on themselves than on Jesus. They only depend on Jesus for their salvation, but thereafter, they look to themselves for success in their families, careers and finances.

"What happens when a believer trusts in his self-efforts and rejects God's grace?"

All believers are redeemed from the curse of the law through Jesus' finished work. But when a believer rejects God's grace and depends on his own works to be blessed, he falls back under the curse of the law. This is the **only** way a believer can fall back under the curse of the law. His rejection of God's grace does **not** mean that he loses his salvation. It just means that he robs himself of enjoying the full blessings that Jesus has purchased for him with His blood, and of becoming the blessed person that we have been discussing in this chapter.

Once you go back to depending on your own works to be blessed, you are going back to the system of the law and you fall back under the curse of the law.

The rejection of God's grace is to fall from grace back into works. Contrary to popular belief, falling from grace does not mean falling into sin. According to the Bible, falling from grace is to fall back into **works** and into the old covenant of law. Galatians 5:4 clearly states that "you who attempt to be justified by law; you have **fallen from grace**."

Once you go back to depending on your own works to be blessed, you are going back to the system of the law and you fall back under the curse of the law. The apostle Paul makes it very clear in Galatians 3:10—"For as many as are of **the works of the law** are under the curse." Let's be very clear here. It is **not** God who curses you. It is the law itself that condemns you. No one can meet the perfect standards of the law. The verse goes on to say, "Cursed is everyone who does not continue in **all things** which are written in the book of the law, **to do them**." The law is an impossible standard and it will bring the worst out of anyone. Nobody can continue to keep the whole law perfectly. The moment you fail in one law, you are guilty of failing in all.

Galatians 3:11–12 continues to say, "But that **no one** is justified by the law in the sight of God is evident, for 'the just shall live by faith.' Yet the law is not of faith…" I really hope that you are coming to a place where you realize that no one can keep the law perfectly and be made righteous. We are only made righteous by faith and that's why the righteous—you and I—shall live by faith. Faith in what? Faith in Jesus' finished work! Let's be the blessed man whose trust is in the Lord and not in his own arm of flesh.

Now, let me show you two very important verses that you need to know. According to Galatians 3:13–14, "**Christ has redeemed us from the curse of the law**, having become a curse for us (for it is written, 'Cursed is everyone who hangs on a tree'), that the blessing of Abraham might come upon the Gentiles in Christ Jesus…" Notice that Jesus had to die on the cross to redeem us from the curse of the law, not the curse of sin. Most people think that they will be cursed when they sin, but that's not what God's Word says. It says that Jesus has redeemed us from the curse of the law.

So even if you fail, the law cannot condemn you because you are forgiven and justified in Jesus. There is hope when you fail and power for you to **fail no more** through Jesus. But what hope is there when you fall back into the system of the law and into depending on your efforts to be justified? The law itself would curse you and the blessing of Abraham cannot flow in your life. Sin is no longer the problem because Jesus dealt with your sins on the cross with His own blood. The problem is man's insistence on trusting in his self-efforts!

King David's Definition Of A Blessed Man

Do you want to know King David's definition of a blessed man? Look at Romans 4:6–8: "just as David also describes the blessedness of the man to whom God imputes righteousness apart from works: 'Blessed are those whose lawless deeds are forgiven, and whose sins are covered; blessed is the man to whom the Lord **shall not impute sin**.'" Can you see the blessedness of this man? The Bible does not say that this man does not sin. It says that his blessing is that even when he sins, that sin will **not** be imputed to him! Why? Because all his sins have already been imputed and punished in the body of Jesus!

"Pastor Prince, are you saying that a believer can still sin?"

Now, before I answer your question, let me share with you the definition of sin. The Greek word for "sin" in the New Testament is the word *hamartia*, which literally means "a failing to hit the mark."[4] Once you understand the definition of sin, you can see that the more appropriate and accurate question to ask is whether a believer can still "miss the mark." The answer is obvious—believers will still miss the mark from time to time.

The more pertinent question then, is whether a believer is still righteous when he misses the mark. David's definition of a blessed man answers this question: "[this is] the blessedness of the man to whom God imputes righteousness apart from works…whose lawless deeds [instances of missing the mark] are forgiven, and whose sins [instances of missing the mark] are covered; blessed is the man to whom the Lord shall not impute [to him] sin [his instances of missing the mark].'"

Now, does knowing that God does not impute your sin to you when you miss the mark make you want to go out and sin? No way! His unmerited favor transforms you and fills your heart with love and gratefulness toward Him. Knowing that you are completely and eternally forgiven by God, you can run boldly to Him and bring every area of need to Him.

Because your trust is in the Lord, you shall not fear when heat comes, but your leaves will be green, and you will not be anxious in the year of drought, nor will you cease from yielding fruit.

You become someone who trusts in the Lord and whose hope is in the Lord. What is the result of that? I declare to you in Jesus' name that you will be like a tree planted by a river, spreading out its roots to the water. Because your trust is in the Lord, you will not fear when heat comes, but your leaves will be green, and you will not be anxious in the year of drought, nor will you cease from yielding fruit. You will find yourself experiencing the blessings of the blessed man in every area of your life!

Chapter 16

Walking In The Blessing Of Abraham

In the previous chapter, I showed you the differences between a blessed man and a cursed man. What a glorious and majestic picture the Bible paints of the blessed man who is like a tree planted by the waters! But the Bible is so rich and exciting. Just by studying the word "bless," we can glean so much more about the Lord's heart for you and me. I believe that as we take a closer look at this word, the Lord is preparing you to step into an even greater and deeper dimension of His blessings for you. Let's dive right in.

The Hebrew word for "bless" is *barak*, while the Greek word is *eulogeo*. According to the *Theological Workbook of the Old Testament*, both these words mean to endue with power for success, prosperity, fecundity (fruitfulness in childbearing) and longevity.[1]

Now, I really don't understand why there are some believers who fight against ministries that proclaim the truth that God wants to give us success, prosperity and health. These believers don't realize that they are essentially fighting to remain sick and poor. Don't they realize that sickness and poverty belong to the realm of the curse? Don't they realize that Jesus has already made a way for us to live by His unmerited favor and to step into the realm of His blessings?

It is time for believers to be like the apostle Paul—stop being apologetic about the good news that we have received. Paul declared, "For I am **not ashamed** of the gospel of Christ, for it is **the** power of God to salvation for everyone who believes, for the Jew first and also for the Greek. For in it the righteousness of God is revealed from faith to faith; as it is written, 'The just shall live by faith.'"[2] The gospel (which means "good news") of Jesus Christ is THE power of God to salvation. This means that there is **no** other power for your salvation except the gospel of Jesus Christ!

By the way, "salvation" here does not just relate to being saved from hell. The Greek word for "salvation" here is the word *soteria*. Its meaning encompasses deliverance, preservation, safety and health.[3] The Lord's salvation in your life is complete and holistic, and it is based on you believing in and depending by faith on **His** righteousness. Don't be ashamed of just how good the good news of Jesus really is. Don't be ashamed that Jesus has the power to give you good success, heal your physical body, cause everything your hands touch to prosper, bless you with children and satisfy you with long life!

The Blessing Of Abraham

Jesus wants you to experience His blessings in your life. God's blessings are part of our inheritance in the new covenant of grace, which Jesus died to give us. God's Word tells us that "Christ has redeemed us from the curse of the law, having become a curse for us…that **the blessing of Abraham** might come upon the Gentiles in Christ Jesus, that we might receive the promise of the Spirit through faith."[4] Isn't it interesting that the Lord is very specific in mentioning that Christ became a curse for us on the cross, so that we can experience and enjoy the blessing of Abraham? He does not want us to simply experience any kind of blessing. He wants us to experience **the blessing of Abraham**. I think it behooves us then to find out what "the blessing of Abraham" is and who can receive it.

Every believer in Christ is an heir.

The Bible tells us that "if you are Christ's, then you are Abraham's seed, and heirs according to the promise."[5] Are you Christ's? Do you belong to Jesus? Then that makes you an heir **according to the promise**. Every believer in Christ is an heir. Whenever you hear the word "heir," it speaks of something good. It speaks of an inheritance that you don't work for, an inheritance that is yours not because of what you do, but because of **whose** you are. In this case, as a new covenant believer in Jesus, you belong to Jesus and you have a blood-bought inheritance in Christ as the seed of Abraham. You, beloved, are an heir according to THE promise!

God's Promise To Abraham

Now, there are many promises in the Bible, but what is THE promise that God made to Abraham? We can't claim this promise if we don't know what it is. We need to go to the Word (use the Bible to interpret the Bible) to establish what the promise is. And we find the answer in Romans 4:13—"For **the promise** that he would be the **heir of the world** was not to Abraham or to his seed through the law, but through the righteousness of faith."

In Christ, you are an heir of the world, its goods, its endowments, its riches, its advantages and its pleasures.

The promise to Abraham and his seed (you and I) is that he would be "the heir of the world"! In the original Greek text, the word "world" here is *kosmos*. Its meaning includes, "the whole circle of earthly goods, endowments, riches, advantages, pleasures."[6] Now, **that** is what you are an heir to through Jesus' finished work! In Christ, you are an heir of the world—its goods, its endowments, its riches, its advantages and its pleasures. This is THE promise that God made to Abraham and his seed. Don't apologize for it. It is your inheritance in Christ!

You Are An Heir Of The World

What does it mean to be an heir of the world? Let's take a look at Abraham's life to see what the Lord did for him. God's Word tells us that Abraham did not just become rich. He became very rich.

"Well, Pastor Prince, being an heir of the world refers to spiritual riches."

Hang on, that is not what my Bible says. According to Genesis 13:2, Abraham was "very rich in livestock, in silver, and in gold."

Now, if financial blessings are not part of the blessings of the Lord, then are you telling me that the Lord cursed Abraham with wealth? I am so glad that God defined Abraham's riches very specifically. God must have foreseen a generation of religious folks who would argue that He is against His people experiencing financial success, so He said clearly in His Word that Abraham was very rich in livestock, silver and gold. Abraham wasn't just rich spiritually. Beloved, God is not against you having wealth, but He is definitely against wealth having you.

The Lord blessed Abraham so that he could be a blessing to others. He told Abraham, "…I will bless you…and you shall be a blessing."[7] Similarly, He will bless you financially, so that **you** can be a blessing to others. You cannot be a blessing to those around you—your loved ones, local church, community and the poor—if you are not blessed by the Lord first.

Suppose you know that God is calling you to do something, such as go for a mission trip, support a ministry, build a church or bless a missionary. But you can't do it because you don't even have enough to take care of your family. Now, what has become bigger in your life? God or money? God says "Go" but your wallet says "No." Which of them is bigger in this situation? Something is clearly amiss here. Yet, there are believers today who settle for traditional religious beliefs that are not biblical instead of seeking God's truth. These beliefs have held the church in bondage for decades and that is why the world sees the church as generally being poor, unable and in debt. That is why the world actually has this saying: "As poor as a **church** mouse." (But in the world, even Mickey Mouse is prosperous and has a magic kingdom!)

Being An Heir Of The World Includes
Having Financial Blessings

The irony is that if you were to examine the lives of those believers who fight against the teaching that God blesses His children with more than enough, you would see that they have no problems with doing their best to secure a nice home and give their children the best education that money can buy. While they do not believe that God wants to bless us financially, you would probably find them looking out for investment opportunities, hoping for promotions in their careers or searching for better job prospects to earn more.

The success that we, as new covenant believers, can believe God for is good, holistic success that permeates every area of our lives!

You see, they have no problem with accumulating wealth for themselves and living well, but they have a problem when we tell them that financial success is from God. They would rather believe in their self-efforts and say that their success is "self-made," than give God the credit. Instead of agreeing with the teaching that God is the source of all blessings, they attack it. But don't be deceived, my friend, every blessing in our lives today, every good and perfect gift, flows directly from the river of God's unmerited favor.[8]

Our heavenly Father wants to make you a success and that success includes financial success. You already know that finances alone don't make you a success. There are a lot of "poor" people in the world today who have a lot of money. They can have fat bank accounts, but their hearts are empty without the revelation of

Jesus' love for them. You and I have something from Jesus that is far more superior. The success that we, as new covenant believers, can believe God for is good, holistic success that permeates every aspect of our lives!

"Well, Pastor Prince... the Bible says that money is the root of all evil. What do you have to say about that?"

The Bible is often quoted wrongly on this. It does not say that money is the root of all evil. It says that "**the love** of money"[9] is the root of all evil. Because of this misquotation and wrong teaching, many believers have been hoodwinked. When the Lord tries to bless them, they shun His blessings because they believe that having more money will lead them to all kinds of evil. Listen carefully to what I am saying. Having more money does not necessarily mean that you love money. Even someone who doesn't have a single cent to his name can be thinking and obsessing about money all the time.

The more occupied you are with Jesus,
the more money follows after you!

What keeps you safe for financial success is when you know that your blessings come by Jesus' unmerited favor. When you have that revelation, you will no longer be preoccupied with having money because you are preoccupied with the Lord. Amazingly, you will realize that the more occupied you are with Jesus, the more money follows after you! Now, why is that? It is simply because when you seek first the kingdom of God, and put Jesus, His righteousness (not your own righteousness), His joy and His peace as your first priority, God's Word promises you that ALL the material things that you need will be added to you.[10] The Lord always gives you money with a mission and prosperity with a purpose. He blesses you and when you are blessed, you can be a vessel to bless others. The gospel of grace can be preached, churches can be built, precious lives can be touched, sinners can be born again, marriages can be restored and physical bodies can be healed when you send out the Word of Jesus with your financial support.

Don't love money and use people. Use money to love people. May it be settled in your heart once and for all that it is God's desire for you to be a financial success and to have more than enough. You are the seed of Abraham and the promise to you is that you will be an heir of the world. It is clear that you cannot be an heir of the world if you are constantly broke and in debt.

Your Blessings Include Health And Renewal Of Youth

Now, let's look at what else it means to be an heir of the world. What other blessings did Abraham receive? We know that Abraham was healthy and strong, and so was Sarah, his wife. The Lord renewed their youth so dramatically that when Abraham was about 100 years old and Sarah about 90, Sarah conceived Isaac after many years of barrenness.

At the beginning of this chapter, I showed you that when God blesses, His blessings include fecundity, which is fruitfulness in childbearing. Nobody can argue that Abraham and Sarah's renewal of youth was merely spiritual. Isaac is proof that the renewal they experienced was physical as well. As an heir of the world, the Lord will likewise cause you to be strong and healthy.

It is not possible to be an heir of the world if you are constantly fatigued, sick and flat on your back. No way! God will make you healthy and keep you in divine health in Jesus' name!

Some years ago, I asked the Lord why the Bible calls every female believer a daughter of Sarah.[11] There were many other women of faith in the Bible, such as Ruth and Esther. So why didn't God choose to refer to female believers as daughters of Ruth or daughters of Esther? The Lord then showed me in His Word that Sarah was the only woman in the Bible who had her youth renewed in her old age. We see evidence of Sarah's renewal of youth when she was pursued twice by two different kings who wanted to include her in their harems.

Do you know how old Sarah was when Pharaoh, the first of these kings, wanted her? She was about 65 years old! Now, if that is not evidence enough for you, do you know how old Sarah was when Abimelech, king of Gerar, wanted her? She was about 90 years old! Hey, these were **heathen** kings. I am sure that they were not captivated by her inner or spiritual beauty. Sarah must have had her physical youth renewed for these kings to desire her in her old age. Ladies, are you getting this? The Lord calls you daughters of Sarah. You can trust the Lord to renew your youth as He did for Sarah!

God's Word promises a renewal of your youth and strength. There are two passages in the Bible that I want you to read for yourself. Psalm 103:1–5 says:

> Bless the Lord, O my soul; and all that is within me, bless His holy name! Bless the Lord, O my soul,

and forget not all His benefits: Who forgives all your iniquities, who heals all your diseases, who redeems your life from destruction, who crowns you with lovingkindness and tender mercies, who satisfies your mouth with good things, **so that your youth is renewed like the eagle's.**

—Psalm 103:1–5

Meanwhile, Isaiah 40:31 promises this:

But those who wait on the Lord shall renew their strength; **they shall mount up with wings like eagles**, they shall run and not be weary, they shall walk and not faint.

—Isaiah 40:31

As in Sarah's case, we can experience a literal renewal in our physical bodies. Let us believe God for this physical renewal of our youth, and that after this renewal, we will have a **brand-new body,** but a **wise and experienced mind**. Now, that is a powerful combination and that's the kind of renewal that God wants to give us.

"Pastor Prince, you keep talking about the blessings of health, wealth and good success. I knew that you were one of those who preach the prosperity gospel... one of those health and wealth preachers!"

My friend, there is no such thing as a "prosperity gospel." There is only the gospel of Jesus Christ. When you have Jesus and depend on His unmerited favor, all these blessings are added to you. What would you rather I preach about? That God wants you to remain sick and poor? Imagine going to your unbelieving friends and telling them, "Hey, God wants you to be sick and poor. Do you want to be a Christian?" Their response would be, "No thanks, I have enough problems on my own now!"

There is no such thing as a "prosperity gospel."
There is only the gospel of Jesus Christ.

It's amazing that there are believers who fight the teaching that God heals today. Don't they realize that they are essentially fighting for the right to be sick? Yet, the moment they fall sick, they have no qualms about seeing a doctor and taking medication, or going to the hospital. Now, if they really believe that it is God's plan for them to be sick and that He is teaching them some lessons, why do they go against His will by trying to get better? Clearly, there are some inconsistencies here.

It is **not** God's plan for you to be sick. Sickness, viruses and diseases are not from Him, and He would certainly not put sickness on you to teach you a lesson, any more than you would put sickness on *your* children to teach them a lesson! Be very clear that God does not and will not discipline you with sicknesses, accidents and diseases. We are on the same side as doctors, fighting the same battle against sickness.

Beloved, it is very important for you to get this doctrine right so that you can believe right. What hope is there and how can you have a confident expectation to be healed if you erroneously think that your condition is from the Lord? It is time for you to stop being deceived by wrong teachings. Just look at the ministry of Jesus to see God's heart for you. Look at the four Gospels. What happened every time Jesus came in contact with a sick person? The sick person got healed! You will never find Jesus going up to a perfectly healthy person and saying, "I want to teach you a lesson on humility and patience. Now, receive some leprosy!" No way! Yet, that is basically what some people are saying about our Lord today.

Jesus wants to bless you with more than enough so that you can be a blessing to others!

Now, tell me, what happened each time Jesus saw lack? When the little boy brought his five loaves and two fish to Jesus, did He gobble them up and say, "I am giving you a lesson in poverty"? Of course not! Jesus took the five loaves and two fish, multiplied them and fed more than 5,000 people with 12 baskets full of leftovers![12] That's my Jesus! That's my Savior! Jesus did not feed the multitudes with just enough food. He blessed them with **more than enough** food. He is the God of more than enough and that is His style. Likewise, Jesus wants to bless you with more than enough, so that you can be a blessing to others!

See God's Blessing On Abraham's Natural Seed

Now, let's look at Abraham's natural seed, the Jewish people. Have you ever wondered how just a tiny nation has produced some of humanity's greatest inventors, thinkers, musicians, entrepreneurs, scientists, doctors, academics and philosophers? Here are just some of the Jews whom you may have heard of:

- The Rothchilds of Europe who revolutionized banking.

- Albert Einstein, whose theories resulted in numerous inventions and breakthroughs, and whose famous equation, $E = MC^2$, revolutionized the scientific world.

- Alan Greenspan, who was the chairman of the Federal Reserve of the United States from 1987 to 2006.

- Steven Spielberg, who is easily Hollywood's most successful director and producer.

- Levi Strauss, whose company is now probably the most recognized jeans manufacturer in the world.

- Stan Lee, whom millions of comic book fans know as the man behind the likes of Spiderman, X-Men, The Incredible Hulk, The Fantastic Four and Iron Man.

- Paul Allen, who co-founded Microsoft with Bill Gates.

- Johann Strauss II, a celebrated composer who composed over 170 waltzes, including The Blue Danube and Emperor Waltz.

- Yehudi Menuhin, who is commonly considered one of the 20th century's greatest violin virtuosi.

Now, I may not agree with the morals of some of these famous Jews, but the fact is that the list of their accomplishments and contributions to humanity just goes on and on! For such a small population of people, they have also produced a disproportionately high number of Nobel Prize winners. According to some reports, out of over 750 Nobel Prizes that were handed out between 1901 and 2008, at least 163 recipients, or over 21 percent, are Jews.[13]

As spectacular as the achievements of the Jews are, they are only experiencing a trickle and a **residue** of the blessing of Abraham. Many of them don't know Jesus and only have the shadow. How much more should you and I, who have **not the residue but the full substance** of Jesus in our lives, expect!

The secret to walking in the blessing of Abraham in your life is to stop trying to deserve it. Instead, exercise your faith to believe that you are righteous through Jesus' finished work.

Why is it then, that there aren't more new covenant believers, the spiritual seed of Abraham, experiencing the full blessing of Abraham? The answer is found in Romans 4:13–16, which says:

> For the promise that he would be the heir of the world was **not** to Abraham or to his seed **through the law, but through the righteousness of faith**. For if those who are of the law are heirs, faith is made void and the promise made of no effect, because the law brings about wrath; for where there is no law there is no transgression. Therefore it is of faith that it might be according to grace [unmerited favor], so that the promise might be sure to all the seed…
>
> —ROMANS 4:13–16

The blessing of Abraham for the new covenant believer is made void and of no effect when you try to earn and deserve it through your efforts. Hence, the secret to walking in the blessing of Abraham in your life is to stop trying to deserve it. Instead, exercise your faith to believe that you are righteous through

Jesus' finished work. The more righteousness-conscious you are, the more blessings you will experience. Begin to experience the Abrahamic blessing of being an heir of the world today, trusting entirely on God's unmerited favor in your life!

Chapter 17

Becoming An Heir Of The World

T he fact that God wants you to be an heir of the world makes clear His desire to see you living an overcoming and victorious life. This means that He wants you to REIGN in life. He wants you to reign over every sickness, disease, financial lack, fear, addiction and anxiety. Whatever it is that you may be struggling with right now, Jesus will help you reign over it! God's Word promises that "those who **receive** the abundance of grace [unmerited favor] and of the gift of righteousness will **reign in life** through the One, Jesus Christ."[1]

My friend, the operative word here is "receive." Reigning in life is not a struggle. The only thing that you need to do is to receive—receive not just unmerited favor, but an ABUNDANCE of unmerited favor, and the GIFT of righteousness! You can never have too much unmerited favor. The Lord wants you to keep on receiving and receiving His unmerited favor until you have an abundance of it to reign in life. That is what this book is about. It is about you having an abundance of Jesus' unmerited favor in your life, and I pray that after reading this book, you will be so saturated with the unmerited favor of Jesus that you can't help but experience good success in every area of your life!

Romans 5:17 states clearly that righteousness is a **gift**. A gift cannot be earned. It can only be received. Anything that you try to earn cannot be called a gift. It goes against the very definition of the word "gift"! The best response to the gift of righteousness is saying a big "Thank You" to Jesus for making you righteous by His blood. Don't try to deserve His gift through your works. That would be an insult to Jesus, who has already freely given it to you. Simply receive the gift!

---

*The promise that you will be an heir of the world is
yours because of who you are in Christ.*

Similarly, there is nothing you can do to deserve God's promise that you will be an **heir** of the world. The promise is yours because of **who you are in Christ**. It is your inheritance. And like a gift, an inheritance can only be received. Today, God wants you to receive your inheritance of all the blessings, promises and benefits that Jesus' finished work has accomplished on your behalf!

In the previous chapter, we looked at why not every believer is experiencing the manifestation of the blessing of Abraham, even though it is supposed to be their inheritance through Christ. We saw that according to the Bible, this blessing was not to Abraham or to his seed through the law, but through the righteousness of faith. This means that access to the blessing of Abraham is not through our performance or our ability to keep the Ten Commandments, but through believing that we are righteous by faith in Jesus. Romans 4:13 says, "For the promise that he would be the heir of the world was not to Abraham or to his seed through the law, but **through the righteousness of faith**." Although the Bible is very clear on this, many believers still think that if they fall sick, for instance, it is because they have failed to obey God in some areas of their lives. That is how the church has been programmed to think today. When something negative happens, believers always look at themselves and ask, "Where have I missed it? What have I done wrong?"

I want you to see that the question we should be asking is this: "Where have I **believed** wrong?" You see, what you believe is critical. Do you believe that you are righteous by works, or do you believe that according to God's Word, you are righteous by faith in Jesus? The Bible is clear about how the blessing of Abraham will occur in your life. If you are not seeing the manifestation of the blessings, whether it is in the area of your health, finances, relationships or career, it is because you are trying to **earn** God's blessings through the law and your performance, when those blessings come only through the righteousness of faith.

Right Living Is A Result Of Right Believing

"But Pastor Prince, don't you think that our performance is important?"

I do, absolutely. But I believe that our performance as husbands, wives, parents, employees and children of God is a **result** of believing that we are righteous by faith. I say this over and over again, and I will never grow tired of saying it: Right living is a result of right believing. There are a lot of people preaching and focusing on right living. For them, right living is always about becoming more holy, fearing God more, doing more, praying more, reading the Bible more, serving in church more or giving more money to help the needy. But my friend, when you focus on external behavior alone, you are only dealing with superficial elements.

While strong preaching on holiness may have a temporal effect on people's behavior, it will not bring about lasting and permanent change. Let me give you an analogy. If you cut off the weeds in your garden but fail to remove their roots, in no time at all, the weeds will grow again in your garden. That is what preaching about right living does in the church. Temporarily, the problem may appear to be resolved, but as long as the roots are still alive, the same wrong behavior, the same evil habits and the same addictions will appear again, just like stubborn weeds.

Believe right and you will live right. The opposite is also true: Believe wrong and you will live wrong.

For decades, the church has preached about "right living," with no results of long-lasting or permanent change in people's behavior. It is time for us to go after the root, and the root is not in preaching right living, but in preaching **right believing**. Believe right and you will live right. The opposite is also true: Believe wrong and you will live wrong. Christianity is not about behavior modification. It is about inward heart transformation. Start addressing the root instead and get hold of good teachings that are full of Jesus and righteousness by faith in Him. When you are anchored on these unshakable foundations, your outward behavior will come in line with His Word and you will begin to be transformed into His image from glory to glory! You will produce the fruits of righteousness!

Just in case there is any misunderstanding, let me state this clearly in black and white: I, Joseph Prince, **hate sin** and wrong living. As a pastor of a local church for over two decades now, I have witnessed firsthand the devastating effects of sin. It destroys marriages, breaks up families, brings diseases and basically tears a person apart from the inside out. I am on the same side as those who preach against sin and teach on the need to live right. However, where I differ is that I believe that the solution to stopping sin is not found in focusing on right living. It is found in **right believing**.

I believe the best of God's children. I believe that true born-again believers in Jesus are not looking for opportunities to sin, but are looking for the power to **overcome** and reign over sin. Even if their actions may not be altogether there yet, I believe that they already know how they *should* be living, and desire to do so. So I believe my part as a pastor is to help them believe right first. When they believe right, and know that they are righteous by faith and not by their works, they *will* live right.

We see in the Bible that the traits of right living include self-control, perseverance, brotherly kindness and love.[2] But did you know that the Bible also tells us why some believers lack these qualities? 2 Peter 1:9 says, "For he who lacks these things is shortsighted, even to blindness, and **has forgotten that he was cleansed from his old sins**." Wow! This verse is essentially telling us that the reason someone does not manifest these qualities of right living is that he has forgotten that all his sins have been forgiven and that he is righteous by faith in Jesus.

So start believing right, and you will live right! If you don't see right living in a particular area of your life—perhaps you are struggling with a secret addiction—check what you believe in that area. Somewhere along the way, you have believed a lie. But here's the good news: When you start confessing your righteousness through Jesus in that area, your breakthrough is just around the corner. Jesus wants to free you!

Use Your Faith To Believe That You Are Righteous In Christ

You can use your faith for many areas of your life, such as your family, health, material needs and career. But the most important area to use your faith in is in the area of righteousness. When you seek first the kingdom of God and His righteousness, not your own righteousness, the Bible says that "all these things"— the blessings that you are believing Him for—will be added to you.[3] Most of the time, when faith is mentioned in the New Testament, especially in the writings of the apostle Paul, it is in the context of using your faith to believe that you are righteous in Christ. It is mostly about righteousness by faith.

Do you know what the opposite of faith is? A lot of believers think that it is fear. But that is not a scriptural answer. The opposite of faith is actually **works**. You can see the contrast between works and faith in Galatians 2:16—"a man is not justified by the **works** of the law but by **faith** in Jesus Christ." We also know that the promise that Abraham would be the heir of the world was through the righteousness of **faith** and not the **works** of the law.

By the way, if faith is not the opposite of fear, do you know what is? The Bible tells us in 1 John 4:18 that "**perfect love** casts out fear." This means that the opposite of fear is love. Jesus' perfect love for you is the antithesis of fear! If you are experiencing any inordinate fear in your life right now, learn to replace that fear with the perfect love and acceptance of Jesus. You don't have to fear man's opinions or struggle for man's approval when you are filled with Jesus' perfect love. With His love, you become complete and secure as a righteous child of God.

See The End Of The Devil's Influence Over You

Do you know that the moment the blessing of Abraham is activated in a believer's life, the devil's influence over him is over? Now, imagine then, if you were the devil. What strategy would you use, knowing that the promise that a believer would be an heir of the world comes not through the law, but through the righteousness of faith? You would, of course, promote the law as much as possible, and transform all your demons into marketers and advertisers of the law. God's Word tells us that "Satan himself transforms himself into an angel of light. Therefore it is no great thing if his ministers also transform themselves into ministers of righteousness, whose end will be according to their works."[4] And you wouldn't stop there. You would launch an all-out attack against the message of righteousness by faith, and at the same time, attempt to assassinate the reputation of those who preach this message. You would do all that you can to short-circuit and sabotage the very channel by which God releases the promise that believers would be heirs of the world.

My friend, open your eyes to the devil's devices and don't allow yourself to be robbed anymore! When the Lord first opened my eyes to the gospel of grace years ago, I really felt that I had been cheated in my Christian walk. It is so clear in the Bible and yet, I had suffered for years because of wrong believing. How I wish someone had taught me about the truths that I rejoice in today, truths like I am righteous by faith in Jesus and not by my own works!

The law is about doing, whereas faith is about speaking.

By the way, it is important that you know that righteousness by faith is not a "basic teaching." No, it is a powerful one. And even if you think that you already know all about this teaching, I challenge you to take a closer look at the areas of your life where the blessing of Abraham seems to be void and of no effect. I challenge you to really take time to look at those areas and ask yourself this question: "Do I really understand righteousness by faith?" I also want to challenge you to start speaking your righteousness by faith in those areas.

The Righteousness Of Faith Speaks

Let me say something about faith. You cannot have faith without speaking it. When you study Romans 10, you will notice that it says that "the righteousness which is of the law...**does**...But the righteousness of faith **speaks**."[5] The law is about doing, whereas faith is about speaking. It is not enough to just know in your mind that you are righteous. It is not enough to just read this chapter or hear a sermon on righteousness and mentally agree that you are righteous. You need to open your mouth and say by faith, "I am the righteousness of God in Christ." This is where many believers are missing out on the blessing of Abraham. They are not speaking their righteousness by faith.

When you fail and fall short of the law's perfect standard,
that is the time you should exercise your faith to say,
"I am the righteousness of God in Christ."

Our first response to a trying situation is very important. Our first response when we discover a symptom in our body, when we receive a bad report or when we are faced with a trial, should always be to say, "I am the righteousness of God in Christ." Come on now, this is where the rubber meets the road. This is when we need to speak it. You need to not only know that you are righteous, you need to believe and speak your righteousness in Christ. It is not faith until you speak it! Paul said, "And since we have the same spirit of faith, according to what is written, 'I believed and therefore I spoke,' we also believe and therefore speak…"[6] The spirit of faith is clearly about believing and speaking. So it does not matter how many sermons or books on righteousness you have heard and read. You need to speak it.

When you fail and fall short of the law's perfect standard, that is the time you should exercise your faith to say, "I am the righteousness of God in Christ." At that very moment when you are seething in anger at your spouse, or when you have just lost your cool on the road, it takes faith to say that you are righteous because you know that you have missed it. And you know what? The moment you say it, even if you are still in the midst of your anger, you will feel like you have ushered something good into that situation. You take a step back and start to relax, and the anger dissipates as you begin to realize your true identity in Christ.

Men, if you see a scantily clad woman on television or on the cover of a magazine and you are tempted, what is your first response? Are you sin-conscious or righteousness-conscious? Sin-consciousness will draw you to succumb to your temptation, whereas righteousness-consciousness gives you the power to overcome every temptation. That is why the enemy wants to keep you sin-conscious. Confessing your sins all the time keeps you sin-conscious. It is as if Jesus did not become your sin on the cross. Righteousness-consciousness keeps you conscious of Jesus. Every time you speak it, you magnify the work of Jesus on the cross.

You Can't Lose Fellowship With God

There are some Christians who believe that you can lose fellowship with God when you sin, and you need to confess your sin to God and obtain forgiveness to become righteous again. They claim that your **relationship** with God is not broken when you sin, but **fellowship** with Him is, so you need to confess your sin to restore fellowship with Him.

It sounds very good. But believing that your fellowship with God is broken when you sin will affect your ability to come boldly to His throne of grace to receive from Him. In reality, both the words "relationship" and "fellowship" share the same Greek root word *koinonia*.[7] This means that even if you fail, relationship and fellowship with God are **not** broken. Why? Because your sins and failures have all been paid for at the cross. How can you ever lose your righteousness in Christ when it is based entirely on His perfect work and not your imperfection?

Today, as a new covenant believer, you are righteous not only until your next sin. You have everlasting righteousness!

To see how we have everlasting righteousness in Christ, look at the prophecy in the Book of Daniel about Jesus' work at Calvary. This scripture describes His mission in no uncertain terms: "…to finish the transgression, to make an end of sins, to make reconciliation for iniquity, to bring in **everlasting righteousness**."[8] Beloved, we can rejoice today because Jesus has fulfilled every iota of this prophecy! The blood of bulls and goats in the old covenant only provided limited and temporal righteousness for the children of Israel, and that is why with every new failing, the sacrifices had to be repeated.

But in the new covenant, the blood of Jesus put an **end** to sin and gave us everlasting righteousness! Listen carefully to this: Jesus does not have to be crucified repeatedly whenever you fail because every sin has already been paid for on the cross. We need to trust in just how complete and perfect His finished work is. Today, as a new covenant believer, you are righteous not only until your next sin. You have **everlasting righteousness**!

Be Righteousness-Conscious And Experience The Blessing Of Abraham

There is a powerful verse in the Bible that is commonly quoted: "No weapon formed against you shall prosper."[9] Do you want to know the secret to unleashing this promise of protection in your life? This verse is rarely quoted in full: "No weapon formed against you shall prosper, and every tongue which rises against you in judgment you shall condemn. This is the heritage of the servants of the Lord, and **their righteousness is from Me**,' says the Lord." When you know that your righteousness is from the Lord, then no weapon formed against you will prosper, and every tongue of accusation, judgment and condemnation that rises against you will fail!

If you maintain your belief and confession that you are righteous in Christ, the promise to Abraham and all the blessings of being an heir of the world will be unleashed into every aspect of your life.

For many of us, it is easy to confess that you are righteous when everything is going well. But let's talk about the times when you are faced with a crisis at work, when you have made a mistake, when you are sick, when you are tempted or when you are depressed. That is when the devil, who is the "accuser of our brethren,"[10] will come against you and scream accusatory thoughts of condemnation in your ears: "You call yourself a Christian? You think that God will hear your prayer this time?"

My friend, **that** is the time to start speaking your righteousness, and no weapon formed against you shall prosper. The accuser wants you to focus on your performance, and if you go into the realm of the law, faith is made void and the promise made of no effect.[11] But if you maintain your belief and confession that you are righteous in Christ, the promise to Abraham and all the blessings of being an heir of the world will be unleashed into every aspect of your life.

The accuser is very subtle. He has no problems with you using your faith for other things, like a new car or promotion, as long as you don't use your faith for the most important thing—believing that you are righteous by faith in Jesus. Once you focus and channel all your faith in that direction, not only will the accuser lose his power over you, all the blessings that you desire will also be added to you! As God's Word promises, "... seek **first** the kingdom of God and His righteousness, and all these things shall be **added** to you."[12]

Good things just happen to us when we are using our faith to believe that we are righteous!

I love it that the Lord makes things so simple for us. He wants us to just focus on using our faith to believe that we are righteous before Him. That is all we need to do. When we do that, God's blessings will come after us. When we use our faith to believe that we are righteous in Christ, we will experience good things in our lives. We will experience amazing increases and opportunities that we are not even believing God for. Good things just happen to us when we are using our faith to believe that we are righteous!

Psalm 128:2–4 says, "...you shall be happy, and it shall be well with you. Your wife shall be like a fruitful vine in the very heart of your house, your children like olive plants all around your table. Behold, thus shall the man be blessed..." This verse is talking about YOU. You are the blessed man. When you are blessed, your career is blessed, and like Joseph in the Bible, everything that your hands touch will prosper. Furthermore, if you are believing God for children, your wife shall be a fruitful vine, and your children will be obedient and anointed (olive plants speak of anointing). See yourself as this blessed person!

"But Pastor Prince, I . . . I don't deserve this blessing."

You are absolutely right, my friend. None of us deserve the blessing of Abraham and that is why it is important that we know that we are righteous by faith. We are not getting what our own righteousness deserves. We are getting what Jesus' righteousness deserves. We did nothing right, but Jesus did everything right on our behalf. *This* is grace—God's undeserved, unearned and unmerited favor. His grace is the key to becoming an heir of the world and to experience the full blessings of Abraham.

You need to read this portion of the Scriptures for yourself:

> For if Abraham was justified by works, he has something to boast about, but not before God. For what does the Scripture say? "Abraham believed God, and it was accounted to him for righteousness." Now to him who works, the wages are not counted as grace but as debt. **But to him who does not work but believes on Him who justifies the ungodly, his faith is accounted for righteousness.**
>
> —ROMANS 4:2–5

The secret to Abraham's blessings is found in verse five. What did Abraham believe? He believed that God justifies the ungodly. Take some time to meditate on this. God wants you to use your faith to believe that even when you have failed, He is a God who justifies the ungodly and makes them righteous. This is grace.

My friend, put your faith in His unmerited favor instead of your works. Being righteous is not based on your perfect performance. It is based on His perfect work. Your part is to use your faith to believe that you are indeed righteous by faith, so that you will reign in this life, become an heir of the world, and live an overcoming and victorious life.

I would like you to put your hand on your heart right now. Let's say this before the Lord and I believe that miracles will happen. Are you ready? Say this:

"Father God, I thank You that in Your great love plan, You want me blessed in every area of my life. Your heart's desire, according to 3 John 1:2, is for me to prosper and be in health even as my soul prospers. I thank You that my children, marriage, career and ministry will all be blessed with the blessing of Abraham. I know that it comes because it's Your promise and not because of my efforts or works. So Father, in Jesus' name, deliver me from performance-oriented Christianity and give me Your grace to be established in the righteousness of faith. I confess before You that I **am** the righteousness of God in Christ. Therefore, every blessing that belongs to the righteous is mine. This is my call. This is my destiny. The devil is under my feet. I am above the evil one because I am in Christ, who is my righteousness. I have everlasting righteousness. I am not righteous today and unrighteous tomorrow. I am righteous forever. The Holy Spirit dwells in me to show me how righteous You have made me. In

Jesus' name, I declare that I shall reign in life and be an heir of the world. Amen!"

As you focus on and confess your righteousness in Christ, get ready to see His blessings coming after you. It may not happen overnight, but if you keep confessing by faith that you are the righteousness of God, you are honoring what Jesus did to make you righteous, and God will make good His promise in your life!

Chapter 18

Self-Occupation Versus Christ-Occupation

*I*t is wonderful to know that God does not measure and judge you based on your performance today. Instead, He looks at Jesus, and as Jesus is, that is how He sees you. His Word declares that "love has been perfected among us in this: that we may have boldness in the day of judgment; because **as He is, so are we in this world.**"[1]

As new covenant believers, we do not have to fear the day of judgment simply because all our sins have been completely judged at the cross, and as Jesus is, so are we! Notice that it does not say that "as Jesus **was** on earth, so are we in this world." That would have been amazing enough because during Jesus' ministry on earth, healing, blessings and abundance followed Him everywhere He went. Yet, that is not what the Word says. What it says is, "as Jesus **is**" (notice the use of the present tense); in other words, as He is **right now**, so are we in this world.

What a powerful revelation! Just consider where Jesus is today. The Bible tells us:

He [God] raised Him [Jesus] from the dead and **seated Him at His right hand** in the heavenly places, far above all principality and power and might and dominion, and every name that is named, not only in this age but also in that which is to come. And He put all things under His feet, and gave Him to be head over all things to the church, which is His body, the fullness of Him who fills all in all.

—Ephesians 1:20–23

Jesus is seated at the Father's right hand today, in a position of power and authority. If I were you, I would take some time to meditate on this passage because the Bible tells us that as Jesus is, so are we right now, in this world. Meditate on how as Jesus is "far above all principality and power and might and dominion, and every name that is named," so are we! See it in God's Word for yourself.

As Jesus is far above all principality and power and might and dominion, and every name that is named, so are we!

In case you are not convinced, the Bible also makes it clear that by God's unmerited favor, we are seated together with Christ at the Father's right hand:

But God, who is rich in mercy, because of His great love with which He loved us, even when we were dead in trespasses, made us alive together with Christ (by grace you have been saved), and raised us up together, and **made us sit together in the heavenly places in Christ Jesus**, that in the ages to come He might show the exceeding riches of His grace [unmerited favor] in His kindness toward us in Christ Jesus.

—Ephesians 2:4–7

Resting In Jesus' Finished Work

What does it mean to be seated together in the heavenly places in Christ Jesus? It means that today, we are in a position of rest in Jesus' finished work. To be seated in Christ is to rest, to trust in Him, and to receive everything our beautiful Savior has accomplished on our behalf. My friend, God wants us to take the position of relying on Jesus for good success in every area of our lives, instead of relying on our good works and human efforts to achieve success. What a blessing it is to be in this position of dependence on our Savior!

But instead of looking at Jesus, believers are misled by the devil into **looking at themselves**. For thousands of years, the devil's strategy has not changed. He is a master at accusing you, pointing out all your flaws, weaknesses, mistakes and blemishes. He will keep on reminding you of your past failures and use condemnation to perpetuate the cycle of defeat in your life.

When the apostle Paul found himself sinking into self-occupation, he became depressed and cried out, "O wretched man that I am! Who will deliver me…?"[2] In the very next verse, he sees God's solution and says, "I thank God—through Jesus Christ our Lord!" Likewise, beloved, it's time for you to step out from being self-conscious and self-occupied, and begin to be Christ-occupied instead.

Today, you should no longer be asking yourself, "Am I accepted before God?" This question puts the focus back on you and this places you under the law. I know that there are people who will encourage you to ask yourself this question, but it is an error to ask yourself if you are accepted before God. The correct question to ask is, "Is Christ accepted before God?" because as Christ is, so are you in this world. Don't ask, "Am I pleasing to God?" Instead, ask, "Is Christ pleasing to God?" Can you see the difference in emphasis? The old covenant of law is all about **you**, but the new covenant of grace is all about **Jesus**! The law places the demand on you to perform and makes you self-conscious, whereas grace places the demand on Jesus and makes you Jesus-conscious.

Your loving heavenly Father wants you rooted, established and anchored in His unwavering love for you.

Can you imagine a young child growing up and always wondering in his heart, "Am I pleasing to Daddy? Am I pleasing to Mummy? Do Daddy and Mummy accept me?" This child will grow up emotionally warped if he does not have the security and assurance of his parents' love and acceptance. That is why your loving heavenly Father wants you rooted, established and anchored in His unwavering love for you. He demonstrated His love for you when He sent Jesus to become your sin on the cross so that you can become His righteousness. Our part today is to turn away from ourselves and to look at Jesus!

The Power Of Looking To Jesus

"Pastor Prince, you are always preaching about looking at Jesus and being Christ-occupied instead of being self-occupied, but what is the value of seeing Jesus? How does this put money in my bank account and food on my table? How does this help my children in their studies?"

Believers who have asked me these questions think that they are being pragmatic, but they don't realize that miracles happen when they keep their eyes on Jesus. Look at what happened to a fisherman called Peter, who was one of Jesus' disciples, in Matthew 14:22–33. When his boat was in the middle of a lake, the most practical thing for a seasoned fisherman to do was to stay in the boat. Science tells you that when you step out into the water, you will sink!

But the greatest miracle that Peter experienced happened one night when he stepped out of his boat in the middle of a storm at Jesus' word. That night, the winds were boisterous, but as long as Peter kept his eyes on Jesus, he did the impossible—he walked on water. Jesus was walking on the water and when Peter looked at Jesus, he became like Jesus and did the supernatural. God's Word declares that "we all, with unveiled face, **beholding** as in a mirror the glory of the Lord, are being **transformed into the same image** from glory to glory, just as by the Spirit of the Lord."[3]

Beloved, as Jesus is, so are you in this world. When you keep your focus on Jesus, you are transformed into His image from glory to glory. You are transformed by beholding, not by working. When you see that Jesus is above the storms of your life, you will effortlessly rise above the storms of your life. No amount of self-effort could have helped Peter walk on water. When he did, it happened simply because he was looking at Jesus.

Now, observe what happened the moment Peter turned his eyes away from Jesus, and started to look at the wind and the waves around him. In that instance, Peter became natural and he began to sink. Now, let's imagine that there was no storm, no howling winds and no crashing waves that night. Let's imagine that it was a perfectly calm evening and the Sea of Galilee was as still as a mirror without a single ripple on its surface. Could Peter have walked on water then? Of course not!

Keep your eyes on Jesus. While it may sound impractical, it is the most powerful thing you can do, and Jesus will cause you to reign over every storm in your life!

Walking on water is not something anyone can do whether or not the water is calm. The wind and waves actually made no difference to Peter's ability to walk on the water. The best thing Peter could have done was to keep his eyes on Jesus and not look at the storm. In the same way, instead of looking at how insurmountable your circumstances and challenges are, turn away from them and keep your eyes on Jesus. While it may sound impractical, it is the most powerful thing you can do, and Jesus will cause you to reign over every storm in your life!

Let me share with you a testimony from a lady in our church. She went for a mammogram one morning and the doctors found some lumps in her breast. They told her to return to the clinic in the afternoon so that they could perform further tests to determine if the lumps were cancerous. But this lady was fresh from hearing me teach that as Jesus is, so are we in this world. So before she returned to the clinic for the biopsy, she actually wrote on her medical report, "Does Jesus have lumps in His breast? As He is, so am I in this world." That afternoon, she went for further tests and guess what! The doctors told her that there must have been a mistake—they could find **no** lumps! Do you know why? Because as He is, so is she!

You have just seen the power of looking to Jesus. If you think that simply looking to Christ is impractical, I am challenging you today to see that it is not. In fact, it is the most practical thing you can ever do. Keep your eyes on Jesus and you will become more and more like Him.

Make Jesus Your Priority And See Blessings Added To You

"Well, Pastor Prince, that is not going to help my business. My business is in trouble and I need help now."

Beloved, you can worry all you like about your current crisis, but it will not improve or change your situation one bit. Please understand that I am not making light of what you are going through. I am just offering you the best solution I know that works. Your breakthrough will not come as a result of your struggling. It will come when you rest in the person of Jesus and His finished work.

Jesus said, "…do not worry about your life, what you will eat or what you will drink; nor about your body, what you will put on..."[4] Now, Jesus was not saying that these things—food, drink, clothing—are not important. In fact, He says that "your heavenly Father knows that you need all these things."[5] But what Jesus wants us to do is to "seek first the kingdom of God and His righteousness," and He promises that "all these things shall be added to you."[6]

The Lord loads us with benefits daily!

Now, who is God's righteousness? Jesus Christ. And who is the king of the "kingdom of God" that we are to seek? Jesus Christ![7] Jesus was actually referring to Himself when He was preaching this. When you seek Him first in your life and make Him your priority each day, all these material provisions—what you will eat, drink and wear—will be added to you. God is not about taking things away from you. He is all about adding to you, increasing you, promoting you and enriching you. Psalm 68:19 says, "Blessed be the Lord, who **daily** loads us with benefits." The Lord loads us with benefits daily! That is how good our Savior is. His mercies and His unmerited favor are new every morning. That is the way to live and enjoy life, knowing that Jesus is *with you* and *for you* every step of the way.

Put Jesus first in everything that you do. Honor Him and give Him preeminence in your daily life. Partake of His finished work daily by reading His living words to you. Practice the presence of Jesus and be conscious that He is with you, the same way that Joseph in the Bible was conscious that the Lord was with Him (see chapters one and two for our discussion on this). Jesus will bless the works of your hands, and everything you touch will indeed prosper and bring good success into your life.

Jesus is the bread of life and bread must be eaten fresh each day. We see this as a principle in the Bible. When the children of Israel were in the wilderness, notice that God instructed them to gather fresh manna every morning, and to eat the manna on the same day it was collected. (The only exception was on the sixth day, when they were supposed to gather a double portion so that they could rest on the Sabbath the next day.[8]) Look what happened when some of the Israelites did not heed God's instruction and left some manna overnight—it bred worms and stank.[9] You cannot live on yesterday's manna. Manna needs to be gathered and eaten fresh every day.

How To Eat Of The Bread Of Life Every Day

Now, remember, Jesus is in the Old Testament **concealed**, and in the New Testament **revealed**. Manna in the Old Testament is a shadow of Jesus, but in the New Testament, Jesus is our substance and our bread of life.[10] Hence, in the same way that manna had to be gathered and eaten fresh every day, we need to have a fresh revelation of Jesus every day! This comes by reading His Word, listening to anointed messages that point you to His finished work, reading resources that are full of Jesus, and spending time with Him and feeding on His love daily. Don't be mistaken. This is not your religious duty. When you have a revelation of Jesus' personal love for you, you will want to feed on Him not because you have to, but because you **want** to. To do something good because you have to is to be back under the law. To do something good because you **desire** to—now, that's grace. In any case, if you have not been reading the Word for a stretch of time, you should **not** be feeling **guilty**. You should be feeling **hungry**.

For example, if you are just reading the Bible because you think that you have to in order to be blessed, there is no doubt that you will still be blessed because of His living Word, but you will run out of steam. Under grace, you read His Word because you want to see more of Jesus. It's the same action, but one is motivated by legalism, while the other is motivated by Jesus' love and unmerited favor. One stems from self-occupation, whereas the other is moved by Christ-occupation. One depends on your grit and willpower, while the other depends on His power working mightily in you.[11] When you read God's Word out of legalistic obligation, you will find that five minutes can seem like an eternity. And if you are reading it in bed, before you know it, you will be in dreamland. Have you experienced this before?

On the other hand, when you are consumed by Jesus' love, time passes really quickly without you even realizing it. You are simply immersed in and enjoying His presence, His Word and His favor. Although the actions appear to be the same on the surface, you experience a world of difference. Why? Because one is born of religion while the other is born of a living, dynamic relationship with the Savior Himself!

Do The One Thing That Is Needful

Let's come back to the questions that we were looking at earlier. Do you think that it is practical to be occupied with Jesus? Does it help you? Does it put food on the table? Does it prosper your finances? Does it make your physical body healthy? We have looked at what it did for Peter. Now, let's take a look at what it did for Mary. You can find this story of Mary and her sister, Martha, in Luke 10:38–42.

Mary was seated at Jesus' feet when the Lord came to visit them. Martha, the elder sister, was busy working in the kitchen, making sure that everything was in order and ensuring that there was enough food and drink for their guest. Who was Martha busy serving? Jesus. And while Martha was frantically running in and out of the kitchen, what was her younger sister Mary doing? In the midst of all the busyness and activity, Mary was sitting at Jesus' feet, beholding His beauty, beholding His glory and hanging onto every word that proceeded from His lips. While Mary was resting and drawing living water from Jesus, her sister Martha was restless, frantic and stressed from serving Jesus. One sister was focused on serving, while the other was focused on receiving.

Look what happened after a while. Martha's stress from serving finally led to this outburst of frustration: "Lord, do You not care that my sister has left me to serve alone? Therefore tell her to help me."[12] In one moment of anger, she blamed two persons: The Lord Jesus, as well as her sister Mary. Now, listen closely to Jesus' response, and you may just find yourself in the Lord's description of Martha: "Martha, Martha, you are worried and troubled about many things. But one thing is needed, and Mary has chosen that good part, which will not be taken away from her."[13]

This is an amazing response. In Middle Eastern culture, it was right for Mary to be in the kitchen preparing food and serving her guest. Now, it would have been a shameful thing for Mary to sit at Jesus' feet and not help Martha if Jesus was just an ordinary guest. But Mary knew something that Martha had missed. Jesus was no ordinary guest. He was God in the flesh and the greatest way you can minister to God when He is in your home is to sit at His feet and keep drawing from Him! That is what delights our Lord.

The one thing that is needful is for you to sit at Jesus' feet and keep your eyes, ears and heart on Him.

When you come to Jesus to draw as much as you can from Him, He loves it. That is why Jesus was pleased with Mary. That is why He defended Mary's action, saying, "…one thing is needed, and Mary has chosen that good part…" What is the "one thing" that is needful? Is it to busy yourself in serving the Lord? Is it to be troubled about many things? No, the one thing that is needful is for you to sit at Jesus' feet and keep your eyes, ears and heart on Him. One sister saw Jesus in the natural, needing her ministry. The other sister saw Him as God veiled in flesh with a fullness to draw upon. Which sister do you suppose complimented Jesus and made Him feel like the God that He is? Mary. Martha obviously forgot that this God-Man multiplied loaves and fishes to feed a multitude. **He has not come to be fed but to feed!**

Unfortunately, sometimes, the hardest thing for us to do is to sit down! Sometimes, the most challenging thing we can do is to cease from our own efforts and rest solely on Jesus' unmerited favor. Often, we are like Martha—worried, busy and troubled about many things. It can all be legitimate things that we are worried about. In Martha's case, she was trying her best to serve the Lord. She ended up doing many things that day but missed out on doing the **one** thing that was actually needful.

When you do the one thing that is needful, you will end up doing the right thing at the right time, and God will cause all that you touch to be amazingly blessed.

Believers who do that one thing that is needful are not worried about anything else. On the other hand, believers who fail to do that **one** thing end up being troubled about **many** things. Do you believe that only one thing is needful—to rest at Jesus' feet and receive from Him?

Hear The Now-Word God Has For You

My friend, you did not pick up this book to hear what Joseph Prince has to say. You picked it up to see more of Jesus, to hear His words and to receive the "now-word" that He has for you. A thousand words from a mere man will do nothing for you. But just one word from Jesus can change your life forever. In writing this book, my prayer is that the person of Jesus will be exalted and glorified in these pages as He speaks through me. I am only a vessel. I am always praying that the Lord will give me the supernatural ability to proclaim and unveil His beauty, loveliness and perfect work in a fresh and powerful way.

Now, is it practical to just be occupied with Jesus? Absolutely. We find that later, in the Gospel of John, Mary took a pound of very costly oil of spikenard, anointed the feet of Jesus and wiped His feet with her hair to prepare him for his burial.[14] On resurrection morning, some women came with ointment to anoint Jesus' body, but it was too late then. They were doing the right thing, but at the wrong time. The Lord had already risen. But Mary did the right thing at the right time. This shows us that when you do the one thing that is needful, you will end up doing the right thing at the right time, and God will cause all that you touch to be amazingly blessed.

Like Mary, choose to focus on the beauty, glory and love of Jesus. Choose not to be troubled about many things or constantly occupied with yourself. Like Peter, turn away from the storm and look at Jesus, and you will start walking above the storm. Beloved, choose to focus on the Lord and rest in His finished work. As Jesus is, so are you in this world!

Chapter 19

The Prayer Of The Unnamed Servant

We concluded the last chapter by showing that when you do **the one thing needful**—resting at Jesus' feet and drawing from Him—you will end up doing the right thing at the right time. To take it one step further, I want to share with you how you can depend on Jesus' unmerited favor to be found **at the right place at the right time**. Turn with me to Ecclesiastes 9:11, which says:

> The race is not to the swift, nor the battle to the strong, nor bread to the wise, nor riches to men of understanding, nor favor to men of skill; but time and chance happen to them all.
>
> —ECCLESIASTES 9:11

This is a very interesting passage, written by the wisest man who ever walked the earth (other than Jesus). His name is Solomon and he is the son of King David.

In the system of the world, the race goes to the swift, the battle to the strong, bread to the wise, riches to men of understanding and favor to men of skill. The world's system of reward is based on meritocracy and achievement. In other words, you will succeed in life based on how swift, strong, wise, knowledgeable and skillful you are. It is based entirely on you and your abilities.

As a new covenant believer in Christ, while you are living in the world's system that is based on meritocracy, you have a supernatural advantage because you have the unmerited favor of Jesus.

Listen closely to what I am saying. There is essentially nothing wrong with this system of reward in the world. Meritocracy is a good system and it has caused nations to flourish, communities to prosper, and given people the incentive to create opportunities for themselves. However, as new covenant believers in Christ, while we are living in the world's system that is based on meritocracy, we have a supernatural advantage because we have the unmerited favor of Jesus.

God Chooses The Weak To Bring Down The Mighty

God is interested in your success. Even if you are not the swiftest, strongest, wisest, most knowledgeable and most skillful in the natural, God can still bless you with good success when you depend on His grace. You can rise above the system of meritocracy through His undeserved, unearned and unmerited favor. The system of the world only rewards the strong, while those who are weak are neglected and in some cases, even despised. But, in Jesus, there is hope for the weak. God's way is completely opposite from the world's way. According to 1 Corinthians 1:26, "not many wise according to the flesh, not many mighty, not many noble, are called." Isn't it fascinating to discover that while the world looks favorably upon the wise, mighty and noble, God does not? Let's see in the next verse what God chooses instead: "God has chosen the **foolish things** of the world to put to shame the wise, and God has chosen the **weak things** of the world to put to shame the things which are mighty."

Isn't it amazing? God has chosen the foolish and weak things to qualify for His abundant blessings. But the verse does not say that the foolish and weak things will remain foolish and weak. Instead, by God's unmerited favor, they will put to shame the so-called wise and mighty things in this world. In His hands of grace, the foolish and weak things become even wiser and mightier than the wise and mighty things of the world.

This is something I have experienced personally. In high school, I was a stutterer. I watched the other kids talking and reading aloud in class effortlessly while I had serious trouble getting words out of my mouth.

I remember how there was this teacher who would come into class, and always get me to stand and read aloud in class. He did this just for the sheer pleasure of watching me stammer and stutter, knowing full well what would happen. And true enough, while I tried to get the first word out—"th- th- th- th- the," my classmates (especially the girls) would laugh, this teacher would laugh, and my ears would burn and turn red. This would happen every time he asked me to read in class.

Honestly, if you had told me then that I would be preaching to thousands of people every week, I would have run for cover under the table and said, "Get thee behind me, Satan!" If there was an area anyone who knew me back then believed I would fail in, it would have to be public speaking. But God looked down and said, "I am going to make a preacher out of this boy."

One day, when I was tired of being miserable, I told the Lord, "Lord, I don't have much to give You, but whatever I have I give You." I remember how my voice was the thing that embarrassed me the most, so I said, "Lord, I give You my voice." When I said that, I pitied Him for getting someone like me who had so many weaknesses.

To cut a long story short, after I gave all my weaknesses to the Lord, something supernatural happened. I stopped being conscious of my stuttering and it supernaturally disappeared. In the area of my weakness, God supplied His strength. About two years ago, one of the teachers from my high school days came to my church and sat in one of the services I was preaching in. After the service, she wrote me a note that said, "I see a miracle. This must be God!"

I believe that the reason God chose someone like me to preach the gospel is so that others (especially those who had known me before) would look at me and say, "This must be God!" and God gets the glory. Now, seeing how God has used my voice, my main weakness, to bring life transformation and miracles not only to people in Singapore but also around the world through our television broadcasts, I feel humbled because I know what I was like before God touched me. My friend, when you look at yourself and see only weaknesses, bear in mind that God can use you. It is those who are proud and who depend on their human strength that God cannot use.

Why does the Lord choose foolish and weak things to confound the wise and mighty things of this world? The answer is simple. It's so that **"no flesh should glory in His presence."**[1] God chooses the things that are weak in the natural so that no man can boast of his **own** ability. All glory redounds to the Lord and as the Bible tells us, "He who glories, let him glory in the Lord."[2]

It is Jesus, His wisdom in your life, His righteousness and His perfect redemptive work on the cross that make you a success. So when you boast of your success, you can boast only in Jesus. Without Jesus, you have nothing to boast about. But with Jesus in your life, you can boast in Him and Him alone for every success and blessing that comes through His unmerited favor. If you are strong, mighty and wise in yourself, then God's unmerited favor cannot flow. But when you realize your weaknesses and foolishness, and depend on Jesus instead, *that* is when His unmerited favor can flow unhindered in your life.

We see this in the story of Moses. In his first 40 years as an Egyptian prince who was looked up to and admired, he thought that he knew everything. The Bible says that in this first 40 years, Moses was "mighty in words and deeds,"[3] but God could not use him. However, in the next 40 years, something happened to Moses. He had fled Egypt after killing an Egyptian who was beating a Hebrew, and went to dwell in the Midian desert. He became a shepherd and was no longer considered mighty in words nor deeds. Indeed, he had even become a stutterer.[4] And at this point in his life, when he probably thought that he was a has-been, insignificant compared to what he had been, and that his glory-days were behind him, God appeared to him and said, "…I will send you to Pharaoh that you may bring My people…out of Egypt."[5]

Forty years earlier, at the zenith of his ability, Moses could not even properly bury one Egyptian whom he had killed—he was found out and forced to flee.[6] But now, stripped of his dependence on his human strength and mindful of his weaknesses, he stepped into his call, dependent solely on the unmerited favor of God. And this time, when Moses waved his rod over the sea, the sea covered tens of thousands of Egyptians perfectly.[7]

The Bible tells us that "God resists the proud, but gives grace [unmerited favor] to the humble."[8] Beloved, God will not impose His unmerited favor on us. Whenever we want to depend on ourselves and our wisdom, He will allow us to do so. His unmerited favor is given to those who humbly acknowledge that they cannot succeed in their own strength and ability.

God Sent A Shepherd Boy To Defeat A Philistine Warrior

When God wanted to bring down a mighty giant who was terrorizing the nation of Israel, He sent someone who was weak in the flesh. Think about it. In the eyes of the world, what could be weaker against a trained and fearsome soldier than a young boy who had no formal military training, no armor, was dressed in a humble shepherd's garb, and did not even carry any real weapons other than a sling and five smooth stones from a brook? It is no wonder that Goliath mocked this young shepherd boy and his strategy. When David stepped into the battlefield, Goliath asked him sarcastically, "Am I a dog, that you come to me with sticks?"[9]

The implications of this battle were massive. It was not just a duel or contest between two individuals. The Israelites and Philistines had agreed to each send a warrior who would represent their nation. The defeated warrior would commit his entire nation to become servants to the other nation. It would be an understatement to say that a whole lot was riding on this one fight. And who does God send to represent Israel? In natural terms, He sent possibly the most unqualified person on that battlefield in the Valley of Elah.

David was not even a soldier in the army of Israel! Do you remember how this shepherd boy ended up at the battlefield to begin with? David was there to deliver bread and cheese to his brothers who were in the army![10] And yet, David found himself standing on the battlefield as Israel's representative against the haughty Goliath. From delivering bread and cheese, he was now called upon to deliver the entire nation of Israel.

Don't Despise The Day Of Humble Beginnings

David was at the right place at the right time because he humbled himself and submitted to his father's instructions to deliver bread and cheese to his brothers. Young people, this is something you need to understand. Submission to your parents and God-appointed leadership will always cause God's favor to flow in your life, and you will find yourself, like David, at the right place at the right time!

The Bible says that we should not despise the day of humble beginnings.[11] There is nothing glamorous about delivering bread and cheese, but David did not despise it. And that put him right in the Valley of Elah, the wind blowing in his hair—a young shepherd boy with no military experience representing the nation of Israel against a mighty giant who was a man of war from his youth.

God loves to take the foolish and weak things to shame the wise and mighty things of the world.

This is what God loves to do. He loves to take the foolish and weak things to shame the wise and mighty things of the world. Pay attention to this young shepherd's words when he stepped into battle: "You come to me with a sword, with a spear, and with a javelin. But I come to you in the name of the Lord of hosts, the God of the armies of Israel, whom you have defied. This day the Lord will deliver you into my hand, and I will strike you and take your head from you."[12] What strong and bold words from a young shepherd boy!

God's Definition Of Humility

"But Pastor Prince, didn't you just say that God gives unmerited favor to the humble? David's speech certainly doesn't sound very humble."

That's a great question. When I was a young Christian, I used to think that to be humble meant that you always had to be soft-spoken and that you should always give in to others. There was a leader in the church that I was attending then who always got onto the speaking platform with a slight bow. He was always very gentle, almost apologetic in the way he spoke, and to me, that was the picture of a humble man. But in reality, humility has nothing to do with whether you are soft-spoken or walk around with a hunch. That is how the world defines humility.

The clearest way to identify humility is to see if the person is Christ-occupied or self-occupied. When somebody is arrogant, proud and self-confident, he is clearly self-occupied. At the other extreme, someone who is always fearful also has a problem with pride even if he appears to be very soft-spoken and gentle. Instead of looking to Jesus, this person is self-conscious and constantly looking at himself. Both extremes are manifestations of pride. While one extreme manifests pride in terms of arrogance, the other extreme manifests pride in terms of self-consciousness. As long as a person is occupied with self, that is still pride. Humility then, is being Christ-occupied. This person knows that without the Lord, he cannot succeed, but with the Lord, all things are possible.

> *As long as a person is occupied with self, that is still pride. Humility then, is being Christ-occupied.*

When you look at David's speech, you will see that he didn't boast in himself. His boast was not in his prowess and skill with weapons. No, he went to battle "in the name of the Lord of hosts." David was completely occupied with the Lord, whom he was confident would deliver the nation of Israel. He made no mention of his own abilities. He went on to make this even more explicit when he said to Goliath, "Then all this assembly shall know that the Lord does not save with sword and spear; for **the battle is the Lord's,** and He will give you into our hands."[13]

I love the spirit of this young man. David knew that the battle was not his but the Lord's, and that was what gave him such boldness in standing up against Goliath, while the rest of the Israelite army cowered in fear. It is beautiful to see how this young shepherd boy had the wisdom not to touch the Lord's glory. Even before the battle took place, David declared that victory belonged to Israel and that all credit went to the Lord. It is clear then, that even though David spoke boldly and courageously, he was not arrogant. He didn't suffer from pride or lack of humility. In fact, his boldness and courage came directly from his humble dependence on the Lord. What a glorious difference between a person who boasts in his own arm of flesh and a person like David, whose boast is in the Lord's mighty arm to deliver him!

True humility is to be occupied with Christ, and then you will be filled with His boldness and courage to overcome your giant!

My friend, whatever battle you may be in right now, you can trust, as David did, that the battle belongs to the Lord. Whatever your giant may be, be it a marital situation, financial debt, problems at your workplace or a sickness that you are battling with, know this: You may be weak, but **He** is strong. You may be unable, but **He** is more than able! Whatever fight you are facing, the battle belongs to Him. True humility is to be occupied with Christ, and then you will be filled with His boldness and courage to overcome your giant!

Right Place Right Time

Never forget that "the race is not to the swift, nor the battle to the strong…but **time and chance happen** to them all" (Ecclesiastes 9:11). God wants you to have the right timing—His timing, and nothing is left to chance because you are God's child. Psalm 37:23 says, "The steps of a good man are ordered by the Lord." You are that "good man" because you are the righteousness of God in Christ.

Now, look at the word "happen." In the original Hebrew text, it is the word *qarah*, which means "to encounter, to meet (without pre-arrangement), to chance to be present."[14] In a nutshell, it means "right happening." My friend, you can depend on God to cause you to be at the right place at the right time, to have right happenings happen in your life! I am sure that you would agree that being at the right place at the right time is a tremendous blessing. You certainly don't want to be at the wrong place at the wrong time. That can lead to disastrous results.

A delay can turn out to be God's protection from an accident ahead.

But even if you find yourself at the wrong place at the wrong time, such as when you are caught in a traffic jam or when you miss your train, don't be too agitated. A delay can turn out to be God's protection from an accident ahead. Sometimes, a delay of just a few seconds can mean the difference between life and death!

In 2001, a brother in my church wrote in to share that his son's office was in the twin towers in New York. On one particular morning, his son's alarm clock did not go off and he ended up missing his regular train to work, and was late arriving at work. Had he been on time that morning, he would have been in his office when the planes plowed into the building during the devastating terrorist attacks on September 11.

In 2003, another brother from my church was in Jakarta, Indonesia, for a business trip. He was staying at the Marriott Hotel and he was in the lobby when a bomb went off just outside the hotel. The bomb tore through the lobby and he saw a body flying past him as the deafening blast reverberated all around him.

After the dust had settled, he found blood spattered on him and debris strewn all around, but amazingly, he was completely unhurt. At the very moment when the bomb exploded, he **happened** to walk behind a pillar and it protected him from the impact of the blast. Just think what would have happened to him if he had reached that pillar just a few seconds before or after the bomb went off!

No matter how intelligent you are, how fat your savings account is or how prestigious your family name may be, there is no way you can know beforehand when to position yourself behind a pillar just as a bomb that you are unaware of explodes near you. Only God can put you at the right place at the right time. It was the Lord who placed this brother behind the pillar at the precise moment. His steps were literally ordered by the Lord. All glory to Him! Jesus is our true pillar of protection!

God's faithfulness in protecting His beloved by putting them at the right place at the right time was demonstrated even more recently. Two massive explosions rocked Jakarta, Indonesia, again on the morning of July 17, 2009, and this time both the Marriott and the Ritz-Carlton hotels were the target of terrorist attacks.

A lady from our church was in the lobby of the Ritz-Carlton

when one of the bombs was detonated in the nearby restaurant where guests were having breakfast. The force of the explosion sent glass shards flying past her, ripping into the flesh of other guests who were standing in front of her. Amazingly, she was completely unharmed!

She shared that she had initially planned to have breakfast at that very restaurant at the time when the bomb had exploded. That would certainly have been the wrong place at the wrong time. If she had done so, she could have been killed by the blast in the restaurant. However, she shared that the reason she missed her usual breakfast time that morning was that she was caught up in reading a few devotional entries from my *Destined To Reign Devotional* and spending time with the Lord in her hotel room. The "delay" she experienced in reading my book kept her away from the restaurant and saved her life! Praise Jesus!

Put your trust in the Lord and believe that He causes all things to work together for good. Being at the right place at the right time is not always about protection from some evil occurrence. Perhaps the Lord wants to connect you with somebody that you have not met in years, and there is just an opportunity of blessing waiting for you.

I don't know how many times the people in my church just **happened** to bump into old acquaintances or meet new people who later turned out to be a blessing to them. We have had testimonies of supernatural connections that resulted in amazing business opportunities, as well as testimonies from people who had been given job opportunities after bumping into friends whom they had not seen in years.

My friend, nothing happens by chance—the Lord knows how to place you at the right place and the right time! You can depend on Jesus for right happenings. They all come by His unmerited favor and are beyond your ability to get them through careful planning and strategizing. The world says, "When you fail to plan, you plan to fail." But you can't plan for *qarah*. This is evident in the testimonies you have just read about.

Nothing happens by chance—the Lord knows how to place you at the right place and the right time!

Hey, I am not against planning. All I am saying is that you should not be stressed out and uptight when things don't go as you have planned. Don't stick so rigidly to your plans that you forget to make room for Jesus' unmerited favor to flow, protect and position you. In the new covenant of grace, the Bible says that the Lord Himself writes His laws on your heart.[15] He can speak to you and guide you in everything that you do. Allow Him to lead you supernaturally!

I received another testimony from a couple in my church who experienced just that. It was 2004 and they had decided to spend their Christmas holidays in Penang, Malaysia. They had originally intended to spend the whole day lounging around on the beach, but one of them unexpectedly felt a strong craving to eat something that was only available on the other side of the island. They decided to flow with that desire and headed in search for that dish. Later, they realized that just a short while after they had left, the Asian tsunami hit the beachfront where they had been relaxing and destroyed everything in its path.

You see, my friend, there are no fixed formulas here. The Lord will do whatever it takes to get His children to safety. Involve Jesus in your plans and allow Him to lead you!

First Mention Of *Qarah* In The Bible

There is a principle in interpreting God's Word known as "the principle of first mention." Every time a word is mentioned for the first time in the Bible, there is usually a special significance and lesson that we can learn. Let's take a look at the first occurrence of the word *qarah*. It is found in Genesis 24, when Abraham sent his unnamed servant[16] to look for a bride for Isaac, his son.

The unnamed servant arrived at a well outside the city of Nahor in the evening and decided to stop there. There were so many young women gathered to draw water there that he did not know who would be the right woman for Isaac. So the unnamed servant prayed this prayer: "O Lord God of my master Abraham, please give me **success** this day, and show kindness to my master Abraham."[17]

The word "success" here is the Hebrew word *qarah*, and this is the first time it appears in the Bible. The servant essentially prayed, "Give me *qarah* this day." It goes without saying that with the Lord's *qarah* or positioning for right happenings, the servant found a beautiful virtuous woman named Rebekah, who became Isaac's bride.

We need the Lord to give us *qarah* every day. I encourage you to pray the prayer of that unnamed servant. Tell the Lord, "Give me success—*qarah*—this day," and depend on His unmerited favor to lead you to be in the right place at the right time!

The Story Of Ruth

There is a beautiful story of a Moabite woman named Ruth in the Bible. In the natural, Ruth had everything against her. She was a very poor widow, and she was a Moabite, a Gentile in the Jewish nation. But even after her husband died, Ruth remained with her mother-in-law Naomi. She left her family to follow Naomi back to Bethlehem, and made Naomi's God—the God of Abraham, Isaac and Jacob—her God.

Now, because of their poverty, Naomi and Ruth could not afford to buy grain, and Ruth had to go out to the field to perform the menial task of gleaning whatever the reapers had left behind. I want you to notice that Ruth was depending on the Lord's favor for she said to Naomi, "Please let me go to the field, and glean heads of grain after him in whose sight I may find **favor**."[18] Ruth was confident that God would give her favor even though she was a foreigner and had no connections with anyone in the field. She didn't even know whose part of the field she would be able to glean in.

Look at the Bible's account of what happened next: "And she went, and came, and gleaned in the field after the reapers: and her **hap** was to light on a part of the field belonging unto Boaz, who was of the kindred of Elimelech."[19] Of all the spots in the field that Ruth could have wandered into, her **"hap"** was to come to the part of the field that belonged to Boaz, who was a man of great wealth, and who also **happened** to be Naomi's relative.

Hap is an old English word and it means "to happen" to be at the right place. However, in the original Hebrew text, the root of this word is the word *qarah!*[20]

When Ruth trusted in God's unmerited favor, she *qarah-ed* or happened to come to the part of the field that belonged to Boaz. To cut a long story short, Boaz saw Ruth, fell in love with her and married her. Ruth was possibly at the lowest point of her life before she met Boaz. All the natural factors were against her. But because she put her trust in the Lord, who put her at the right place at the right time, her situation was turned around completely. In fact, she became one of the few woman to be mentioned in the genealogy of Jesus in Matthew 1:5, which states that "Boaz begot Obed by Ruth." What an honor to be included in the genealogy of Jesus Christ. Talk about being at the right place at the right time!

Have faith in God's grace in your life. Your blessings are just around the corner!

My friend, no matter what natural circumstances may be against you today, have confidence in the unmerited favor of Jesus and the Lord will give you what I call "*qarah* success." He will cause you to be positioned at the right place at the right time to experience success in all areas, such as physical protection, relationships, career and finances.

It does not matter if you do not have the right educational qualifications or the necessary experience. You may be born in a poor family, you may be a divorcee or a single parent, but whatever the case may be, don't give up on God's abundant grace in your life to turn your situation around. All you need is one *qarah* moment and for God's unmerited favor to place you at the right place at the right time. Have faith in His grace in your life. Your blessings are just around the corner!

There is a lady in my church who was an orphan and a foreigner. She did not have much when she first joined us and nobody knew who she was. After hearing the gospel of grace, she began to depend on the unmerited favor of Jesus and to believe God for big things. She attended a business convention in Israel where she met with some scientists who had a special membrane technology for water treatment, and that was her *qarah* moment.

Because of God's unmerited favor upon her, these scientists wanted to work with her. She went on to start a business in the water treatment industry, and in a short time, was able to take the company public. When she decided to do so, the timing was perfect as the scarcity of water was all over the media, and it resulted in her company being oversubscribed several times when it was listed. Talk about being at the right place at the right time!

Her success did not end there. By the unmerited favor and wisdom of Jesus, she went on to build a company that is worth several hundred million dollars today. She also won several major awards and is now recognized as the richest woman in Southeast Asia.

Not too long ago, some of my key leaders and I met up with her. As I listened to her speak, it was obvious to me that this businesswoman was not only humble, but she was also someone who understood and walked in the unmerited favor of Jesus. She travels extensively for work and she shared with me that wherever she goes around the world, she would bring along my sermon DVDs and watch them in her hotel room. She emphasized to me how vital it was for her to keep hearing the gospel of grace to stay grounded on and rooted in the unmerited favor of Jesus. Hearing her say that made me feel like watching my own DVDs when I got home! She truly caught a revelation of making the gospel of Jesus a priority in her life, no matter how busy she got with her business. She is a fine example of a person who is safe for success. She has no illusions about the source of her blessings. Like Joseph in the Bible, she is conscious of the Lord's presence and knows that everything she touches will be blessed because of His unmerited favor upon her. This is what I call good success!

Don't look at your natural circumstances. This businesswoman started with literally nothing, and in the natural, the odds were stacked up against her. However, as she depended on God's grace (unmerited favor), the Lord turned everything around for her in one *qarah* moment. Beloved, Jesus can do the same thing for you. Pray the prayer of the unnamed servant and ask the Lord to give you *qarah* today!

Chapter 20

Divine Wisdom To Succeed

*I*n this chapter, I want to talk about how you can depend on God's wisdom to succeed. Wisdom from the Lord comes by God's unmerited favor. It is not something that you can study for or acquire with your own efforts. Wisdom from the Lord is something that the world cannot have. This is not to say that the world does not have wisdom. Step into any bookstore today and you will find shelves full of books containing experts' theories and methods on all sorts of subjects. The great majority of these, however, stem from **human wisdom**, which strengthens and builds up only the flesh. Whether they know it or not, the people of the world are crying out for true wisdom from the Lord. Just look at the constant demand for self-help books. But what we need is not more "self-help." What we need is the Lord's help! Read books that are written by Spirit-filled believers and Christian leaders who encourage you to look to Jesus and not to yourself.

Psalm 1:1 tells us this from the start: "Blessed is the man who walks not in the counsel of the ungodly." This means that there *is* counsel in human wisdom. But the man who does *not* walk according to the wisdom of the world is the man who is blessed.

At the same time, if his delight is in Jesus, and he meditates on Jesus day and night, Psalm 1:3 says, "He shall be like a tree planted by the rivers of water, that brings forth its fruit in its season, whose leaf also shall not wither; and whatever he does shall prosper." Sounds familiar? God's Word is very consistent. The promises in Psalm 1 are the same as those we covered in Jeremiah 17 about the blessed man!

When Jesus was on earth, He was never in a situation where He lacked wisdom.

My friend, make a decision to walk in the counsel of the godly and not in the counsel of the world, and you will see whatever you do prosper. God has raised up men and women who are established in the truths of the new covenant, and who will help you keep your eyes on Jesus. In Him, you will find all the wisdom that pertains to life. The Bible tells us that in Him "are hidden all the treasures of wisdom and knowledge"[1] for your success.

See The Wisdom Of Christ In Action

See the wisdom of Jesus in action for yourself. When Jesus was on earth, He was never in a situation where He lacked wisdom. Look at what happened when the Pharisees brought the woman caught in adultery to Him. The Pharisees came to Him and quoted from the law, saying, "Teacher, this woman was caught in adultery, in the very act. Now Moses, in the law, commanded us that such should be stoned. But what do You say?"[2]

They thought that they had succeeded in trapping Jesus because if He told them to stone her, then they would accuse

Him of not demonstrating the forgiveness and grace that He had been preaching about. If Jesus were to say that they should not stone her, then the Pharisees would accuse Him publicly of breaking the law of Moses and bring a charge against Him.

The Pharisees were probably confidently gloating over the clever trap that they had devised. That is why they confronted Jesus with this woman in the public area around the temple. They wanted to embarrass Him in front of the multitudes that had come to hear Him teach. Now, observe the wisdom of Jesus in operation. He simply told them, "He who is without sin among you, let him throw a stone at her first."[3]

What majesty! They came to Jesus with the law of Moses and Jesus gave them the perfect standard of the law. Without flinching, He simply challenged the person who was perfect before the law to cast the first stone. The Pharisees who had come to ensnare Jesus began to walk away one by one, completely silenced. This same Jesus, with all His wisdom, is today our ascended Christ, who is seated at the Father's right hand, and whom the Bible says is "made unto us wisdom!"[4]

Before we leave this story of Jesus and the woman caught in adultery, I want you to see something important. Who was the only person on the scene who was without sin? It was Jesus Himself. But instead of condemning the woman, He silenced her accusers and showed her His grace, asking, "Woman, where are those accusers of yours? Has no one condemned you?... Neither do I condemn you; go and sin no more."[5]

Isn't it amazing to know that the most powerful being in the universe is also the kindest, most gracious and forgiving One?

It is vital that you know that "God did not send His Son into the world to condemn the world, but that the world through Him might be saved."[6] Jesus did not come to condemn us. He came to save us! By extending the gift of no condemnation to the woman caught in adultery, He gave her the power to "go and sin no more." In the same way, that is how Jesus' unmerited favor toward us brings us to repentance, and gives us the power to overcome the failures in our lives!

Our Savior is altogether lovely. He is never early, never late. He is always at the right place at the right time. He is always in perfect peace and there is no sense of hurry about Him. When it was time to be tender, He was infinitely gentle. When it was time to overturn the tables of the money changers, He did it with passion. He was never frazzled by the Pharisees' attempts to trip Him up and He was always flowing with divine wisdom. He is steel and velvet, meekness and majesty, perfect manhood and deity. This is Jesus, and you are **in Him**!

You Are In Christ

Now, what does it mean to be in Christ? It means that we are new creations.[7] When we are in Christ, we are blessed with every blessing.[8] When we are in Christ, we are in the secret place of the Most High[9] and we are protected. When we are in Christ, we are the head and not the tail, above only and not beneath.[10] Don't be like the world and say things like "I am doing okay under the circumstances." You don't have to be "under" the circumstances. The Lord can cause you to rise over and above all your circumstances!

God's Word tells us that "you are **in Christ Jesus,** who became for us wisdom from God—and righteousness and sanctification and redemption."[11] When we are in Christ, God makes Jesus to become for us wisdom, righteousness, sanctification and redemption. Throughout this book, we have been talking about righteousness, holiness and your redemption through the finished work of Jesus. By now, I hope you know that the question to ask today is no longer if you are righteous or holy in God's eyes. The questions to ask are, "Is Christ righteous in God's eyes?" and "Is Christ holy in God's eyes?" When you are in Christ, as Christ is, **so are you!**[12] Is Christ healthy, full of favor and well-pleasing to God today? Then, so are you!

You don't have to be intimidated by your circumstances. Whether you are facing giants of financial lack, sickness or depression, they are all bread for you.

All the blessings of the righteous that are recorded in God's Word are yours today. When the Bible says, "The effective, fervent prayer of a righteous man avails much,"[13] you don't have to wish that you were a righteous man, or go around looking for a righteous man to pray for you. My friend, you are in Christ. Christ has made you righteous. As He is righteous, so are you. Based on God's Word, that means that you can pray and have a confident expectation that your prayers will avail much! God will hear and answer your prayers. The Bible says that you have not because you ask not.[14] So be bold and very courageous, and ask God for big things!

Here is another description of the righteous: "the righteous are bold as a lion."[15] That's describing *you*, beloved. You don't have to be intimidated by your circumstances. You are bold and you have the courage to face off with any giant in your life. Whether you are facing giants of financial lack, sickness or depression, they are all bread for you.

But you know what? The greatest boldness you can have when you are established in righteousness is to stand before God with no fear or consciousness of sin, and to receive His unmerited favor. When you are confident of your righteous standing based on Christ's righteousness, you don't have to be afraid that God will come after you to judge or condemn you. You are free to be bold with the Lord and claim His promises for you even when you have failed, or I should say **especially** when you have failed.

God wants us to "come boldly to the **throne of grace** [unmerited favor], that we may obtain mercy and find grace [unmerited favor] to help in time of need."[16] Notice that for the believer, God's throne is not a throne of judgment. It is a throne of grace, a throne of unmerited favor. You can have the courage to believe for God's favor in your life only when you are secure in your righteousness in Christ. So make sure that you are believing right today.

Wisdom Is The Principal Thing

Now, notice that in 1 Corinthians 1:30, Christ is made unto us **wisdom first**, then righteousness, holiness and redemption. Wisdom comes first! Jesus as our wisdom is given first importance. There is a difference between wisdom and knowledge. Knowledge puffs up.[17] It can make one proud and arrogant. But wisdom will make you humble and teachable. You can read extensively and accumulate a lot of knowledge, but still lack wisdom. You also don't become wise just by growing older and having more experience in life. Wisdom is not natural. It does not matter if you are young or old, experienced or inexperienced, highly educated or not. Wisdom comes from God's unmerited favor.

Promotion and honor all come as a result of receiving Jesus as your wisdom.

Listen to what God's Word says about the importance of wisdom: "Wisdom is the principal thing; therefore get wisdom. And in all your getting, get understanding. Exalt her, and she will promote you; she will bring you honor, when you embrace her. She will place on your head an ornament of grace [unmerited favor]; a crown of glory she will deliver to you."[18] You see, promotion and honor all come as a result of receiving Jesus as your wisdom.

I remember how the key thing that I would pray for every day in the early days of our church was for the wisdom of God to guide us in everything that we did. That was my focus. I did not want to manage the church with my own wisdom. I wanted to depend on Jesus' wisdom. In fact, it was during this time of believing for God's wisdom that the Lord opened my eyes to the gospel of grace!

When my eyes were opened to the gospel of Jesus' unmerited favor, lives began to be radically changed and transformed, and from just a few hundred people in the mid-nineties, our highest attendance for our Sunday services to date was more than 22,000 precious people. Whenever I am asked to explain how we grew the church, my answer is plain and simple—it was and is entirely by the unmerited favor of Jesus. I know that it is grace and grace alone that caused our church to experience such explosive growth.

Before our church experienced such an explosion in numbers, the Lord asked me if I would do something. As I was spending time in His presence and reading His Word one day, He asked me if I would preach Jesus in every sermon. To be honest, my first thought then was that if I preached only Jesus in every message, many people would stop coming and the size of our church would shrink. Then, the Lord asked me, "If people stop coming, will you still preach Jesus in all your messages?" Like all young pastors, I was ambitious and wanted to grow the church, but I submitted to the Lord and said, "Yes, Lord, even if the church grows smaller, I will keep on preaching Jesus!"

Wisdom will always lead you to the person of Jesus and the cross!

Little did I know that this was actually a test from the Lord, because from the moment I began preaching Jesus, unveiling His loveliness and the perfection of His finished work every Sunday, as a church, we have never looked back. I didn't realize that throughout all those years of praying for wisdom, the wisdom of God would lead me to the unveiling of the gospel of grace—the gospel of grace that is unadulterated by the law and man's works, and based entirely on the finished work of Jesus. That is what wisdom does. It will always lead you to the person of Jesus and the cross!

Today, the same gospel of grace that we preach every Sunday in our church is being broadcast into millions of homes across America, Europe, the Middle East and the Asia Pacific region. We started as a little church in Singapore that nobody had heard of, but God's unmerited favor has blessed us to become an international ministry that is impacting the world with the good news of His unmerited favor. We take no credit for it because this wisdom is from Jesus, and our boast is in Him and Him alone.

The Spirit Of Wisdom

We have talked about how wisdom is the principal thing, but do you know what the "spirit of wisdom" is? Look at the prayer that the apostle Paul prayed over the church in Ephesus:

> That the God of our Lord Jesus Christ, the Father of glory, may give to you the **spirit of wisdom and revelation in the knowledge of Him**, the eyes of your understanding being enlightened; that you may know what is the hope of His calling, what are the riches of the glory of His inheritance in the saints, and what is the exceeding greatness of His power toward us who believe, according to the working of His mighty power
>
> —Ephesians 1:17–19

Are you getting this? The spirit of wisdom and revelation is in the **knowledge of Jesus**! The more you know Jesus and have a revelation of His unmerited favor in your life, the more you will have the spirit of wisdom. I challenge you to pray this prayer for wisdom on a regular basis because when you increase in the knowledge of Jesus, He will surely lead you to good success in every aspect of your life.

The more you know Jesus and have a revelation of His unmerited favor in your life, the more you will have the spirit of wisdom.

Note that when Paul was praying this prayer for the believers in Ephesus, they were already filled with the Holy Spirit. But Paul still prayed that God would give them a spirit of wisdom and revelation in their knowledge of Jesus. It is one thing to have the Holy Spirit inside you, but it is another thing to let the Holy Spirit inside you flow as the spirit of wisdom and revelation. When the Holy Spirit leads you in the wisdom of Jesus, there will be no impossible situation, no insolvable problem and no insurmountable crisis. The wisdom of Jesus in you will help you to successfully navigate all your trials and cause you to prevail over all your challenges.

The Secret To Solomon's Wisdom

Let's take a look at the life of Solomon. When Solomon became king, he was only a young man of about 18 years old and had big shoes to fill as David's successor to the throne. Solomon was not filled with wisdom when he first ascended the throne, but he was clearly very earnest. He went to Mount Gibeon, where the tabernacle of Moses was, to offer a thousand burnt offerings to the Lord. At Mount Gibeon, the Lord appeared to Solomon in a dream and said, "Ask! What shall I give you?"[19]

Now, think about this for a moment. What would you have asked for if you were in Solomon's position? Solomon did not ask for riches. Neither did he ask to be honored by all men. Instead, he told the Lord, "...give me **wisdom and knowledge**, that I may go out and come in before this people; for who can judge this great people of Yours?"[20] The Bible records that Solomon's request "pleased the Lord"[21] and the Lord replied, "Because this was in your heart, and you have not asked riches or wealth or honor or the life of your enemies, nor have you asked long life—but have asked wisdom and knowledge for yourself, that you may judge My people over whom I have made you king—wisdom and knowledge are granted to you; and I will give you riches and wealth and honor, such as none of the kings have had who were before you, nor shall any after you have the like."[22]

The Book of 1 Kings tells us that Solomon told the Lord, "Therefore give to Your servant an **understanding heart** to judge Your people, that I may discern between good and evil. For who is able to judge this great people of Yours?"[23] So when Solomon asked for wisdom and knowledge, he was asking for an understanding heart. Let's go deeper. The word "understanding" here is the Hebrew word *shama*, which means "to hear intelligently."[24] In other words, Solomon had asked for a **hearing** heart—one that hears from and flows with the leading of the Spirit of God, who leads us into all truth.[25] You need a hearing heart for God's wisdom to flow through you in every aspect of your life!

I believe that the same request that pleased the Lord then pleases Him today. God is pleased when we ask Jesus for wisdom. To ask Him for wisdom is to put ourselves in a posture of trusting and depending on His unmerited favor. Only the humble can ask Jesus for wisdom and a hearing heart. Although Solomon only asked for wisdom, the Lord added "riches and wealth and honor" to him. Too many people are chasing riches, wealth and honor, not realizing that they come through the wisdom of Jesus. Even if someone were to come into sudden wealth, without the wisdom of Jesus to manage it, the money would be squandered away. But with the wisdom of Jesus, you won't only be blessed, you will also be able to hold on to the blessings in your life. Jesus makes you safe for good success that produces lasting and abiding fruit from generation to generation.

Jesus makes you safe for good success that produces lasting and abiding fruit from generation to generation.

Coming back to Solomon, let's see what he did right after receiving wisdom from God. David had instituted worship at Mount Zion, not at Mount Gibeon. What were left in the tabernacle of Moses at Mount Gibeon were merely the religious structure and form. It had the lampstand, table of showbread and altar of incense. But the most important furniture in the tabernacle was missing—the ark of the covenant, which had the presence of God.

King David had a special revelation of the ark of the covenant and had brought it back to Jerusalem and placed it on Mount Zion. We see that for some reason, Solomon was into religion before he received wisdom. While he was sincere in seeking the Lord at Mount Gibeon, the Lord's presence was actually at Mount Zion. The tabernacle of Moses only had the form, but the substance of the presence of the Lord was with the ark of the covenant in Jerusalem. But notice this: Once Solomon had received wisdom from the Lord, **the first thing** that he did when he awoke was to go to Jerusalem where he "stood before the ark of the covenant of the Lord, offered up burnt offerings, offered peace offerings, and made a feast for all his servants."[26]

Wisdom Makes You Value Jesus' Presence

How can you tell if somebody has received wisdom from the Lord? The first thing that he will do is value the presence of Jesus! Once Solomon was inundated with God's wisdom, he left the religious structure in the tabernacle of Moses and went to look for the Lord's presence in Jerusalem. After receiving wisdom and a hearing heart, he valued and treasured the Lord's presence. In the same way, when you receive God's wisdom, it will not draw you away from church. Instead, it will cause you to want to receive even more from God's Word and from the presence of Jesus.

"Pastor Prince, what is so significant about the ark of the covenant?"

The ark of the covenant is a picture of Jesus. It is made of wood, which speaks of Jesus' humanity,[27] and it is overlaid with gold, which speaks of Jesus' divinity.[28] Jesus is 100 percent Man and 100 percent God. In the ark are three items: The stone tablets of the Ten Commandments, Aaron's rod, which had budded, and a golden pot of manna. These items represent man's failure and rebellion against God's perfect law, His appointed leadership and His provision, respectively.[29]

Now, look at God's heart for His people. He gave instructions that these symbols of man's rebellion be placed inside the ark and covered with the mercy seat! The mercy seat is where the high priest would sprinkle the blood of the offering to cover all the failings and rebellion of the children of Israel.

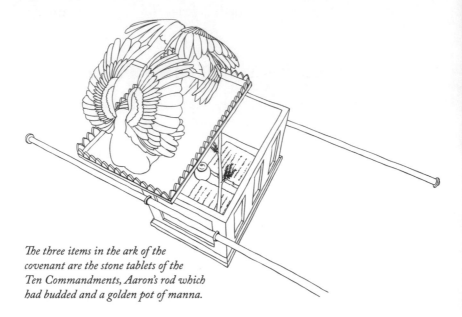

The three items in the ark of the covenant are the stone tablets of the Ten Commandments, Aaron's rod which had budded and a golden pot of manna.

The ark of the covenant is but a shadow. Today, we have the substance of the finished work of Jesus at the cross, where the blood of God's own Son, not the inferior blood of bulls and goats, was shed to blot out **all** our sins, failings and rebellion **once and for all**!

It is no wonder that in battles in which the children of Israel **appreciated the value** of the ark, they emerged victorious. In the same way today, it is a clear indication of God's wisdom upon your life when you value and appreciate the person of Jesus and what He did for you at the cross. And because the true ark of the covenant is with you all the time, you can't help

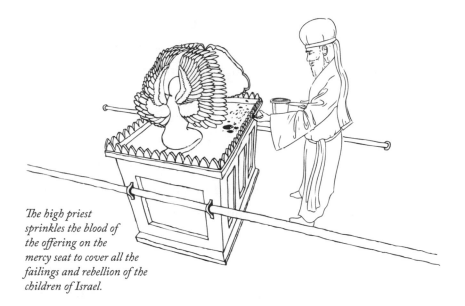

The high priest sprinkles the blood of the offering on the mercy seat to cover all the failings and rebellion of the children of Israel.

but be triumphant, successful and victorious in any battle that you may be in. Solomon realized this and immediately pursued the presence of the Lord after he awoke from his dream. My friend, go after the presence of Jesus in your life. He is your wisdom and victory over every battle today!

Wisdom And Length Of Days

The Bible promises something else when you have wisdom: "Happy is the man who finds wisdom ... **Length of days is in her right hand**, in her left hand riches and honor."[30] Unfortunately for Solomon, he only had the left hand of wisdom, which holds riches and honor. The Lord had said to him, "...**if** you walk in My ways, to keep My statutes and My commandments ... then **I will lengthen your days**."[31]

For Solomon, who was under the old covenant of law, the

blessing of length of days was a conditional one, which he could receive only if he was able to keep the law perfectly. However, Solomon failed to do so and he did not enjoy length of days, which is in wisdom's right hand. But, because we are under the new covenant of grace today, Jesus is the Father's right hand and our wisdom. And when we have Jesus, we can be blessed with the two hands of wisdom because of His finished work on the cross. This means that riches and honor, as well as length of days, belong to us! What an awesome God we serve!

Beloved, pursue Jesus and you will experience wisdom in every area of your life. You cannot try to earn, deserve or study to acquire God's wisdom. It comes by His unmerited favor. His wisdom will give you good success in your career. It will cause you to succeed as a student, parent or spouse.

God's wisdom always leads to promotion and good success.

For instance, if you are facing some problems in your marriage, God will not just "zap" your spouse and make him or her do a moonwalk and come back to you! The same thing that drove your spouse away from you in the first place will just drive him or her away again. What you need is wisdom for your marital situation!

If you are faced with a crisis in your business, depend on the Lord for His wisdom. There are no "money problems," only "idea problems." Trust that the Lord will bless you with the wisdom from heaven to cause everything that you touch at your workplace to prosper. God's wisdom always leads to promotion and good success.

God's Wisdom Brings Promotion

In Genesis 39:3–4, we see how when Potiphar saw that the Lord was with Joseph, and that everything he touched prospered, Potiphar immediately promoted Joseph and placed him in charge over all the affairs of his house. Similarly, when Pharaoh saw that the Spirit of God was in Joseph and that there was none who was as wise and as discerning as Joseph, Pharaoh placed him in charge of the whole of Egypt.[32] But you need to note this: Joseph **knew** that God was the source of his wisdom. When Pharaoh said, "I have had a dream, and there is no one who can interpret it. But I have heard it said of you that you can understand a dream, to interpret it," Joseph immediately replied, "It is not in me; God will give Pharaoh an answer of peace."[33] Joseph knew that his wisdom was a result of the Lord's unmerited favor and would not take any personal credit for it. Clearly, here was a man who understood grace, and could be trusted with increase, promotion and more good success.

Observe the wisdom of Joseph in action. Joseph did not just interpret Pharaoh's dream. He went on to advise Pharaoh on how to take advantage of the seven years of abundance to prepare for the seven years of famine that were revealed in his dream. Did you notice how Joseph's wise advice led to the creation of a position of influence for himself? That is how the wisdom of the Lord operates. Proverbs 18:16 says, "A man's gift makes room for him, and brings him before great men." Joseph knew that his wisdom was a gift from the Lord. He knew that he did not earn it and that it flowed from the Lord's unmerited favor toward him.

The Lord's ways are amazing. See the extent of Joseph's

promotion in Genesis 41. In the space of less than an hour, he rose from a lowly prisoner to the highest possible office in all of Egypt. That, my friend, is the unmerited favor of God! No striving, no self-effort, no compromises and no manipulation, just pure grace and grace alone made all the difference in Joseph's life!

Don't forget what we covered at the beginning of this book. When the Lord is with you, you are a successful person. It may feel like you are in a prison now, stuck in a hopeless situation, cast away and forgotten like Joseph was, but the story is not over yet! The Lord's promotion is around the corner. Whatever situation you are in right now, do not give up.

As you receive God's wisdom, riches and honor,
as well as long life, will follow after you.

If you are caught in a situation and you don't know what to do, it is time to humble yourself and ask the Lord for wisdom. The Bible says, "If any of you lacks wisdom, let him ask of God, who gives to all liberally and without reproach, and it will be given to him."[34] To ask the Lord for wisdom is to say, "I can't, Lord, but You can. I give up on my own efforts and depend entirely upon your unmerited favor and wisdom." As you receive His wisdom, riches and honor, as well as long life, will follow after you. Run to Him right now!

Chapter 21

Greatly Blessed, Highly Favored, Deeply Loved

We have taken an exciting journey to understand the Lord's unmerited favor and we are now at the penultimate chapter of our journey. I pray that God has opened your eyes to the exceeding riches of His grace (unmerited favor) in His kindness toward us in Christ Jesus, and given you a revelation of what it truly means to be righteous by faith and not works.

We are washed by the blood of Jesus, filled with His Spirit and clothed with His righteousness. When Jesus died on the cross for our sins, the veil that separated us from the Lord's holy presence was rent in two,[1] and a new and living way to God's holy presence was opened. Today, we can enter **boldly** into the holy of holies with no fear or trepidation because we are not standing in our own holiness, but Christ's. Beloved, do you know what an awesome privilege this is? To do this was impossible under the old covenant of law.

Under the old covenant of law, the only person who could enter the holy of holies where the ark of the covenant stood was the high priest of Israel. And even the high priest could not enter anytime he wanted. He was only allowed into the presence of God **once a year,** on the Day of Atonement. But today, you and I have free and complete access into Jesus' presence any time. Jesus is with us all the time. This means that we can be a success at all times, in everything that we do!

Jesus is with us all the time. This means that we can be a success at all times, in everything that we do!

The Divine Exchange At The Cross

As we prepare to wind down, I want to make sure that before you close this book, you will have full assurance of your perfect standing in Christ today. Let me reiterate what the new covenant is in very simple terms to you. In the old covenant of law, God told the nation of Israel that unless they kept His commandments perfectly, He could not accept them. But God Himself found fault with the old covenant because man could never fulfill its requirements, and He decided to make a new covenant that was based entirely on the perfect work of Jesus.

In the new covenant of unmerited favor, God essentially said, "I have a better way. Let Jesus keep perfectly all the laws on your behalf. And even though there is no sin in Him, let Him pay the price for all your law-breaking. Let Him carry all the punishment that you deserve. Once all your sins have been judged on Jesus' body on the cross, I will never punish you for those sins again. All you need to do is to accept Jesus and believe all the good things that He has done, and I will put all that He has accomplished to your account, and give you all the blessings, favor and success that My Son deserves.

"As for all the wrong things that you have done and will ever do, I will put them all to His account—on the cross, He will bear all the judgment, condemnation and punishment that you deserve for your sins. This way, all the good things that He has done become yours, and all the bad things that you have done and will do become His at Calvary!"

This is why we call it the gospel of grace. "Gospel" means "good news," and this is GOOD NEWS indeed! Even if you don't fully understand the theological differences between the old and new covenants, you simply need to understand the divine exchange that occurred at the cross and you will already have a profound and intimate understanding of the gospel of Jesus. What am I saying here? I am telling you that you do not need to be a Bible scholar to understand the gospel. You simply need to know the person of Jesus and all that He has done for you! You need to know that the moment you accepted Jesus, God gave you an eternal "A+" for your right standing with Him. You need to know that today, you can enjoy favor with God. It is completely undeserved and unmerited, and it is yours because of what Jesus did on the cross!

How To Increase In God's Unmerited Favor

God's Word tells us that "Jesus **increased** in **wisdom** and stature, and in **favor** with God and men."[2] This is a good verse to pray and speak over your children—that they first increase in favor with God, and then in favor with man. Your "vertical relationship" with God should always be given priority over your "horizontal relationship" with the people around you.

Like Jesus, you can increase in wisdom and in God's unmerited favor. How? You have probably noticed that some believers seem to experience a lot more unmerited favor than others. I believe that this is because these believers understand the key to accessing God's favor. Romans 5:2 clearly spells out that "we have access **by faith** into this grace [unmerited favor] in which we stand." To gain access to your computer or your bank account, you need a password. To gain access to and increase in God's unmerited favor, the "password" or the key that we need to have is faith, faith to believe that YOU, _____ (insert your name), **are** highly favored!

One of the things that I have taught my church members to do is to declare over themselves that they are **greatly blessed, highly favored and deeply loved**.

"How do we know that we are greatly blessed, Pastor Prince?"

Read Hebrews 6:13–14 for yourself. God wanted us to be so anchored in the sure and steadfast knowledge that He **will** bless us, the seed of Abraham, that He swore by Himself, saying, "Surely blessing I will bless you, and multiplying I will multiply you."

"How can we say that we are highly favored?"

Ephesians 1:6 tells us that by God's grace (unmerited favor), God "made us **accepted** in the Beloved." In the original Greek text, the word "accepted" is the word *charitoo*, which means "highly favored."[3]

"And are we really deeply loved by God?"

God didn't just love us. John 3:16 says that "God **so** loved the world that He gave His only begotten Son." He demonstrated how He SO loved us when He sent Jesus to die on the cross for us.

I pray that the verses that I have shown you here and throughout this book will help you believe that through Jesus, **you** are indeed greatly blessed, highly favored and deeply loved. If these truths are still not established in your heart, start speaking them. Look at yourself in the mirror every morning and declare boldly, "Because of Jesus' perfect work on the cross, I am righteous by His blood, and I am greatly blessed, highly favored and deeply loved! I expect good things to come my way. I expect good success and I have a confident expectation of good!"

Because of Jesus' perfect work on the cross, you are righteous by His blood, and you are greatly blessed, highly favored and deeply loved!

Once you receive Christ, you are standing on favor ground. You are no longer on condemnation ground. God looks on you as His favorite child!

"But Pastor Prince, how can God have so many favorites?"

Hey, He is God. Don't try to limit an infinite God with your finite mind. The Bible tells us that God counts the very hairs on each of our heads.[4] (I love my daughter very much, but I have never counted the number of strands of hair on her head.) His love for each of us is intimate and deeply personal. In His eyes, we are all His favorites!

The Story Of Esther

When you know that you are greatly blessed, highly favored and deeply loved, you don't have to depend on your self-efforts. Look at the story of Esther, for example. When King Ahasuerus was looking for a new queen, the most beautiful women in the land were all brought into the palace. All the women were given the opportunity to adorn themselves with whatever they desired from the women's quarters before they were brought for an audience with the king. But when it was Esther's turn, she "requested nothing but what Hegai the king's eunuch, the custodian of the women, advised." And look at the results: "Esther **obtained favor** in the sight of all who saw her,"[5] and the king "loved Esther more than all the other women, and **she obtained grace and favor in his sight** more than all the virgins; so he set the royal crown upon her head and made her queen."[6]

While the other women grabbed the best garments, perfumes and accessories to beautify themselves, Esther did not rely on her own abilities but submitted herself to Hegai, the official who had been appointed by the king to oversee the women. There was so much wisdom and humility in her decision. Can you see the beauty of Esther? She did not trust in her own efforts. While the women tried to outdo one another by relying on their own efforts, Esther wisely submitted to the one person who would know the king's preferences best, and the results speak for themselves.

This incident also demonstrates to us that Esther depended entirely upon the Lord's unmerited favor. When you depend entirely upon the Lord's unmerited favor, you are in a position of rest, trust and ease. Esther did not have to struggle. When she rested in the Lord and humbled herself, the Lord promoted her and exalted her above all the other beautiful women. God resists the proud and gives unmerited favor to the humble.[7] When you humble yourself and cease from your own efforts to promote yourself, and depend on Jesus and Jesus alone, the Lord Himself will be your promotion and increase. Like Esther, you will stand out in a crowd and obtain grace and favor with God and man.

When the Lord promotes you, He gives you the influence to be a blessing and protection to the people around you.

Do you know why the story of Esther is so important? Read the details in the Book of Esther. Because Esther was promoted to become the queen, she was in a favored position to protect all the Jewish people in the kingdom from being killed. When the Lord promotes you, He gives you the influence to be a blessing to the people around you. There are no coincidences, only God-incidents. The Lord will bless you to be a blessing!

Having Favor Does Not Mean That You Won't Face Problems

When God's unmerited favor is shining on you, good things **will** happen to you. However, at the same time, I want you to be aware that you might also face some problems that arise because of the favor on your life. For example, if you are a businessman, you will have more business than you can handle. If you are a doctor, patients will be forming long lines to be treated by you. But these are "good problems" to have.

As the Lord continues to bless our church, our problem is that we keep running out of space to accommodate the precious people who come every Sunday to hear the gospel of grace and the "now-word" that God has for them. As it is, we already have four services every Sunday being broadcast "live" at several overflow venues, with many standing in line for more than an hour each week to get a seat in our main auditorium. Our largest overflow venue currently accommodates more than 2,000 people. It's a "good problem," but securing new overflow venues remains a constant challenge as we await the completion of the much bigger venue that we are currently building at the time of this writing.

So unmerited favor does not mean that you won't have any problems in your life. But remember, even in the midst of those problems, God's almighty grace is sufficient for you, and in your weakness, His strength is made perfect![8]

Having Favor Does Not Mean That Everybody Will Like You

Enjoying God's unmerited favor in your life also does not mean that everybody you meet will like you. I believe that you will have favor with a large majority of people, but there might be a handful of people whom you just don't seem to have favor with. Let's look at Jesus' life because the same favor that is on His life is on yours today.

When Jesus began His ministry at 30 years old, multitudes flocked to Him everywhere He went. For example, Matthew 4:24 says that "His fame went throughout all Syria; and they brought to Him all sick people who were afflicted with various diseases and torments, and those who were demon-possessed, epileptics, and paralytics; and He healed them."

Jesus had so much favor that when He stood before Pontius Pilate, Pilate actually tried various means to release Jesus. In fact, Jesus had to keep His mouth shut in order to have Himself crucified. He knew that if He opened His mouth and spoke with God's favor and wisdom, He would have been released.

Listen, my friend, Jesus was not murdered! He laid down His life willingly. He chose to be led like a lamb to the slaughterhouse. He had the power at any time to stop the soldiers who held Him. In fact, the men who had gone to arrest Him in the Garden of Gethsemane fell to the ground when He said, "I am..."[9] Jesus had to wait for them to get up to arrest Him!

Jesus **chose** to be subject to the beatings, abuse and scourging. He **chose** to be crucified on the cross at Calvary. Through it all, you and I were on His mind. He endured every act of torture, so that He could wash away all our sins and reconcile us to God. How can we help but love and worship our Savior, who paid such a heavy price for our salvation?

While Jesus had favor with pretty much everyone, there was one group of people He did not have favor with—the self-righteous, self-seeking, religious Pharisees. Similarly, when you look at Joseph's life, you will see that he had so much favor with his father Jacob that Jacob gave him an exquisite coat of exquisite fine linen. But Joseph did not have favor with his elder brothers. They were filled with such envy and hatred for Joseph that they threw him into a pit and sold him as a slave.

Unfortunately, the self-righteous Pharisees and the jealous "older brothers" are still around today. Their dependence is on their own flesh and they operate under the system of "deserved favor" based on the law. That is why they hate and envy people who walk under God's grace, which is unmerited, undeserved and unearned favor. So don't be surprised that you do not have favor with self-righteous people when you are walking in God's favor. In fact, you may find that as you grow in the favor of God, some people will write terrible things about you, attempt to assassinate your character and drag your name through mud.

God's favor is like a shield encircling you, protecting you from those who come against you.

Nonetheless, don't worry about them. They are fast becoming a small minority. There is a revolution of the gospel all over the world as people are rediscovering the gospel that our Savior died to give us. Just focus on the Lord's favor in your life and believe that indeed, "No weapon formed against you shall prosper, and every tongue which rises against you in judgment You shall condemn."[10] You don't have to try to defend yourself because God's protection surrounds the righteous. The psalmist says, "For You, O Lord, will bless the righteous; with favor You will surround him as with a shield."[11] What a beautiful promise in God's Word. God's favor is like a **shield** encircling you, protecting you from those who come against you. Picture that for your own life and experience His loving protection!

Personalizing God's Favor In Your life

I used to think that among Jesus' 12 disciples, John was the Lord's favorite disciple and the one who was the closest to Him because the Bible calls John "the disciple whom Jesus loved."[12] I was under the impression that John had a special favor with Jesus, and always wondered what made him so special that he stood apart from the other disciples. Don't you want to be known as the disciple whom Jesus loves? I do!

Then one day, when I was reading God's Word, the secret of John's favor dawned on me. The Lord opened my eyes and showed me that the phrase "the disciple whom Jesus loved" is actually found only in John's *own* book! Check it out for yourself. You will not find this phrase being used in the Gospels of Matthew, Mark and Luke. It is found only in the Gospel of John. It is a phrase that *John* used to describe himself!

Now, what was John doing? He was **practicing and personalizing the love that Jesus had for him**. We are all God's favorites, but John knew the secret of accessing Jesus' unmerited favor for himself. It is your prerogative to see yourself as the disciple whom Jesus loves, and to call yourself that!

When I started to teach that the secret of John's favor lay in his personalization of God's love, the people in my church literally stepped into a new dimension of experiencing God's unmerited favor in their lives. I have seen how some of them really took this revelation and ran with it. Some of them customized the wallpapers of their cell phones to say "The disciple whom Jesus loves," while others signed off their text messages and emails with the phrase.

As they kept reminding themselves that they are the disciple whom Jesus loves, they began to grow in the consciousness of the Lord's love for them. At the same time, they began to grow in being favor-conscious! I have piles of praise reports on how our congregation members have been so blessed just by being conscious of Jesus' favor in their lives. Some of them have been promoted, some have received spectacular increments to their paychecks and many have won various prizes at company functions and in other contests, including all-expense-paid vacations.

A brother from my church signed up for a certain credit card during a special promotion in which new applicants stood to win a range of prizes. There were probably hundreds of thousands of people who participated in this promotion, but this young man just believed that *he* was highly favored, and because of that, *he* would win the top prize.

For the believer, there is no such thing as luck.
There is only the unmerited favor of Jesus!

The day of the draw came and true enough, this young man won the top prize—a stunning black Lamborghini Gallardo! When he wrote to the church to share his testimony, he enclosed a picture of himself smiling from ear to ear, posing with his brand-new Lamborghini. He said that he knew that he had won the car by the unmerited favor of God, and after he had sold off the car, he brought his tithe to the church, giving all glory and honor to Jesus. The world calls this "luck," but for the believer, there is no such thing as luck. There is only the unmerited favor of Jesus!

How God's Favor Rescued Me

I thank God for revealing the truth of God's unmerited favor to me even when I was in my late teens. During my military service, which is mandatory for all male citizens in Singapore, something happened to me that really established me in the favor of God.

When I was undergoing jungle training, I was placed under a section commander who was known to be a sadist. He worked us to the bone. Each night, long after other sections had completed their training, he would still be pushing us with one exercise after another. The punishing regime battered our bodies, and this section commander would heap verbal abuse on us at the same time, crushing whatever esteem we had left in our sweat-drenched, aching bodies.

On one particular evening, the section commander forced us to charge up a hill over and over again until I really felt I could not take it anymore. I saw other sections already getting ready for bed while we were forced to continue the grueling exercise. After charging up and down the hill countless times, it finally occurred to my lightning-fast mind to call on Jesus. So gasping, I cried out for favor! Before then, I had never called upon God in this way, but God was just waiting for me to open my mouth to release His favor upon me. That night finally ended, but something unexpected was in store for us the next day.

The next morning, the section commander gathered us together. As we sat on the ground, looking uniformly exhausted, he told us this, "Last night, I had a dream. One of you appeared in my dream and when I saw this face, I felt something happen in my heart…and I realized that I have been treating all of you very badly. Do you want to know who I saw?"

He pointed his sun-browned finger right at my face.

From that time, the section commander went to the other extreme. When our section was alone with him, he would always tell us to relax and not train so hard. Instead of forcing us to complete hundreds of sit-ups, he now sat down with all of us, telling us story after story. We didn't particularly care about the stories he had to tell about his father, his grandfather, and people from goodness knows how many other generations in his family, but we had absolutely no complaints. Military life was suddenly a breeze!

Anyway, soon after that incident, I was sent to several other military training programs, and did not see that section commander for almost a year. But on the last day of my military service, our paths happened to cross and he called out my name from afar. Knowing that he has hundreds of trainees each year who all looked the same (we all wore the same uniforms and had the same crew-cut hairstyle), I knew that it must have been *some* dream that he had of me. By that time, I was fully convinced that the favor of God works!

The more you are conscious of how precious you are to Jesus and how favored you are because of Him, the more you will increase in favor with God and man.

Beloved, I pray that you will learn to **personalize God's favor** in your life. When you realize that you are not just a face in the crowd, but someone whom God—the Creator of all heaven and earth—is passionately in love with, you can't help but want to live a life that glorifies your Abba. And the more you are conscious of how precious you are to Jesus and how favored you are because of Him, the more you will increase in favor with God and man. Get ready to see good success in your life as you become more and more Jesus-conscious. And remember, you are greatly blessed, highly favored and deeply loved!

Chapter 22

The Secret Of The Beloved

My friend, we have come to the last chapter of this book and before we close, I want to make sure that you know the secret of the beloved, which is to know that you are deeply, deeply loved by Almighty God. Knowing this truth will cause you to be established in the unmerited favor of God and to always carry a sense of favor-consciousness wherever you go.

All Christians probably believe that God has the **power** to bless, heal, protect, prosper and make someone a success. However, we know that not all Christians believe that God is **willing** to do all that for them. Matthew 8:1–3 records the story of a leper who came to Jesus for healing. He said, "Lord, if You are willing, You can make me clean." The leper did not doubt Jesus' ability to heal him, but he was unsure if Jesus was **willing** to heal **him**, a leper who was ostracized by all. In other words, he believed in God's omnipotence, but was not sure if God's heart was one of love and unmerited favor toward him. I am sure that you know believers who are like that. They may believe in God's power, but they are unsure of God's heart toward them. They know that God can, but they are not sure if He is willing.

This is one of the biggest tragedies in the church today. When these believers hear testimonies of believers being healed by the Lord, they are unsure if God is also willing to heal them. When they read praise reports of the Lord blessing others with promotions and financial blessings, they privately question if God is also willing to do the same for them. They wonder what these people **did** to get their blessings.

More tragically, they look at their own lives, imperfections and failings, and start to disqualify themselves from receiving God's blessings. They think, "Why would God bless me? Look at what I've done. I am so undeserving." Instead of having faith to believe God for their breakthroughs, they feel too condemned to be able to believe in God's goodness and receive anything good from Him.

My friend, don't be like that leper who completely misread Jesus! Let's see how Jesus responded to him. This is important because it would be the same response that Jesus would give you if you approached Him today.

"I Am Willing"

Matthew 8:3 records that "Jesus put out His hand and touched him, saying, 'I am willing; be cleansed.'" Can you see how personal Jesus' ministry is? He did not touch every person that He healed. At times, He simply spoke and the sick were healed. But in this case, Jesus stretched out His hand and touched the leper tenderly. I believe that Jesus did this to heal him not just of his leprosy, but also of the emotional scars that he had received from years of rejection.

Leprosy was a highly contagious disease and the law forbade lepers from coming into contact with anyone. This means that for years, this leper had been shunned by everyone who saw his condition, even his own family members. He probably stank of decaying flesh and neglect, and his appearance must have been repulsive.

Whatever breakthrough you are believing Jesus for, He says to you, "I AM WILLING."

But without flinching, Jesus touched him, giving him the first human touch he had since he contracted the disease. The Bible tells us that immediately, his leprosy was cleansed and the man received his healing.

Jesus is the same yesterday, today and forever.[1] Whatever breakthrough you are believing Him for, He says to you, "I AM WILLING." Don't doubt His heart of love for you any longer. Stop being occupied by your own disqualifications and be completely absorbed in His love and grace (unmerited favor) toward you!

Come To Jesus As You Are

"But Pastor Prince, why would God want to bless me? My life is a mess."

My friend, you are favored and accepted by God today because of **His** unmerited favor. He can take your mess and make it into something beautiful. Come to Him just as you are.

Years ago, one of my church members suddenly stopped

coming to church for a long time. I met up with him to find out how he was doing and to see if everything was alright. He was very honest with me and told me that he was going through a lot of problems in his marriage, and that he was now addicted to alcohol. Then, he said this: "Let me get my life right, then I will come back to church."

I smiled and asked him, "Do you clean yourself before you take a bath?" I could tell from his expression that he was taken aback by my question, so I told him, "Come **as you are** to the Lord. He is the bath. He will cleanse you. He will get your life in order for you, and He will cause every addiction to lose its hold on you. You don't have to use your own efforts to clean yourself before you take a bath!"

I am glad to share that this precious brother soon returned to church and Jesus turned his life around. Today, he is happily married, blessed with a beautiful family and is one of my trusted, key leaders. That is what the Lord does when you come to Him as you are, and allow Him to love you into wholeness. He will make all things beautiful in your life.

There are many people today who are like this brother. They want to get their lives together by themselves before they come to Jesus. They are under the impression that they need to make themselves holy before they can step into God's holy presence. They feel like they are being hypocrites if they don't sort out their lives first before coming to church.

Nothing could be further from the truth. You will **never** be able to make yourself holy enough to qualify for God's blessings. You are made holy, righteous and clean by the blood of Jesus

Christ, and it is **His** righteous standing that qualifies you— nothing more and nothing less. So stop trying to clean yourself before you go to the Lord. Come to Jesus with all your mess, all your addictions, all your weaknesses and all your failures. God loves you just as you are. However, He also loves you too much to let you stay the same. My friend, when you come to Jesus, He becomes your "bath." He will wash you clean, whiter than snow! Jump into the bath today and allow Jesus to make you perfect, righteous and holy in God's eyes!

Highly Favored In The Beloved And Well-Pleasing To God

Ephesians 1:6 says, "to the praise of the glory of His grace [unmerited favor], by which He made us **accepted** in the Beloved." It is not possible for us to make ourselves accepted. We are made accepted by the glory of the Lord's unmerited favor. In the previous chapter, we learned that the word "accepted" in Ephesians 1:6 is the Greek word *charitoo*. Now, the root word for *charitoo* is *charis*,[2] which means "grace." So *charitoo* simply means "highly graced" or "highly favored." In other words, you are highly favored in the Beloved!

Now, we know that "the Beloved" in Ephesians 1:6 refers to Jesus. If you read on, it says in the next verse that "In Him [Jesus the Beloved] we have redemption through His blood, the forgiveness of sins, according to the riches of His grace [unmerited favor]." Now, why didn't the Bible just say that we are highly favored in Jesus or in Christ? (There are no insignificant details in the Bible.) Why did the Holy Spirit choose specifically to say that we are highly favored **"in the Beloved"**?

"Beloved" is a warm and intimate term that was used by God at the Jordan River to describe Jesus. The Bible tells us that when Jesus was baptized in the Jordan River, as soon as He came up from the water, "He saw the heavens parting and the Spirit descending upon Him like a dove. Then a voice came from heaven, 'You are My **beloved Son**, in whom I am **well pleased**.'"[3] In these scriptures, you can see the triune God—God the Father, the Son and the Holy Spirit. This tells us that there is something very important for us to learn here.

God the Father spoke publicly and His words were recorded for you to know that to be "accepted in the Beloved" means that God is **well pleased** with **you** today. See yourself sandwiched right smack in the midst of Jesus, God's Beloved. When God looks at you, He doesn't see you in your failures and shortcomings. He sees you in Jesus' perfection and loveliness! Because you are in Christ, God says to **you**, "You, _____ (insert your name here), are My beloved, in whom I am well pleased." Jesus is well-pleasing to God because He kept the law perfectly. You and I are well-pleasing to God because we are accepted and highly favored in the Beloved, who took all our sins and fulfilled the law on our behalf!

Always Remember That You Are God's Beloved

Immediately after Jesus was baptized, He was led into the wilderness to be tempted by the devil. The devil came to Jesus and said, "If You are the Son of God, command that these stones become bread."[4] Now, don't forget that Jesus had just heard the voice of His Father affirming Him with the words "You are My beloved Son." Years ago, as I was studying Jesus' temptations by the devil, the Lord asked me, "Did you notice that the devil dropped one word when he came to tempt My Son?"

For the devil's temptations to work, he cannot remind you that you are God's beloved.

I had never heard anyone preach this before or read this in any book, but God opened my eyes to see that the devil had omitted the word "beloved"! God had just told Jesus, "You are My **beloved** Son." But shortly after that, the devil came to Jesus, saying, "If You are the Son of God…" The word "beloved" is missing! The serpent had deliberately left out the word "beloved"!

The Lord then showed me that for the devil's temptations to work, he cannot remind you that you are God's beloved. The moment you are reminded of your identity as God's beloved in Christ, he will not be able to succeed! It is no wonder that the devil wants to rob believers of their sense of being God's beloved.

God Will Never Be Angry With You

A warning is issued in 1 Peter 5:8—"Be sober, be vigilant; because your adversary the devil walks about **like a roaring lion**, seeking whom he may devour." I know that a lion roars to intimidate and to bring fear, but I used to wonder what kind of fear the devil tries to instill in the believer. But we must **let the Bible interpret the Bible**. We can't base our interpretations on our denominational backgrounds or our experiences.

One day, I was reading Proverbs 19 when I came across verse 12: "The king's wrath is like the **roaring of a lion**, but his favor is like dew on the grass." Who is the king that this verse refers to? It is our Lord Jesus! So when the devil goes about **like a roaring lion**, he is trying to impersonate the King. He is trying to make you feel as if God is angry with you. Every time you hear preaching that leaves you with a sense that God is angry with you, guess what? You have just been roared at! But know this, beloved: God will NEVER be angry with you ever again. He only has to tell us this, but He wanted us to be so sure that He **swore** in His Word that He would never be angry with us again. I want you to read these scriptures for yourself:

> "For this is like the waters of Noah to Me; for as I have sworn that the waters of Noah would no longer cover the earth, **so have I sworn that I would not be angry with you**, nor rebuke you. For the mountains shall depart and the hills be removed, but My kindness shall not depart from you, nor shall My covenant of peace be removed," says the Lord, who has mercy on you.
>
> —Isaiah 54:9–10

This passage in Isaiah 54 is right after the famous messianic chapter of the sufferings of Christ in Isaiah 53. Therefore, Isaiah 54 is spelling out the triumphs and spoils of His sufferings.

Do you know why God will never be angry with us again? It is because of what Christ has accomplished for us! On the cross, God poured out all His anger on the body of His Son. Jesus exhausted all the fiery indignation of a holy God against **all** our sins, and when all of God's judgment of our sins had been completely exhausted, He shouted, "It is finished!"[5] And because our sins have already been punished, God, who is a holy and just God, will **not** punish us today when we believe in what Christ has done. God's holiness is now on your side. His righteousness is now **for** you, not against you. You are His beloved, in whom He is well pleased!

When you know that you are God's beloved, you will be able to take down all the giants in your life!

What a powerful revelation. It means that whenever you are full of the revelation that **you** are highly favored in the Beloved, you can overcome any temptation thrown at you. The next time the devil tries to rob you of your sense of being beloved by making you think that God is angry with you, ignore him. Ignore him when he says, "How can you call yourself a Christian?" You are God's beloved! By the way, did you know that David's name in Hebrew means "beloved"? When you know that you are God's beloved, you will be able to take down all the giants in your life!

Nearness To God In The Beloved

After Joseph revealed himself to his brothers, he tells them to return to their father and to tell him, "...come down to me, do not tarry. You shall dwell in the land of **Goshen**, and you shall be **near to me**, you and your children, your children's children, your flocks and your herds, and all that you have."[6] The name "Goshen" means "drawing near."[7] God wants you to be in

"Goshen," which is a place of nearness to Him, and there is no place nearer to Him than being in the Beloved. God's heart of love is not satisfied with just removing your sins from you. No, He wants more. He wants you in His presence. He wants you in the place where He can lavish the bountiful love in His heart on you!

When you draw near to Jesus, look what happens. Joseph tells his brothers to also tell their father, **"There I will provide for you**, lest you and your household, and all that you have, come to poverty; for there are still five years of famine."[8] When you draw near to your heavenly Joseph, He will provide for you and your little ones. In the midst of financial famine in the world, in the midst of rising fuel and food costs, do not despair. Draw near to Jesus, for there in "Goshen," in that place of nearness, He will provide for you and your household. Your God shall supply ALL your needs according to HIS riches (not according to your bank account balance or to the world's economic situation) in glory by Christ Jesus![9]

Protection In The Beloved

That's not all, my friend. Another blessing that you can enjoy when you are in the Beloved is divine protection. In recent years, new strains of deadly viruses have been making headlines. But whatever the virus may be, whether it's the bird flu or swine flu or some other new plague, you can safely claim Psalm 91 for yourself. You can declare, "A thousand may fall at my side, and ten thousand at my right hand; but it shall **not** come near me, God's beloved!"[10]

When there were plagues and pestilences all over Egypt because Pharaoh refused to let God's people go, look at what God said about the children of Israel: "...I will set apart the land of **Goshen**, in which My people dwell, that no swarms of flies shall be there, in order that you may know that I am the Lord in the midst of the land. I will make a difference between My people and your people..."[11] There is a difference between God's beloved people and the people of the world. Although Egypt was plagued by swarms of flies and other pestilences, the children of Israel were safe in the land of Goshen, completely untouched by the troubles!

So even if there are bad things happening in the world today, remember that as God's beloved child, you are **in** the world, but not **of** the world.[12] No plague, no evil and no danger can come close to you and your dwelling place because you are safe in the secret place of the Most High. As the children of Israel were kept safe and protected in Goshen, so will you and I, whom God calls His beloved!

Daily Nourishment In Knowing That You Are God's Beloved

Now, let's look at Jesus' response to the devil's temptation in the wilderness. Jesus said, "It is written, 'Man shall not live by bread alone, but by every **word** that proceeds from the mouth of God.'"[13] There is a powerful revelation hidden in Jesus' reply. In the original Greek text, the word used for "word" here is *rhema*, which means "that which is or has been uttered by the living voice, thing spoken."[14] I call this the "now-word" or "the word in season." Jesus was referring to a very specific word. Can you recall what it was? The now-word for Jesus was what the Father had just said to Him at the Jordan River—"You are My beloved Son, in whom I am well pleased." Every single word uttered by the Father here was bread for Jesus. They are also bread for us to live by. And because Jesus was conscious that He was His Father's beloved Son, He was able to overcome every temptation the devil brought.

Live each day feeding on God's love, grace, perfect acceptance of and unmerited favor toward you.

Jesus said that man "shall not live by bread alone, but by every word that proceeds from the mouth of God." "Bread" here speaks of physical nourishment. Jesus was saying that it is not enough to just eat physical food. We need to draw nourishment from and live by *rhema* too. We need to know what the specific now-word from God to us is. Just as it is important for us to get physical nourishment from food, it is important for us to get spiritual nourishment from Jesus and His words to us.

My friend, God wants you to live each day knowing that you are His beloved child, in whom He is well pleased. That is your daily nourishment from Him—to know, believe and confess that you are His beloved and that you are well-pleasing to Him all the time.

So live each day feeding on God's love, grace, perfect acceptance of and unmerited favor toward you. When you do so, you are reminding yourself that you are His beloved no matter what happens to you. When you are constantly full of the consciousness of His favor on your life, nothing can get you down. You will have such a confidence of God's goodness toward you that even when the devil starts throwing lemons at you, you know that God will turn those lemons into refreshing lemonade for you! You begin to have a confident expectation of good even when circumstances in the natural don't look so great. That is walking by faith in Jesus' goodness, and not by sight. You are no longer looking at your challenges. You are looking at Jesus' face shining upon you and imparting grace into your situation.

If it matters to you, it matters to God.

When you are confident that you are God's beloved, not only will you overcome the devil's temptations, you will dare to ask Him to bless you even in the little things. Many years ago, Wendy and I went to a restaurant for dinner when she was pregnant with Jessica. As we were about to order our food, a man seated not too far away from us took out a pack of cigarettes and prepared to take a smoke. I really didn't want Wendy to take in any of that secondhand cigarette smoke, but there was no nonsmoking section in that restaurant. So guess what I did? I prayed! Under my breath, I told the Lord, "Lord, I know that I am your beloved. Please stop that man from smoking in this restaurant." That was all I said—a quick and simple prayer.

Guess what happened? That man tried to light his cigarette, but he just could not get his lighter to work! He persisted and kept trying, but no matter what he did, the lighter simply would not work. After some time, he shoved his cigarettes back in his shirt pocket in frustration. Praise Jesus! Even in the little things,

God hears and answers the prayers of His beloved. Nothing is too big or too small for your Daddy God. If it matters to you, it matters to Him. When you know that you are His beloved, you can walk in constant expectation of His unmerited favor in every situation!

For God So Loved You

Some years ago, I was taking a cab in New York and I took the opportunity to share the love of Jesus with the driver. Her response was quite typical. She said flippantly, "God loves everybody, man!"

It is absolutely true that God loves everybody, but to experience His love firsthand in your life, you have to personalize His love **for you.** Jesus died for you and do you know that even if you were the only person on earth, God would still have sent His Son to die on the cross for you? That is how precious YOU are to Him!

You need to personalize John 3:16 by declaring, "For God so loved _____ (insert your name), He sent His only begotten Son to die on the cross for _____ (insert your name)." Be like John, who personalized the Lord's love for him by calling himself "the disciple whom Jesus loved."

The sun shines on every blade of grass in a field. But if you put a magnifying glass over one particular blade of grass, it will center the heat from the sun over that blade, and that blade of grass will burn.

That is what I have been hoping to do with this book. I have been putting the magnifying glass of Jesus' love and unmerited favor over your life. I want you to be so conscious of Jesus' unmerited favor that your heart can be set ablaze with His unconditional love for you.

God, who loves you deeply, is on your side, and because of that, you can enjoy good success in all that you do!

Jesus said in Matthew 8:20, "Foxes have holes and birds of the air have nests, but the Son of Man has nowhere to **lay** His head." The Greek word for "lay" here is *klino*.[15] It is the same word used in John 19:30—"So when Jesus had received the sour wine, He said, 'It is finished!' And **bowing** His head, He gave up His spirit." The Greek word for "bowing" here is *klino*. In other words, after Jesus said, "It is finished!" He laid His head to rest. He finally found His rest in LOVING YOU.

As you close this book, may you burn with the revelation that God, who loves you deeply, is on YOUR side. And because of that, you **can** enjoy good success in all that you do!

Closing Words

Throughout this book, I have endeavored to show you how it is God's delight to bless you with good success in every area of your life through His unmerited favor. While success to the world comes by one's self-effort, willpower and striving by one's own strength, God's way to supernatural, effortless success is for you to depend totally on His unmerited favor. This unmerited favor, which you do not deserve and cannot earn for yourself, will perfect every imperfection in your life and transform every area of weakness and struggle that you are facing now into testimonies of His grace and power.

Many believers are living lives of defeat today because they are depending on their own obedience to the law to be blessed. They do not know that Jesus' unmerited favor IS the new covenant that we can enjoy today, made possible only through the cross and the obedience of Jesus Christ. This means that we can move from merely experiencing a little bit of His unmerited favor here and there to seeing it permeate every aspect of our lives.

I believe with all of my heart that as you have taken this exciting journey with me into the heart of our heavenly Father to bless you through the finished work of Jesus, God has been laying a strong foundation in you that will set you up for every success in life. More and more will you see Jesus' unmerited favor manifest in your family life, career and relationships, and less and less will you settle for what is less than God's best for you.

It is my heart's desire to see God's grace and peace multiplied in every aspect of your life. Once more, let me bring your attention to 2 Peter 1:2. It says, "Grace [unmerited favor] and peace be multiplied to you in the knowledge of God and of Jesus our Lord." The more you know and see Jesus, the more God's unmerited favor and peace will be multiplied in your life. That is why I have, from chapter to chapter, sought to unveil the person of Jesus and the perfection of His finished work. The more you see Him, the more you will move from self-occupation that brings stress, frustration and defeat, to Christ-occupation that releases the peace, joy, divine wisdom and supernatural ability to handle every challenge in life.

I want your life to be radically blessed, and this can only happen if the unmerited favor of God is radically preached to you, and I pray I have done that in this book. What the Lord said to me in 1997 as I was vacationing with my wife in the lovely Swiss Alps is still as vivid to me as ever: "If you don't preach grace (unmerited favor) radically, people's lives will never be radically blessed and radically transformed."

My friend, I hope you have enjoyed reading this book as much as I have enjoyed writing it. If you have been blessed by the many truths that I have shared, and hunger for more, you can find more of these powerful foundational truths and revelations about the grace (unmerited favor) of God laid out in my earlier book, *Destined To Reign*. In it, I explain in greater detail how to rightly divide God's Word, how our new covenant of grace gives abundant life, and how we can reign in life simply by receiving an abundance of God's grace and His gift of righteousness. And like many whose lives have been wonderfully blessed and transformed through reading *Destined To Reign*, may you also be tremendously blessed by the foundational and life-changing truths that you will find in that book.

As expressed in my previous book *Destined To Reign*, all that I have shared works most powerfully and effectively within the environment of the local church. These truths are for the greater good of the body of Christ and should never result in you becoming a law unto yourself. Beloved, I want to see you enjoying the safety of the covering of a local church where there is accountability and submission. This is where our blessings are tremendously multiplied.

What a journey it has been! I have truly enjoyed your company. I pray that I have deposited in your heart a strong sense of being greatly blessed, highly favored and deeply loved by our Lord. Remember that He is with you as He was with Joseph in the Bible. And when He is with you, He will cause everything that your hands touch to prosper. As He did for Joseph, He will cause you to see good success in every area of your life to the glory of God. I look forward to hearing from you about how the words in this book have blessed you, empowered you and given you good success in life.

Till we meet again,

Joseph Prince

Notes

Introduction
1. Luke 12:32; Psalm 35:27
2. John 8:7
3. John 8:10–11
4. Mark 4:37–39
5. Hebrews 9:13–14
6. Hebrews 8:7
7. 1 Corinthians 15:10

Chapter 1
The Definition Of Success
1. Matthew 1:19
2. Matthew 1:20–21
3. Matthew 1:22–23
4. Joshua 6:20
5. Hebrews 13:5

Chapter 2
Everything You Touch Is Blessed
1. Philippians 4:6–7
2. *Jamieson, Fausset, and Brown Commentary*, Electronic Database. Copyright © 1997, 2003, 2005, 2006 by Biblesoft, Inc. All rights reserved.
3. Genesis 37:8
4. Genesis 37:19–20
5. Psalm 127:1
6. Galatians 5:4, NLT
7. Hebrews 13:5

Chapter 3
Becoming Safe For Success
1. 1 Timothy 6:10
2. Genesis 12:2
3. Galatians 3:29
4. Isaiah 53: 5
5. 2 Corinthians 8:9
6. 2 Corinthians 3:18
7. Luke 5:6–7
8. John 6:13
9. Matthew 6:33
10. Matthew 6:25–32
11. Genesis 39:4–5
12. Genesis 39:10
13. Genesis 39:9
14. Exodus 20:14, KJV
15. Hebrews 8:10

Chapter 4
Success Beyond Your Circumstances
1. Mark 2:1–12
2. Isaiah 54:17
3. Proverbs 3:5–6
4. Hebrews 13:5
5. Psalm 37:23–24
6. Proverbs 18:24
7. Matthew 27:46
8. Hebrews 13:5–6
9. NT:3364, Biblesoft's New Exhaustive Strong's Numbers and Concordance with Expanded Greek-Hebrew Dictionary. Copyright © 1994, 2003, 2006 Biblesoft, Inc. and International Bible Translators, Inc.
10. Genesis 41:39–41

Chapter 5

Practicing The Presence Of Jesus

1. Psalm 97:5
2. Psalm 3:3
3. 1 Peter 5:7
4. Luke 12:7
5. John 10:3, 14
6. Exodus 15:25
7. 1 Samuel 16:18
8. Proverbs 22: 1
9. James 1:17
10. Psalm 34:3
11. Psalm 68:1

Chapter 6

Your Right To God's Unmerited Favor

1. 1 John 4:17
2. Galatians 2:21, KJV
3. Isaiah 53:5
4. Philippians 3:8–9

Chapter 7

God's Peace For Your Success

1. Psalm 91:1, 4
2. Isaiah 54:17
3. John 6:35
4. Proverbs 4:20–22
5. John 14:27
6. OT:7965, The Online Bible Thayer's Greek Lexicon and Brown Driver & Briggs Hebrew Lexicon, Copyright © 1993, Woodside Bible Fellowship, Ontario, Canada. Licensed from the Institute for Creation Research
7. 1 John 4:18
8. Isaiah 54:9–10
9. Philippians 4:7

Chapter 8

Covenanted To Succeed In Life

1. Hebrews 8:7–8, TLB
2. 1 Samuel 13:14; Acts 13:22
3. Psalm 103:1–5
4. 2 Timothy 2:15
5. Hebrews 10:12–14
6. Matthew 8:16–17
7. Romans 8:3
8. Galatians 3:24–25
9. Hebrews 13:5
10. Hebrews 8:6

11. Mark 2:22
12. Coverdale's Dedication and Preface, *Coverdale's Bible*. Retrieved 23 April 2009 from www.bible-researcher.com/coverdale1.html

Chapter 9

God's Covenant Of Unmerited Favor With Us

1. Exodus 14:11
2. Exodus 15:23–25
3. Exodus 16:3
4. Romans 4:2–3
5. Exodus 19:4–6
6. Exodus 19:8
7. Exodus 19: 9–13
8. Exodus 20:3
9. 1 Corinthians 15:56
10. Numbers 21:6
11. Deuteronomy 28:13–14
12. Hebrews 10:1
13. Colossians 2:17
14. Exodus 20:25
15. Exodus 20:26
16. John 19:30
17. Proverbs 25:2
18. Romans 6:23

Chapter 10

Perfected By Unmerited Favor

1. Exodus 29:38-39, KJV
2. Mark 15:25; Luke 23:44–46
3. James 2:10
4. Matthew 5:22
5. Matthew 5:28
6. Matthew 5:29–30
7. Romans 7:7–8
8. Romans 7:24
9. Romans 7:25
10. Romans 8:1, NAS
11. Romans 4:6
12. John 8:10–11

Chapter 11

Transforming The Next Generation

1. Matthew 22:37–40; Mark 12:29–30
2. John 3:16
3. Romans 5:7–9
4. 1 John 4:10

5. Romans 13:10
6. Genesis 39:9
7. 2 Timothy 2:22
8. Galatians 1:6–7
9. Galatians 3:2–3
10. Carl Stuart Hamblen, "Is He Satisfied With Me?" *I Believe*, Hamblen Music Company, 1952.
11. John 19:30
12. Hebrews 8:7–9
13. Hebrews 8:13
14. Karen Lim, "I'm Held By Your Love," *You Gave*, CD album by New Creation Church, Singapore, 2005.
15. Hebrews 13:5

Chapter 12
Our Part In The New Covenant
1. Hebrews 8:11
2. Philippians 2:13
3. Exodus 20:5
4. Hosea 8:7
5. Luke 8:11
6. Hebrews 7:27

Chapter 13
How Unmerited Favor Is Cheapened
1. Romans 14:23
2. James 2:10
3. James 2:13
4. 1 Corinthians 6:19
5. Ephesians 1:1
6. 1 Corinthians 1:2
7. 2 John 1:1–3
8. 3 John 1:1 2
9. Romans 3:23
10. 1 John 1:3
11. 1 John 2:1–2
12. Hebrews 10:2
13. Matthew 22:36–38

Chapter 14
The Secret To Good Success
1. Deuteronomy 6:10–11
2. Hebrews 3:11
3. Exodus 18:21
4. Matthew 4:10
5. Numbers 14:7–9
6. Numbers 13:31–33

7. Numbers 14:24
8. Joshua 1: 6–7, 9, 18
9. Romans 6:14
10. Joshua 1:8
11. OT:1897, The Online Bible Thayer's Greek Lexicon and Brown Driver & Briggs Hebrew Lexicon, Copyright © 1993, Woodside Bible Fellowship, Ontario, Canada. Licensed from the Institute for Creation Research.
12. Psalm 39:3
13. Romans 10:17
14. NT:5547, Biblesoft's New Exhaustive Strong's Numbers and Concordance with Expanded Greek-Hebrew Dictionary. Copyright © 1994, 2003, 2006 Biblesoft, Inc. and International Bible Translators, Inc.

Chapter 15
The Blessed Man Versus The Cursed Man
1. Hebrews 5:13
2. Proverbs 10:22
3. NT:1680, Thayer's Greek Lexicon, Electronic Database. Copyright © 2000, 2003, 2006 by Biblesoft, Inc. All rights reserved.
4. NT:266, Thayer's Greek Lexicon, PC Study Bible formatted Electronic Database. Copyright © 2006 by Biblesoft, Inc. All rights reserved.

Chapter 16
Walking In The Blessing Of Abraham
1. *Theological Wordbook of the Old Testament*. Copyright © 1980 by The Moody Bible Institute of Chicago. All rights reserved. Used by permission.
2. Romans 1:16–17
3. NT:4991, Thayer's Greek Lexicon, Electronic Database. Copyright © 2000, 2003, 2006 by Biblesoft, Inc. All rights reserved.
   NT:4991, Biblesoft's New Exhaustive Strong's Numbers and Concordance with Expanded Greek-Hebrew Dictionary. Copyright © 1994, 2003, 2006 Biblesoft, Inc. and International Bible Translators, Inc.

4. Galatians 3:13-15
5. Galatians 3:29
6. NT:2889, Thayer's Greek Lexicon, Electronic Database. Copyright © 2000, 2003, 2006 by Biblesoft, Inc. All rights reserved.
7. Genesis 12:2
8. James 1:17
9. 1 Timothy 6:10
10. Matthew 6:33
11. 1 Peter 3:6
12. Matthew 14:20
13. Jewish Virtual Library, A Division Of The American-Israeli Cooperative Enterprise. (n.d.). *Jewish Nobel Prize Winners*. Retrieved 22 May 2009 from www .jewishvirtuallibrary.org/jsource/Judaism/ nobels.html

Chapter 17
Becoming An Heir Of The World

1. Romans 5:17
2. 2 Peter 1:5–7
3. Matthew 6:33
4. 2 Corinthians 11:14–15
5. Romans 10:5–6
6. 2 Corinthians 4:13
7. NT:2842, Biblesoft's New Exhaustive Strong's Numbers and Concordance with Expanded Greek-Hebrew Dictionary. Copyright © 1994, 2003, 2006 Biblesoft, Inc. and International Bible Translators, Inc.
8. Daniel 9:24
9. Isaiah 54:17
10. Revelation 12:10
11. Romans 4:14
12. Matthew 6:33

Chapter 18
Self-Occupation Versus Christ-Occupation

1. 1 John 4:17
2. Romans 7:24
3. 2 Corinthians 3:18
4. Matthew 6:25
5. Matthew 6:32
6. Matthew 6:33
7. Revelation 19:16
8. Exodus 16:5
9. Exodus 16:20

10. John 6:35
11. Colossians 1:29
12. Luke 10:40
13. Luke 10:41–42
14. John 12:3–8

Chapter 19
The Prayer Of The Unnamed Servant

1. 1 Corinthians 1:29
2. 1 Corinthians 1:30–31
3. Acts 7:22
4. Exodus 4:10
5. Exodus 3:10
6. Exodus 2:11–15
7. Exodus 14:26–28
8. 1 Peter 5:5
9. 1 Samuel 17:43
10. 1 Samuel 17:17–20
11. Zechariah 4:10
12. 1 Samuel 17:45–46
13. 1 Samuel 17:47
14. OT:7136, The Online Bible Thayer's Greek Lexicon and Brown Driver & Briggs Hebrew Lexicon, Copyright © 1993, Woodside Bible Fellowship, Ontario, Canada. Licensed from the Institute for Creation Research.
15. Hebrews 8:10
16. The unnamed servant is probably Eliezer of Damacus, Abraham's chief servant.
17. Genesis 24:12
18. Ruth 2:2
19. Ruth 2:3, KJV
20. OT:4745, Biblesoft's New Exhaustive Strong's Numbers and Concordance with Expanded Greek-Hebrew Dictionary. Copyright © 1994, 2003, 2006 Biblesoft, Inc. and International Bible Translators, Inc.

Chapter 20
Divine Wisdom To Succeed

1. Colossians 2:2–3
2. John 8:4–5
3. John 8:7
4. 1 Corinthians 1:30, KJV
5. John 8:10–11
6. John 3:17
7. 2 Corinthians 5:17
8. Ephesians 1:3

9. Psalm 91:1
10. Deuteronomy 28:13
11. 1 Corinthians 1:30
12. 1 John 4:17
13. James 5:16
14. James 4:2, KJV
15. Proverbs 28:1
16. Hebrews 4:16
17. 1 Corinthians 8:1
18. Proverbs 4:7–9
19. 2 Chronicles 1:7
20. 2 Chronicles 1:10
21. 1 Kings 3:10
22. 2 Chronicles 1:11–12
23. 1 Kings 3:9
24. OT:8085, Biblesoft's New Exhaustive Strong's Numbers and Concordance with Expanded Greek-Hebrew Dictionary. Copyright © 1994, 2003, 2006 Biblesoft, Inc. and International Bible Translators, Inc.
25. John 16:13
26. 1 Kings 3:15
27. Isaiah 55:12; Mark 8:24
28. Isaiah 2:20; Song of Solomon 5:11, 14–15
29. Prince, Joseph. (2007). *Destined To Reign*. Singapore: 22 Media Pte Ltd. p.208–209.
30. Proverbs 3:13–16
31. 1 Kings 3:14
32. Genesis 41:38–41
33. Genesis 41:15–16
34. James 1:5

Chapter 21
Greatly Blessed, Highly Favored, Deeply Loved

1. Matthew 27:51
2. Luke 2:52
3. NT:5487, Biblesoft's New Exhaustive Strong's Numbers and Concordance with Expanded Greek-Hebrew Dictionary. Copyright © 1994, 2003, 2006 Biblesoft, Inc. and International Bible Translators, Inc.
4. Matthew 10:30
5. Esther 2:15
6. Esther 2:17
7. 1 Peter 5:5
8. 2 Corinthians 12:9
9. John 18:6
10. Isaiah 54:17
11. Psalm 5:12
12. John 21:20

Chapter 22
The Secret Of The Beloved

1. Hebrews 13:8
2. NT:5485, Biblesoft's New Exhaustive Strong's Numbers and Concordance with Expanded Greek-Hebrew Dictionary. Copyright © 1994, 2003, 2006 Biblesoft, Inc. and International Bible Translators, Inc.
3. Mark 1:10–11
4. Matthew 4:3
5. John 19:30
6. Genesis 45:9–10
7. Hitchcock's Bible Names Dictionary, PC Study Bible formatted electronic database Copyright © 2003, 2006 Biblesoft, Inc. All rights reserved.
8. Genesis 45:11
9. Philippians 4:19
10. Psalm 91:7
11. Exodus 8:22–23
12. John 17:11, 16
13. Matthew 4:4
14. NT:4487, Thayer's Greek Lexicon, PC Study Bible formatted Electronic Database. Copyright © 2006 by Biblesoft, Inc. All rights reserved.
15. NT:2827, Biblesoft's New Exhaustive Strong's Numbers and Concordance with Expanded Greek-Hebrew Dictionary. Copyright © 1994, 2003, 2006 Biblesoft, Inc. and International Bible Translators, Inc.

Salvation Prayer

If you would like to receive all that Jesus has done for you, and make Him your Lord and Savior, please pray this prayer:

> Lord Jesus, thank You for loving me and dying for me on the cross. Your precious blood washes me clean of every sin. You are my Lord and my Savior, now and forever. I believe that You rose from the dead and that You are alive today. Because of Your finished work, I am now a beloved child of God and heaven is my home. Thank You for giving me eternal life, and filling my heart with Your peace and joy. Amen.

We Would Like To Hear From You

If you have prayed the salvation prayer, or if you have a testimony to share after reading this book, please send us an email at info@destined2reign.com.